A SPECIAL RELATIONSHIP

A SPECIAL RELATIONSHIP

BRITAIN COMES TO HOLLYWOOD AND HOLLYWOOD COMES TO BRITAIN

ANTHONY SLIDE

University Press of Mississippi / Jackson

www.upress.state.ms.us

Designed by Peter D. Halverson

The University Press of Mississippi is a member of the Association of American University Presses.

Manufactured in the United States of America

First printing 2015

∞

Library of Congress Cataloging-in-Publication Data

Slide, Anthony.
A special relationship : Britain comes to Hollywood and Hollywood comes to Britain / Anthony Slide.
pages cm
Includes bibliographical references and index.
ISBN 978-1-62846-087-2 (hardback) — ISBN 978-1-62846-088-9 (ebook)
1. Motion pictures—United States—History—20th century. 2. Motion picture industry—United States—History—20th century. 3. Motion pictures—Great Britain—History—20th century. 4. Motion picture industry—Great Britain—History—20th century. I. Title.
PN1993.5.U6S5535 2015
791.430973—dc23
2014042234

British Library Cataloging-in-Publication Data available

CONTENTS

ACKNOWLEDGMENTS VII

A NOTE ON STYLE IX

INTRODUCTION 3

CHAPTER ONE
British Pioneers in America and an American Pioneer in Britain 23

CHAPTER TWO
The O'Kalems 34

CHAPTER THREE
The American-Anglo-Irish 50

CHAPTER FOUR
American Silent Stars to the Rescue of British Cinema in the 1910s and 1920s 69

CHAPTER FIVE
American Cinematographers of the 1920s and 1930s in Britain 91

CHAPTER SIX
The 1930s and the Golden Age of the Hollywood Has-beens 105

CHAPTER SEVEN
Hollywood Producers and British Film Production in the 1930s 134

CHAPTER EIGHT
Diversity—Female Filmmakers, African American Performers, and Others 164

CHAPTER NINE
Technicolor Comes to Britain 183

CHAPTER TEN
A Golden Age for the British in Hollywood 197

CHAPTER ELEVEN
British Cinema at War 219

CHAPTER TWELVE
The Postwar Renaissance 246

CHAPTER THIRTEEN
The New International Cinema 263

NOTES 271

BIBLIOGRAPHY 285

INDEX 292

ACKNOWLEDGMENTS

PRIMARY RESEARCH WAS UNDERTAKEN AT THE MARGARET HERRICK Library of the Academy of Motion Picture Arts and Sciences. Additional research was conducted at the University of Southern California (including the Warner Bros. Archives and the Jack Warner Archives), and at the British Film Institute and the Cinema Museum (London), with special thanks at the last to Ron Grant and Martin Humphries.

Many thanks to Marty Kearns, who provided me with DVDs of vast numbers of British films, no matter how obscure. Thanks also to Stacey Behlmer, Stephen Bourne, Kevin Brownlow, Ned Comstock, Robert Gitt, Patricia King Hanson, Steve Hanson, Janice Healey, Eric Honnefer, Don Lee, Patrick Reynolds, Gary Rhodes, Lea Whittington, and most especially Tony Williams (for his critical commentary).

Through the years, I have had the good fortune to speak with many individuals who appear in this book, all of whom sadly are no longer with us: Edward Bernds, Mary Brian, Phil Brown, Davina Craig, Constance Cummings, Bebe Daniels, Walter Forde, Adelaide Hall, Joyce Howard, Alexander Knox, Laura La Plante, Anna Lee, Ben Lyon, Helena Millais, Joan Morgan, Anna Neagle, Ronald Neame, Esther Ralston, Charles Rosher, Harold Schuster, Phil Tannura, Bernard Vorhaus, Elisabeth Welch, Herbert Wilcox, and Fay Wray.

I appreciate the conversations that I have had on the subject of this book with Samantha Eggar, Marsha Hunt, and Norman Lloyd.

I would be remiss if I did not acknowledge the debt that anyone writing on British film history owes to historian Rachael Low. I was lucky to have known her back in the late 1960s, and I remember with fondness her generosity in inviting me to view films with her at the British Film Institute at 81 Dean Street while she was working on the 1930s volumes of her definitive history of British film. The British Film Institute is much changed, and those of us who knew it back then can only feel nostalgic for those good old days when the institute was located in the heart of Soho.

At the University Press of Mississippi, I am grateful, as always, to Leila Salisbury for her help, support, and friendship. I must also acknowledge a debt to Valerie Jones, Anne Stascavage, John Langston, Shane Gong, Clint Kimberling, and copy editor Peter Tonguette.

Chapter Two, "The O'Kalems," was originally published in a slightly different format in the Summer 2013 issue of *Post Script*.

All illustrations are from either the author's collection or from the Margaret Herrick Library of the Academy of Motion Picture Arts and Sciences.

A NOTE ON STYLE

UNLESS OTHERWISE INDICATED, THE DATES GIVEN FOR BRITISH FILMS discussed in the text are release dates in the United Kingdom. Where two film titles are given, the first is the original British release title and the second is the American release title. There are variant British and American spellings throughout, depending upon the context in which the word is used.

A SPECIAL RELATIONSHIP

INTRODUCTION

AT A SPEECH IN FULTON, MISSOURI, ON MARCH 5, 1946, WINSTON Churchill used a phrase (actually first used a year earlier) which has become a mantra for politicians ever since. There was, said Churchill, a fraternal association of the English-speaking peoples—"a special relationship." While there are many Britishers who look askance at American politics and wonder about the worth of such a relationship, it remains steadfast in at least one area of British and American society and culture: the film industry. Just as Britishers have flocked to Hollywood in search of work, international fame, and fortune, so have members of the Hollywood community come to the British Isles, bringing American filmmaking techniques to the Mother Country. The cross-ocean journeys, by sea and later by air, began during the silent era, when it mattered little if those involved were English-speaking, and continue through to the present. It has been maintained through two World Wars, driven by economic, political, and even patriotic factors. As Iris Barry, the British film critic and founder of the film department at New York's Museum of Modern Art, perceptively wrote in 1926, "films are no respecters of frontiers."[1] And neither are filmmakers both in front of and behind the camera.

The careers, and the lives, of British-born film people on both sides of the camera have been documented in a number of book-length studies. *A Special Relationship*, while acknowledging and documenting the career arc from Britain to America, concentrates more specifically on the journey in the opposite direction. It is a journey taken by a surprising number. Wim Wenders has written that "Americans have colonized our subconscious,"[2] but, in a way, in response to an earlier British colonization, American filmmakers have gone beyond our subconscious and colonized our very lands.

(If I may be allowed to digress, it is obvious that throughout most of its history the British cinema produced films that were generally considered shoddy and cheap. It has been suggested that the British character is responsible for the mediocrity of British films, but what does this say about books on British cinema by British authors? Is the character, or more precisely the dull academic background, of such writers responsible for so many passionless and tedious volumes, published with such painful regularity by the British Film Institute?)

While the cinema today is universal in scope, with films routinely shot outside of the financing country or countries and with technical and creative talent drawn from all over the world, the casual observer might assume that in the past Hollywood talent stayed in Hollywood and did not journey far from home. Films were produced in Hollywood with American financial control and American personnel. If a character had an accent then perhaps an individual with that accent—be it English, French, German, or Italian—from the appropriate country might be tempted to make the trip from Europe to the United States. Some might return home, while others, obviously influenced by financial reward and a pleasant climate, might decide to stay, perhaps gathering together with others of the same nationality to form a small colony, the most well-known of which was the British one. Occasionally, and it was quite occasionally, a Hollywood studio executive might recognize a unique ability in someone from the other side of the camera, a director, a writer, or a cinematographer, and they also would be lured to Hollywood with much the same incentive as the acting fraternity. Alfred Hitchcock is the prime example of a talented British director lured to Hollywood (in 1939 by producer David O. Selznick). Another, and inexplicable, example is mediocre, if indefatigable, British director Maurice Elvey, who was invited to Hollywood by William Fox to make five films there in 1924 and 1925.

In reality, the movement of Americans to the British Isles began almost as soon as the motion picture transformed from a novelty to an industry. The Kalem Company realized the appeal of location shooting abroad and sent a group of actors, a director, and a cinematographer to Ireland, then still part of Britain. By the 1920s, British producers were only too aware that if there was to be a market for their product in the United States, they would need to use popular Hollywood leading players as their stars.

At the same time, there was always a simmering animosity between the British and American film community, and it was not limited to production. It was not only Americans who routinely criticized the primitive quality of British filmmaking and of British studios. In 1926, British leading man Ralph Forbes was one of the stars of Paramount's *Beau Geste* in Hollywood, and he had much that was negative to say about his country's film industry:

> There, the film companies are short-handed. The troupes are small—only the director, sometimes one assistant, a cameraman, and the fewest possible number in the cast. Every one lends a hand. . . .
>
> Remember that the cinema in England is as yet scarcely an industry. The financiers over there are not interested in business possibilities, considering it too hazardous. You Americans, who dare and do, probably would chafe at such conservatism, but it is the backbone of our slow and methodical nation.[3]

Certainly, there was a strong patriotic attitude by the British towards their own films. What the rest of the world found lacking in them was regarded as their strength and *raison d'etre*. Reviewing a minor 1924 film, *The Lilac Sunbonnet*, the British fan magazine *Picturegoer* wrote that it was "quiet, but British and thoroughly wholesome." In the same publication, in August 1924, a fan describing herself as "Patriot" of Cricklewood wrote,

> I suppose my taste is peculiar for, although I hear *Broken Blossoms* and *Way Down East* described as masterpieces and absolutely true to life, they merely leave me with a bad taste in my mouth. I infinitely prefer our wholesome British films.

It is perhaps no exaggeration to claim, as one British screenwriter did in 1916, that the impact of Britain's national life is upon each film.[4]

There was even a British Empire Film Institute, founded in March 1926, with a distinguished patronage and the aim to encourage and officially recognize native screen work on merit. Even as an Englishman, I must confess that the institute must have been hard pressed to meet its goal.

Did English filmmakers really understand how mediocre their work was compared to much that was coming out of America? In 1922, the most famous of pioneering British directors, Cecil Hepworth, whose films might be beautiful to look at but lack dramatic impact and much approaching contemporary film technique, wrote an essay for an American trade paper. He had the audacity to complain of "unnecessary close-ups," which "any fool could make . . . by the hundred." He pointed out that he avoided cuts in his own production, much preferring "a short 'fade,' a blend from one scene to the next."[5]

British exhibitors rallied in 1919 to fight a potential American takeover of British theatres, led by Famous Players-Lasky with financial backing from William Randolph Hearst. There was appropriate outrage at Hearst's pro-German leanings during World War I. "They claim British films are not equal to American. That is a lie," announced one exhibitor who was obviously very out of touch with reality.[6]

In America, *Photoplay* editor James R. Quirk was seeing a conspiracy by British critics to pan American films, notably MGM's *The Big Parade*, which was viewed in Britain as propaganda to the effect that America won World War I. "English picture criticism is on a par with English pictures," Quirk wrote in 1926.

> They just do not know how to make pictures. And they just won't learn. . . .
>
> We are not singing "The Star Spangled Banner" when we put down our money at the box office. And we may not know the German national anthem when we go to see *Variety* and *The Last Laugh*. But we do know a good picture from a bad one. . . .
>
> Take a little bicarbonate of soda, you English critics. Your own folks are giving you the laugh and making *The Big Parade* a great success right under your noses.[7]

Obviously in agreement with James R. Quirk was the editor of the intellectual, Swiss-based publication *Close Up*, who editorialized in its first issue,

> We know that an announcement "British film" outside a movie theatre will chill the hardiest away from its door. . . . Turn to films and you get muck.[8]

With the coming of sound, Hollywood found much that was pleasing with the English accent; producer Sam Goldwyn, who had Englishman Ronald Colman under contract and had just signed London stage star Evelyn Laye, declared that female audiences "prefer the English accent to any other."[9] A group of Hollywood players, including Genevieve Tobin, Edward Everett Horton, Adolphe Menjou, and Hedda Hopper (an unlikely choice in view of her birthplace of Altoona, Pennsylvania), were identified as "Those English Americans."[10] Hedda Hopper would see her position as a leading Hollywood gossip columnist threatened by an Englishwoman, Sheilah Graham, who left her native land to pursue a career first as an actress (like Hedda) and later a writer, and whose column appeared in more than 150 newspapers. In the 1930s, one-time major Hollywood names whose careers had come to a virtual standstill with the coming of sound made the journey to the United Kingdom and to British films with the realization that while the films might not be commensurate with their talent, there was money to continue to be made and there was a free vacation, which might even be lengthened if a suitable billing could be found for them on the stages of the British music halls or even in one of London's West End theatres.

It is a safe assumption that in the 1930s, at least, there were more Americans working in the British film industry than there were British workers in Hollywood. As director Anthony Asquith pointed out, "At one time it could be said with truth that Britain was a branch of Hollywood, and with many British producers and directors making 'quota quickies' for Hollywood companies and scores of Americans working on the production side of our industry, the inevitable had come."[11]

At least one American during that decade, Douglas Fairbanks, Jr., had a more positive attitude towards the notion of Americans in Britain:

> What they are trying to do is specialize. They are making mistakes and they know it. They say, "We want to learn. Send over your technicians and your people and if we get any good ideas developed we will send them over there. Let's get together and make pictures. That is what is important. The cinema, this film medium which has developed out of the century which is so grand—let's get together and build it up."[12]

British commentators were often highly critical of British film production in the 1930s, generally with good reason. Cedric Belfrage, who spent time observing the American film industry as a journalist, asked,

> One gets to wondering if the English are racially fitted for movie-making as one observes how, with a mere extra chew on a rare cigar, the magnates of Hollywood issue orders for expenditure on a single set greater than that spent on the whole on an average English production.[13]

Critic and historian Paul Rotha wrote in 1949 that "the British film lacks honest conception. It has no other aim than that of the imitation of the cinema of other countries."[14] The most obvious of such countries was the United States of America.

Journalist Josie Lederer described the British public as "blinder than a bat" in its inability to spot stars, such as George K. Arthur, Clive Brook, Walter Butler, Ronald Colman, Ralph Forbes, and Victor McLaglen, who were lost to the United States.[15]

The negative image of the British cinema remained in the new millennium. In the November 16, 2001, issue of the *Guardian*, Andy Beckett wrote,

> As long ago as the mid-1960s, François Truffaut and Satyajit Ray and Pauline Kael all decided, respectively, there was a certain incompatability between the terms "cinema" and "Britain," that the British were not "temperamentally equipped to make the best use of the movie camera," and that "English films have always been a sad joke."

Generally, visitors from Hollywood in the 1930s found production methods at British studios to be somewhat unprofessional. In particular, the compulsory tea breaks (enforced by British unions with a severity unmatched by their American counterparts) were a curious anomaly. "Making a film in England was an innovation," wrote Frank Capra's legendary cinematographer Joseph Walker. "Four o'clock each afternoon work halted abruptly, and did not resume 'til cast and crew had had their spot of tea. This costly delay every afternoon infuriated [Columbia studio head] Harry Cohn. 'It's the English temperament,' Leslie Howard explained to him, 'and even you can't change it.'"[16] There were some American visitors who reveled in the obsession with tea breaks; for example, actor Gregory Ratoff in 1934 would host "little tea parties" on the set of *Forbidden Territory*.[17] The tea break was also unfortunately why the British film industry could never compete with that of America; as one commentator had it, you could not make sixty films a year and stop for tea.

British character comedian Sydney Howard tried to explain the tea break to American visitors:

> Whatever may be suggested to the contrary, I can tell you from experience that film work is very fatiguing. There are many times during production when a cup of tea does me all the good in the world. I grudge no man his whisky or beer, and all I ask in return is to be allowed my tea whenever I want it. I have often watched a crowd scene late in the afternoon just before a tea interval. When I have gone back after the interval they were different people, vivacious where they had been flagging. . . . But the greatest value of tea in a studio lies in the sociability it inspires. Visitors from Hollywood have often told me there is a genuinely friendly atmosphere in the British studios than in the American ones. If so, absurd as it may sound, I attribute the improvement largely to tea.[18]

As actress Anna Lee once commented, in comparing her British and American careers, "I always enjoyed stopping for tea."[19]

Just as personal economics played a part in Hollywood's diaspora to Britain in the 1930s, so it was corporate economics that played a seminal role in Hollywood's interest in filmmaking in Britain in the 1940s. The profits that Hollywood companies had earned during the war years were unavailable for transfer to the United States from Britain, and so Hollywood came to Britain to film and to utilize those frozen assets. In the 1950s, politics played a crucial role in the migration of a select few from Hollywood to Britain. As America embarked on an enhanced witch hunt against those it determined might have pro-Communist leanings, so did the likes of Larry Adler, Phil Brown, Alexander Knox, Joseph Losey, Fred Zinnemann, Carl Foreman, and others find a happy and profitable refuge in the United Kingdom. There they were initially welcomed by liberal-leaning American actress Constance Cummings and her British writer/Labor politician husband Benn Levy.

By the 1960s, the movement backwards and forwards between Hollywood and the United Kingdom had become routine, with the lines blurred as to both financial investment in a production and that production's country of origin. It was also an era in which a career in one country might become totally variant in the other. Joyce Howard, for example, had been a leading lady in British films of the 1930s and 1940s, but when she moved to the United States in the 1960s, she took work as an executive assistant at Paramount. Even the most peculiarly British of films, *Follow That Camel* (1967), released in the US as *Carry On in the Legion*, starred American Phil Silvers, best known to audiences in Britain for the *Sgt. Bilko* television series. Producer Peter Rogers paid Silvers 30,000 pounds, the largest salary ever paid to a player in the *Carry On* series at that time, with the idea that the actor's presence would guarantee an American audience—it did not. Similarly, a decade earlier, in 1952, aging Hungarian-born Bela Lugosi had been brought over to play opposite Arthur Lucan's comic character Old Mother Riley in *Mother Riley Meets the Vampire*. Two aging performers, both past their prime, was a sure sign of a flop, coupled with Lugosi's inability to play comedy. It had made far more sense to have Lugosi appear in *The Mystery of the Mary Celeste* (1935), released in the US as *The Phantom Ship*, in which his ominous presence added appropriate sinister gravitas to the storyline.

Oddly, the most obvious difference between the British in Hollywood and American filmmakers in Britain is that the latter did not immediately decide to create a colony in their new land. Once the British started congregating in Los Angeles, they felt the need to identify themselves as "different" from their American hosts. They established a British colony, a Hollywood Raj, as it has been called, where afternoon tea was served and where cricket was the sport of choice. Today, there is a corner of a foreign Southern California field that is forever England, and that is Santa Monica.

A seaside community to the immediate west of Los Angeles, it is still the home of English tearooms and English pubs, and aging Britishers, dressed in white, play bowls on a carefully manicured public lawn. Perhaps what the British have brought to Santa Monica, for which they should be praised, is a liberality seldom found in other American communities. It is not without good reason that the city is popularly known as the People's Republic of Santa Monica. Yet, for all its determined Britishness (and the Irish, Scottish, and Welsh are also well represented here), and the fact that Cary Grant had a beach house there in the 1930s which he shared with Randolph Scott, and Stan Laurel retired there, Santa Monica was not always the center of British life in Southern California.

At their height in the 1930s, the British filmmaking community was scattered, with residences in Bel Air, Beverly Hills, Pacific Palisades, and West Los Angeles. Sir C. Aubrey Smith had a home at the top of Coldwater Canyon in Beverly Hills. Charles Laughton and Elsa Lanchester enjoyed an ocean view from the top of a cliff slightly north of Santa Monica; they also had the experience of their home gradually facing extinction as the cliff slowly eroded away. Ronald Colman and his wife, Benita Hume, also enjoyed an ocean view from their mansion in Pacific Palisades.

When their house disappeared into the ocean, Laughton and Lanchester moved to a home overlooking Wattles Park in Hollywood. A few years earlier, prior to moving to Beverly Hills, Charlie Chaplin had also been a Hollywood resident. His brother, Syd, occupied a substantial mansion next to the Chaplin Studios in Hollywood, built beginning in 1917 in the form of a group of English-style cottages. Prominent British visitors to Los Angeles, including Winston Churchill and Lord Louis Mountbatten, could be assured of a visit to the studios.

From 1970 onwards, actress Anna Lee ruled over a home in the foothills of West Hollywood, very close to the George Cukor estate, her residence identified by a Union Jack waving in the breeze and a banner on her roof on St. Patrick's Day, proclaiming, "Death to the I.R.A."

"I hate the I.R.A.," she told me.

> I used to get into a lot of trouble. You see the I.R.A. has a branch over here called Friends of the Irish. And they have meetings in a pub here, and any

> time they had a chance, they would picket. I used to go out and strike a hammer at the picket lines. I had expressed my feelings, particularly after [Lord Louis] Mountbatten had been killed. I was quite voluble. One day, right after that I attended a memorial service, and I came out and a Union Jack on my car had been ripped off. Then, a few days later, they congregated outside my house in a van. They smeared the Union Jack I had on the front door with red paint and wrote, "Death." I was really worried about them coming up and planting a bomb or something, so I ceased to be quite so voluble about it.

As to how her feelings might go down with professional Irishman John Ford, for whom she made a couple of films and perhaps had an affair, she told me,

> I got in one or two body blows, and then he said, "You can't judge all the Irish alike." I avoided it as much as possible, because he did get very incensed about it. I think John Ford really thought of the Irish as being naughty children. I cannot understand them [the British authorities]. When they finally get these bastards, why don't they shoot them?[20]

Critic John Russell Taylor has pointed out that "Los Angeles has always been a city of strangers."[21] And so, émigrés, almost of a necessity, required a hub around which to gather. The German community in Hollywood congregated around actress Salka Viertel, who had come to America with her husband, Berthold, in 1927. The German émigrés came to Hollywood of political necessity, with the rise of the Nazis in their native land. The British émigrés came in search of fame and fortune, and only displayed any political spirit when Britain declared war on Germany in 1939 and C. Aubrey Smith virtually ordered all eligible young Englishmen to return to their native land and serve their country. David Niven recalled that the "hard core" of the British colony would take tea on Sundays at the homes of either Edinburgh-born Ernest Torrance and his wife or London-born C. Aubrey Smith and his wife. Smith's home was called "The Round Corner," with three cricket stumps and a bat and ball on the roof serving as a weather vane. Some Britishers in Hollywood were "fiercely independent" of the group, and their number included Nigel Bruce, Ronald Colman, Reginald Gardiner, and Basil Rathbone.[22] Nigel Bruce was always very much aware that his first name was unusual in the United States, and would introduce himself to colleagues with the words, "It's Nigel, not 'Niggle.'"[23]

In 1936, the *Christian Science Monitor* offered a fascinating glimpse of the British community in all its determination to remain steadfastly British in an alien environment:

> British customs notoriously prevail among the British colony. Speaking a language which at least approximates that of the Americans, they maintain a stricter aloofness than do most other nationalities, are harder to absorb, even after years. Several English cake shops exist and cater almost exclusively to English trade. Once a year, on New Year's Eve, the principal members of the British colony gather at a Hollywood café to hear the bells of Big Ben ring out over the radio.[24]

So widespread was the British Empire in Los Angeles that its cricket club, founded in 1932 by C. Aubrey Smith, was named the Hollywood Cricket Club and its playing field was located in Griffith Park, Burbank. It was one of some twenty-two cricket clubs to be found in the Los Angeles area in the mid-1930s; indeed, as one commentator points out, "English games, such as rugby and cricket, are becoming common sights on vacant fields."[25] Also to be seen playing cricket with Smith in the 1930s were Nigel Bruce, Boris Karloff, H. B. Warner, and P. G. Wodehouse, while enthusiastic spectators—or as enthusiastic as anyone can get watching a cricket match—included Ronald Colman, Leslie Howard, David Niven, and Merle Oberon. British cinemagoers took their cricket very seriously as displayed on screen. Raffles, the gentleman safecracker, as created by E. W. Hornung, was also something of cricketer, and when, in 1930, for producer Samuel Goldwyn, Ronald Colman introduced the character to the talkies with *Raffles*, there was a brief scene of the actor playing cricket. The scene is described in mind-numbing detail in the fan magazine *Film Weekly*: "Lord Melrose takes middle-and-leg. Raffles, played by Ronald Colman, who looks eleven inches in every twelve a cricketer, puts down a soft one and the old aristocrat gets a run, much to his delight. The next ball, faster and trickier although not exactly a Grimmett googly, gets the last man. Village green cricket this, soft ones to the old men and good stuff for the players."[26] *Film Weekly* went on to praise Hollywood for its verisimilitude but complained that the extras watching the match should have been told not to deliver singularly inappropriate audio encouragement.

As British historian Jeffrey Richards has pointed out, no one represents more the image and spirit of the British Empire on screen than C. Aubrey Smith, who was knighted in 1944 for his services to the Empire performed in

The Hollywood Cricket Club in 1935, with Errol Flynn and Nigel Bruce, front row left, and C. Aubrey Smith, with pipe and blazer, in center of front row.

the studios of Hollywood. He has impersonated virtually the entire British upper class, including two prime ministers, peers, admirals, generals, many officers of the Empire in India, a chief constable, the Lord Chief Justice, and the Chancellor of Oxford University.[27] As a fellow British actor, Sir Cedric Hardwicke, commented, Smith's "craggy manner somehow suggested that he had just completed a ceremonial tour of all four corners of Queen Victoria's Empire."[28] Sir C. Aubrey Smith died, appropriately on a 1947 visit to England, to where he had returned to appear in Alexander Korda's production of *An Ideal Husband* and to watch cricket.

Screenwriter and later producer Charles Brackett records in his diary a visit to a British War Relief Party at Smith's home on top of Coldwater Canyon in Beverly Hills on May 25, 1941:

> It was a large party filled with professional and non-professional character parts, and it was a gravely troubled party—none of the British arrogance so irritating in times past, which would be so welcome now. I had a feeling that it was an odd and touching way to see an Empire shake, if not crumble, at a garden party in Hollywood.

British sexpot Diana Dors, who had a brief American career in the 1960s, demonstrates the correct stance for the wicket keeper in cricket.

Aside from cricket, American filmmakers returning from Britain also introduced darts to their fellow countrymen. It was a popular pastime for Americans working in Britain and, presumably, enjoying the atmosphere in British pubs. While working on the set of *Jericho* at Pinewood in 1937, actor Wallace Ford "succumbed to an overwhelming passion"[29] for the game, reportedly taking back a score of dart boards for friends in Hollywood.[30]

Soccer, or as the rest of the world excluding the US knows it, football[31] does not seem to have had appeal to the British colony. Perhaps it is too working class. Yet as the intellectual film journal *Close Up* editorialized in 1927,

> REALLY the Englishman can only be roused to enthusiasm on the football field. A cup final will evoke tens of thousands of whooping maniacs. One doesn't mind that, but in the face of it one does ask WHY attempt art.[32]

There were a couple of British films of the 1930s devoted to the subject, and both featured the London football club of Arsenal: Anthony Asquith's *The Lucky Number* (1933) and Thorold Dickinson's *The Arsenal Stadium Mystery* (1939). *Variety* (June 6, 1933) reviewed the latter, and found it "not up to the standard of America," but hazarded that "some day young Anthony Asquith will do a picture of magnitude. He has come near it once or twice, but apparently needs Hollywood training."

There were working-class characters in early Hollywood, not only Charlie Chaplin and Stan Laurel, but also forgotten names with British music-hall backgrounds, such as William Austin, Jimmy Aubrey, Eric Campbell, and Dick Henderson. The latter's son of the same name made a swift transformation from working-class background to the upper classes, thanks to his father's sending him to private schools in the US and his being cast as the son of Clive Brook and Diana Wynyard in *Cavalcade* (1933).[33] Luckily for young Henderson, London-born Freddie Bartholomew had yet to immigrate to the United States, where he became known for his upper-class child roles, such as *Little Lord Fauntleroy* (1936). Aside from Henderson, the other representatives of the working class found work with Chaplin, who served, at least in the early years, as almost a father figure to a particular group of British émigrés.

The first representative of the British aristocracy to find meaningful employment in Hollywood—there may have been minor members of the aristocracy working as extras during the same period—was Sir Herbert Beerbohm Tree. One of the great actor-managers of British theatre, Sir Herbert was as much a formidable personality as a great actor, as was evident from his foray into film production with *Macbeth*, shot in 1915 and released the following year. The production company was Fine Arts, whose supervising producer was D. W. Griffith, someone easily swayed by anything connected to the British aristocracy, even a somewhat over-the-hill actor. *Macbeth* was received without enthusiasm on both its American and British release, with *Variety* (June 9, 1916) sarcastically noting that "it is safe to assume that Shakespeare on the screen will never have any great vogue." Tree's contract required that Fine Arts continue his employment, and so he was miscast as a US senator in another 1916 production, *The Old Folks at Home*. The film was little more successful than *Macbeth*, and supposedly, in

Dame May Whitty, with husband Ben Webster, firmly in control of British society in Hollywood.

an effort to force the knight to cancel his contract, Fine Arts informed him that his next production would require his appearance in blackface. Tree hastily left for London, where he died the following year.

Another British theatrical knight, Sir Johnston Forbes Robertson, came to America in 1917, but, like his predecessor, he was not well received in his first and only film appearance.

The British colony in Hollywood, as might be expected, adopted a class system. At its head was Dame May Whitty, who, in June 1942, reminded gossip columnist Louella Parsons that despite Merle Oberon's recent elevation to Lady Korda, it was she who was the ranking Englishwoman in the community. Whitty had been made a Dame Commander of the British Empire in 1918 in recognition of her war work, and was the first actress to be so recognized. Merle Oberon gained her title merely through her marriage to Sir Alexander Korda, honored in 1942 for his war work.

There will always be an England, and there will always be the British class system—even in Hollywood. That same class system, curiously, did not infect the British film industry. There was little snobbery evident between star and technician, in part perhaps because British leading men and women received little recompense for their film work and would, in all probability, be found sharing a drink at the local pub after day's end with their fellow workers. Hollywood visitors to Britain might expect to be treated as stars, but, if so, the British studio fraternity did not oblige. Just as British studios in the 1930s turned out pseudo-American films, which ultimately appealed neither to British nor American audiences, so did they adopt the American notion of a classless society, an equally false concept.

EVERYTHING STOPS FOR TEA

Boris Karloff relaxes while filming *Frankenstein* (1931).

A tea break, captioned in the pages of Britain's *Daily Mail* in October 1933: "At Elstree, where the fight to make British films universally supreme is being fought and won. A break for tea."

The cast and crew of *Sunset in Vienna/Suicide Legion* (1937) take a tea break.

Teatime on location for Merle Oberon and director Tim Whelan, filming *The Divorce of Lady X* (1938).

Robert Donat as William Friese-Greene tells Laurence Olivier as Police Constable 94-B of his invention: "I've only just this minute done it. And there he is, almost as if he were alive."

CHAPTER ONE

British Pioneers in America and an American Pioneer in Britain

DESPITE THE ARGUMENTS PUT FORWARD FOR BIRT ACRES, WORDSWORTH Donisthorpe, Louis Aimé Augustin Le Prince, or William Friese-Greene (celebrated in the personage of Robert Donat in the 1951 biographical film *The Magic Box*), Britain does not have a legitimate claim to the invention of the cinema. (*Pace*, I say to those academics, obsessed with the minutiae and triviality of the origins of the motion picture, all of whom will disagree with me.) However, the British can take substantial credit for America's assertion to have invented the motion picture thanks to two individuals, Eadweard Muybridge and W. K. L. Dickson. Indeed, the British might go even further and point out that a countryman was responsible for the invention of the material that gave the cinema its very *raison d'être*, celluloid—invented as "Parkesine" by Alexander Parkes, working in Birmingham, England, in 1855. To Parkes goes the credit but it was an American company, the Celluloid Manufacturing Company of Albany, New York, which gave the new substance the name by which it is commonly known.

Almost on a par with Alexander Parkes's work, and similarly ignored is the contribution of two brothers from Leicester, Thomas and William Taylor, who first experimented with camera lenses in the 1860s, and with a partner, W. S. H. Hobson, formed Taylor, Taylor & Hobson, Ltd. In the 1890s, H. Dennis Taylor (no relation) of T. Cooke & Sons of York brought to the Taylors' attention his Cooke triplet lens (patented in 1893), which was developed into the finest lens available. In the early 1930s, Arthur Warmisham, who had joined the company in 1911, developed a special lens for use with Technicolor cameras. By 1935, Metro-Goldwyn-Mayer reported that all of its productions were shot with Taylor-Hobson Cooke lenses, and so it was throughout the industry throughout the world, with the company claiming in 1939 that 80 percent of all lenses used at film studios were produced by them. The company has changed names and ownership through the years, and in 2013, at the eighty-fifth presentation, as Cooke Optics, Ltd., it was awarded an award of merit from the Academy of Motion Picture Arts and Sciences "for their continuing innovation in the design, development and manufacture of advanced camera lenses that have helped define the look of motion pictures over the last century."

First in the chronology of pioneers is Eadweard Muybridge (1830–1904), born with the very English last name of Muggeridge, in the Surrey town of Kingston upon Thames. Muybridge was very much the eccentric Englishman, sporting a long white beard and a broad-brimmed hat, and must have appeared so to Americans once he had immigrated here in 1851. He first gained the attention of the press in 1872, when he was sponsored by Central Pacific Railroad president Leland Stanford in an effort to photograph a trotting horse and prove that it might have all four hooves off the ground at the same time, thus winning a wager for Stanford. This was successfully done, if in somewhat primitive fashion. Three years later, Muybridge gained even more prominent attention when he murdered his wife after discovering she was pregnant by another man. He was acquitted by a jury on the grounds of justifiable homicide. After making the wise decision to take an extended trip to South America, Muybridge returned to the United States, and in 1877 he was again working under Stanford's sponsorship, using a series of cameras to show animal and human "locomotion." Using his Zoopraxiniscope projector, Muybridge began to show his photographs in front of a wide audience, attracted no doubt by the fact that, aside from the animals, Muybridge photographed nude or semi-nude female and male students from the University of Pennsylvania performing various acts which, aside from the lack of clothing, might be described as quite innocent. Many of these photographs, particularly those of naked young men wrestling together in a quite amused, not to mention very intimate, fashion can today only be considered homoerotic. Never one to shun the limelight, Muybridge was quite happy to strip down and photograph himself in all his substantial naked glory; with his penis proudly flopping, he walks, ascends steps, and uses a shovel and a pick in front of his cameras. Experiments involving betting, nudity, and sexual crime—on the whole one gets the impression that Eadweard Muybridge must have been a fun character to know. Certainly, Muybridge does not in any way exemplify the stereotypically reserved, quiet, and well-behaved Englishman.

William Kennedy Laurie Dickson.

Muybridge returned to his native land in 1894, publishing two famous volumes, *Animals in Motion* (1899) and the far more titillating *The Human Figure in Motion* (1901). His work is generally considered a precursor to the invention of the motion picture as we know it today.

Compared to Muybridge, William Kennedy Laurie Dickson (1860–1935) is not an entertaining personality, and yet his role is crucial in the invention of the motion picture. His parents were British, but Dickson was born in France, for which we will forgive him. He immigrated to the United States in 1879 and began working for Thomas Edison in 1883. Five years later, under Edison's vague supervision, Dickson became involved in the motion picture. He designed the famous Black Maria studio in 1893, followed by the Kinetoscope, introduced to the world the following year. Unfortunately for Dickson, his ego allowed him to usurp Edison's power and influence and he found himself pushed out of the organization. He subsequently began to work for others, most notably the American Mutoscope and Biograph Company. In 1897, Dickson came to London and set up the British Mutoscope and Biograph Company, one of the largest British production companies until 1907, and the first to film a Shakespearian play: four scenes from *King John*, starring Sir Herbert Beerbohm Tree, in 1899. Dickson's last major achievement was to journey to South Africa in 1899 and shoot what might be described as newsreels of the Boer War, work which he describes in his 1901 book, *The Biograph in Battle: Its Story in the South African War*. It is not Dickson's only published work; with his sister, Antonia, he had produced two earlier volumes, *The Life and Inventions of Thomas Alva Edison* (1894) and *History of the Kinetograph, Kinetoscope and Kinetophonograph* (1895).

Dickson's contributions to Edison's "invention" of the motion picture are still being discussed and analyzed by academics. Whatever the outcome, certainly he is deserving of a prominent place as the only Britisher directly involved in making the motion picture a reality.

Apropos the French connection, it is perhaps worthy of record that Alice Guy, the first female filmmaker and, equally, a pioneering filmmaker alongside her employer, Léon Gaumont, married—in 1907—the British-born Herbert Blaché-Bolton. He took his wife to the United States, dropped the "Bolton" from his name, and ran Gaumont's US operation, while his wife founded the Solax Company. Herbert Blaché directed a number of prominent American features during the silent era, including the Nazimova vehicles, *The Brat* (1919) and *Stronger Than Death* (1920), Buster Keaton's *The Saphead* (1920), and Ethel Barrymore's *The Divorcée* (1919). He continued as a director through 1929.

There has never been acknowledgment that Britain was there at the birth of film exhibition in the United States. The first public showing of films before a paying audience took place on April 24, 1896, at Koster and Bial's Music Hall in New York, and one of the "actualities" presented was *Rough Sea at Dover*, the work of pioneering British cinematographer Birt Acres. The piece is less than a minute in length and had already been screened in London, at the Royal Photographic Society, in January 1896. Thus, at its beginning, film was truly not only an international language but a transatlantic language.

While none of the major studios from Hollywood's so-called "golden era" can claim a British connection in their creation, one of the most important

J. Stuart Blackton (left) and Albert E. Smith, co-founders of the Vitagraph Company of America.

of the earliest pioneering American film companies was founded not by one, but by two Englishmen. The organization was the Vitagraph Company of America, and its founders were J. Stuart Blackton and Albert E. Smith. Both men were farsighted and intelligent, each in his own way. Blackton was obviously the creative genius behind the partnership, whereas Smith was the businessman. One was a dreamer, whose life was illustrative of his mindset; the other had his feet firmly planted on the ground and, equally, proved until his death that he knew the importance of money over much else. James Stuart Blackton was born in Sheffield on January 4, 1875, and was brought at the age of ten to the United States by his parents. In later years, he was to dismiss his humble working-class background and claim to have been educated at Eton. (In reality, actor John Loder would later point out that he was the only Englishman working in Hollywood who could legitimately claim to be an old Etonian.) Albert Edward Smith was born in the Kentish town of Faversham on June 4, 1875, the son of a market gardener. His entire family immigrated to the United States some thirteen years later.

The two men may perhaps have met while apprenticed to a New York carpenter. Whatever the circumstances of their meeting, both had ambitions to be entertainers. A third Englishman, Ronald A. Reader, convinced the two to join with him in forming an act which featured Smith's magic tricks and Blackton's expertise as a cartoonist; it was called The Royal Entertainers. The act was not a success, but the crafts of magic and cartooning led to Smith and Blackton, initially minus Reader, acquiring a camera/projector from Thomas Edison and forming their own production company in the spring of 1897.[1]

Vitagraph, like its fellow pioneering film companies, had humble beginnings, but Smith and Blackton persevered, and their first "major" success owes its origins not only to the couple's backgrounds as entertainers, but also their desire to show their American patriotism. Using primitive miniatures, a water tank, and smoke provided by Blackton's cigar, they made *The Battle of Manila Bay* in May 1898, a celebration of Admiral Dewey's defeat of the Spanish fleet in the Philippines. Blackton became one of the screen's first recognizable characters, portraying "The Happy Hooligan" in a series of short subjects beginning in 1900. Trick films and animated subjects followed. A major studio was opened in the Flatbush area of Brooklyn in 1906, a Paris office to handle European distribution in 1908, and a Hollywood studio in the mid-1910s (which still survives today under the ownership of ABC Television). Blackton left the company in 1917, but it continued in operation through 1925, when it was acquired by Warner Bros.

Vitagraph has many British links. Two of its first stars, Florence Turner and John Bunny made films in England, as did J. Stuart Blackton. In its early years, Vitagraph made good use of Shakespearian (and public-domain) plays as the bases for many of its early one-reel productions. One of the company's last major films, released in 1921, was *Black Beauty*, based on the classic British novel by Anna Sewell, and starring Smith's wife, Jean Paige. Among those associated with Vitagraph, and British-born, are John Bunny's leading lady, Flora Finch, plump character actress Kate Price (born in Ireland), pioneering actor William Shea, and director Wilfred North.

The most important of links between Vitagraph and Britain is the company's production in 1915 of the feature-length *The Battle Cry of Peace*, which argued against American isolationism and its entry on the side of Britain into World War I. The production, now "lost," was aggressive in its attack on American pacifists and isolationists and depicts the country's invasion by an army which appears suspiciously Germanic in appearance and attire. Based on Hudson's Maxim's book, *Defenseless America*, the film was supported by Theodore Roosevelt, Cornelius Vanderbilt, and Admiral Dewey. There were claims that *The Battle Cry of Peace* had been at the least influenced and possibly financed by the British Embassy in Washington, D.C., and to counter some of the accusations of its pro-British stance, Blackton announced concomitant with the film's premiere that he had become an American citizen. As his daughter Marian recalled,

> Born an Englishman, imbued with the love of country so stubbornly characteristic of the British, my father was nevertheless profoundly grateful for the blessings of a way of life that made possible his fabulous leap from poverty to riches. Duly, if a shade belatedly, he embraced United States citizenship.[2]

A second Vitagraph production, *Womanhood, the Glory of a Nation*, released in the spring of 1917, carried much the same message. Blackton completed his pro-British trilogy, if such it may be described, with *Whom the Gods Destroy* (1918), a thinly veiled account of the Easter Rebellion in Ireland and the hanging of Irish patriot, Sir Roger Casement. While *Whom the Gods Destroy* (also no longer extant) might appear on the surface to be pro-Irish, one trade paper, *Exhibitor's Trade Review* (December 16, 1916), explained, "Vitagraph has chosen a neutral path in presenting this story by taking the attitude that while the freedom of Ireland from English sovereignty might be a good thing, it is best accomplished by other means than violence at a time when Britain is facing a great crisis."

The production of these three films was very much Blackton's project, and after he had left the company, Albert E. Smith explained to *Motography* (September 1, 1917),

> Vitagraph, I think, has partially done its duty toward awakening the nation to a sense of its obligation to itself and civilization. Now, I feel, the policy of Vitagraph and of every motion picture manufacturer should be to make pictures than will take the minds of the people off the war and their troubles, make them laugh, and in that way, make them happy. That is to be our policy.

J. Stuart Blackton was married multiple times and also had his share of mistresses. By the mid-1910s, he owned a large mansion in Brooklyn, an estate in fashionable Oyster Bay, with Teddy Roosevelt and Louis Tiffany as his neighbors, and promoted himself as a commodore of the Atlantic Yacht Club. In 1931, he filed for bankruptcy, and ten years later, either by accident or design, he was hit by a car and died within a couple of days in Los Angeles. Blackton was in many regards a sentimental fool, but Smith had little time for personal feeling. He was a businessman who presided over Vitagraph until its sale to Warner Bros., and had no compunction in firing longtime employees when they had ceased to be saleable commodities. After his "retirement" from Vitagraph, he became a successful real estate investor, owning, among other properties, the Chateau Marmont in West Hollywood.

Of the early and original American film producing entities, only one, Lubin, was founded by a Jewish entrepreneur. The remainder was all Gentile-owned and operated, and, perhaps, nothing could be more Aryan than Vitagraph with its two English founders, who, like their colleagues, were decidedly anti-Semitic and resentful of the Jewish element that by the mid-1910s was quickly taking over the industry.

It was another Englishman to whom credit is due for establishing the film industry on a permanent footing in Hollywood, and that is David Horsley, who was born in the coal mining village of West Stanley in the county of Durham on March 11, 1873. In 1888, Horsley lost his left arm as a result of being hit by a locomotive. That same year, his family immigrated to America, and seven years later, Horsley had his first taste of show business—on a very plebeian level—as the operator of a pool parlor in Bayonne, New Jersey. In 1907, he formed a partnership with scenic artist Charles Gorman, and the two set up the Centaur Film Company, also in Bayonne, with its first production being the one-reel short, *The Cowboy's Escape*, released on September 15, 1908. Gorman sold his share to Horsley in 1910, and the latter reorganized the company in partnership with his brother William, and established a second producing entity, Nestor. (Greek mythology was obviously a strong influence in the Horsley household.) Despite opposition from the Thomas Edison-based Motion Picture Patents group, to which the Horsleys did not belong, Centaur and Nestor expanded their operations, taking on Al Christie to produce comedies and building up a stock company that included three future cowboy stars Tom Mix, Hoot Gibson, and Art Accord.

In search of sunshine and year-round filming, Horsley initially tried Florida, but in 1911, the company decided to move to Hollywood. Horsley and Christie acquired land at the corner of Sunset Boulevard and Gower Street, and Hollywood's first permanent studio was opened.[3] Its first Hollywood production was *The Best Man Wins*, released on October 27, 1911, and photographed by Charles Rosher (who was later to work on films in England). Within two years, Horsley had given up ownership of the company and sold it to Carl Laemmle and the Universal interests. David Horsley continued in the entertainment industry with a relative lack of success and died on February 23, 1933. Brother William was put in charge of the building of the new Universal Studios in the San Fernando Valley, and established the William Horsley Film Laboratories in Hollywood, which later became Hollywood Film Enterprises. He died in 1957. Britain's Horsley brothers are forgotten, but, as Paul Mandell has written,

> the fact remains that on a lousy, gray day in 1911, a man with one arm burned his bridges behind him, gambled every buck he could raise, put a throng of thirty-nine on a train west, and single-handedly turned Hollywood into "the movies."[4]

In 1912, Horsley hired a cinematographer named William C. "Daddy" Paley. Lincolnshire-born Paley had built a projector as early as 1897, and the following year, he filmed a version of the *Passion Play* in New York. Also in 1898, Paley was hired as a cameraman by Edison, filming the US invasion of Cuba and gaining the title of "the Kinetoscope Man."

It may well be argued that the films of these Britishers working in the United States have been preserved thanks to the pioneering efforts of another Britisher, Iris Barry. Born in the English industrial city of Birmingham in 1895, Barry was a film critic for the British publications, the *Spectator* and the *Daily Mail*, before immigrating to the United States in 1930. Here, in 1935, she founded the Film Department of New York's Museum of Modern Art, the first film archive in the United States and one of the first in the world.

If Blackton and Smith were of importance to the American film industry, then of equal if not more importance was American Charles Urban to a burgeoning British film industry. Indeed, there are many British film historians who would claim that Charles Urban was the most significant figure in the early British film industry.

Born in Ohio, Charles Urban was involved in the film industry as early as 1894, when he managed a kinetoscope parlor in Detroit. In 1897, he joined the American company, Maguire & Baucus, as its film manager, and he was sent to London to manage the office there on what was described as a three-month trial trip. It was Maguire & Baucus that had opened Britain's first kinetoscope parlor, at 70 Oxford Street, London, on October 17, 1894, in all probability the first commercial film venture in the United Kingdom. Urban did far more than serve as the company's London manager; the following year, he reorganized the company as the Warwick Trading Company, taking its name from its location in Warwick Court in the High Holborn district of London. "Mr. Charles Urban's surname is the aptest imaginable," commented the British periodical, the *Spy*. "He is all urbanity."[5] He also had a "powerful, ebullient personality," according to film historian Luke McKernan,[6] and this helped guide his prominence in the British film industry as he began to produce films as well as sell projectors. Urban also distributed the films of others, most notably James Williamson, George Albert Smith, the Lumière brothers, and Georges Méliès. And the last was asked by Urban to produce a fake news record of the coronation of Britain's Edward VII.

When he left Warwick in 1903, Urban was well on his way to becoming the most important individual—British or American—in the British film industry, founding the Charles Urban Trading Company, the Natural Color Kinematograph Company, the Kineto Company, and the French Eclipse Company.

Utilizing the pioneering work of others, notably George Albert Smith, Urban made commercial use of Kinemacolor, the first major color system, preceding Technicolor. Like the original Technicolor process, Kinemacolor was a two color system, using only the primary colors of red and green, and it required that projectors be run at twice the regular speed for its presentation. It was first demonstrated in May 1908 at Urban's new London headquarters, Urbanora House on Wardour Street, a thoroughfare fast becoming the new commercial hub for the British film industry. A public presentation took place in February 1909 at London's Palace Theatre, and in 1911, Urban took over the lease of another theatre, the Scala, in which to present Kinemacolor productions on a regular basis. Using Kinemacolor, he shot the first color newsreel (of the funeral of Edward VII in 1910), and in 1914 Urban produced the first feature film in color, *The World, the Flesh and the Devil*, directed by F. Martin Thornton and starring, as the Devil, Harry Agar Lyons, who in the 1920s was to become the screen's first Fu Manchu. Urban tried to interest American investors in the system, presenting a demonstration at New York's Madison Square Garden in December 1909. The Americans were not interested and, ultimately, neither were British filmgoers.

Urban had become a naturalized British citizen in 1906, and, like many converts, he became staunchly patriotic. In 1911, in Kinemacolor, he shot the Delhi Durbar, honoring the visit of King George V as Emperor of India to a part of his far-flung empire. The film was released the following year as *With Our King and Queen through India*, and ran for two-and-a-half hours. Urban made many patriotic World War I films and newsreels, notably *Britain Prepared* (1915) and *The Battle of the Somme* (1916). He was also instrumental in the United States in the production of the *Official War Review*.

In 1917, Urban moved his headquarters to the United States, formed Urban Motion Picture industries, and a few years later established new offices at the Urban Institute at Irvington-on-Hudson, New York. By 1922, it was claimed that since 1896, he had made eighty transatlantic crossings.[7] A year later, Urban's business had collapsed and he was declared bankrupt. He returned to England in 1930, and, following his wife's death in 1937, he retired to Brighton, where he died in 1942.

There is no later British producer, not even Alexander Korda, comparable to Charles Urban in terms of the magnitude and scope of his work. He was responsible for fictional films, newsreels (the first being of the 1898 Oxford and Cambridge boat race), nature films (generally in association with Percy Smith),[8] travelogues, patriotic efforts, trick films, and propaganda pieces, advocating both peace and war. There was no end to his talent, and his career ended perhaps because he had been around too long. There is no room in the film industry of the 1920s for pioneers from the 1890s.[9]

As Luke McKernan has noted, Charles Urban represents the first American invasion of the British film industry, part of the influx of American imports, business methods, and cultural influence. He was the human face of a movement to quietly Americanize Britain, "probably the most important happening in the economic history of mankind since the Industrial Revolution in Britain," to quote historian H. C. Allen.[10]

CHAPTER TWO

The O'Kalems

THE FIRST EXTENDED, AND EXTENSIVE, LOCATION TRIP BY AN AMERICAN film company to the British Isles involved not so much the mainland as the province of Ireland, which was, of course, in the 1910s part of Great Britain. Indeed, despite native filmmaking efforts since, if Ireland has a prominent and unique place in the history of world cinema, it is not as a producer but rather as the first country utilized as a regular location by a major American film company. For a period of five years between 1910 and 1915, Ireland—its romantic history, its scenery, its compass—was routinely on display on screens in the United States and elsewhere. It preempted England, which would seem to have more obvious "tourist" attractions for American immigrant audiences and, to a large extent, demonstrated that the potential motion picture viewer in the United States was either an Irish emigrant or an emigrant from elsewhere in Europe who could empathize with all of which this small country was representative. For a brief period, unmatched since independence, Ireland flexed its hegemony over all other countries and nationalities.

The catalyst for all this is not ultimately an American production company but a director who was born neither in the United States nor Ireland, but whose Irish ancestry and patriotic pride drove his creativity. Sidney Olcott was born in Toronto, Canada, on January 20, 1872, shortly after his Irish-born parents arrived there. His birth name was John Sidney Alcott, but, for professional reasons, he changed his last name to Olcott in honor of the "Irish" tenor Chauncey Olcott (1860–1932), who had starred in Irish-based musical dramas, introduced "Mother Machree," wrote and sang "My Wild Irish Rose," and whose real name, in turn, was John Chancellor. If nothing else, both Olcott men demonstrated not only their pride of Irish ancestry but also their understanding of the audience potential in an Irish name.

"Olcott was of Irish birth and possessed all the sparkle and sentiment of that emotional race," wrote his co-worker Gene Gauntier. "His method of direction would not be tolerated today. Shouts, threats, sarcasm, bullying, cajoling, petting, he would try each in turn. But after the scene was over it was always the same—an arm thrown round the shoulder, compliments, enthusiasm. His people adored him, respected him and would (and did) risk their lives for him. He was the sun around which they all revolved."[1]

Sidney Olcott was to become a prominent and reliable, if not innovative, director of the 1910s and 1920s, most closely associated with Famous Players-Lasky. He directed Mary Pickford in *Madame Butterfly* (1915) and *Poor Little Peppina* (1916), George Arliss in *The Green Goddess* (1923), Marion Davies in *Little Old New York* (1923), Rudolph Valentino in *Monsieur Beaucaire* (1924), Pola Negri in *The Charmer* (1925), as well as many other films and many other stars. Olcott directed only one feature-length production with an Irish theme, *The Innocent Lie* (1915), involving an Irish immigrant, amnesia, and mistaken identity. While the film received relatively poor reviews, there are those who claim it is one of his best works, with a leading critic of the time commenting, "Olcott has the art of depicting Irish ways and creating Ireland's atmosphere."[2]

After selling newspapers on the streets of Toronto, Olcott began working in the theatre, appearing in amateur dramatics and eventually moving to New York. In 1904, he entered films as an occasional actor with the American Mutoscope and Biograph Company, prior to D. W. Griffith's joining the company, and eventually moved up to the position of general assistant. He became a full-fledged director when three film executives, George Kleine, Samuel Long, and Frank Marion, the last two of whom had worked with Olcott at Biograph, combined their financial resources, and formed the Kalem Company. The name is an amalgam of the initials of its founders. It was Olcott who directed Kalem's first film, a half-reeler titled *The Runaway Sleighbell*, in a loft at 131 West Twenty-fourth Street, New York, in February 1907, with a cast including himself along with Joseph and Fred Santley, two Irish-American actors with whom he had earlier appeared on stage. Actress Gene Gauntier (1885–1966) had met Olcott in 1906 at the Biograph Company, and she was one of the first to join him at the new organization. Gauntier served not only as the company's leading lady, but also as its screenwriter and co-editor of the films with Olcott. She claimed to have written some 500 scripts for the company, as well as picking locations, supervising sets, co-directing with Olcott, and editing and writing intertitles. It was Gauntier who wrote the script and Olcott who directed Kalem's 1907 production of *Ben-Hur*. There being no precedent for a film company to pay for a screen adaptation, Kalem did not concern itself with such an obvious matter, but the subsequent lawsuit by the estate of the author of the original work, General Lew Wallace, determined the rights of authors and others.

The Kalem Company did not own a studio and generally filmed on location in Coytesville and Fort Lee, New Jersey, and Cos Cob, Connecticut. When weather conditions in the New York area made outdoor filming impossible, beginning in 1908, Kalem moved its company to Florida for the winter months. When the company returned to New York after the 1909–10 winter season down south, Kalem's executives decided that some members of the company would continue filming in and around New York, while others would go abroad.

Sidney Olcott and Gene Gauntier vie for boasting rights as to which persuaded Kalem initially to choose Ireland as a film location. The director's story has a simplicity to it, if not total verisimilitude. He maintained that one day in the spring of 1910, Frank Marion called him into his office, pointed to a map of the world on his desk, and asked where Olcott would like to make films. Without hesitation, the director pointed to the country of his ancestors. Ireland it was.[3]

As documented in her published 1928 autobiography, Gene Gauntier's account is far more detailed (though somewhat odd). She had visited Europe for the first time in the spring of 1909, accompanying her younger sister to Berlin, where she was to undertake operatic training. Gauntier considered staying in Germany, but became homesick, and when she received an offer from Kalem to return to the company as scenarist and leading lady, she paid brief visits to Paris and London before returning to the United States in August 1909. Back with Kalem, and without even a hint of logic, Gauntier broached the idea of filming not in Germany but in Ireland, "a country which, though I had never seen it, appealed tremendously to my imagination."[4]

The company showed no interest in the idea, but, suddenly, in May 1910, Gauntier's mother arrived in New York, with passage booked to visit her daughter in Germany and anxious to have her other daughter journey with her. Perhaps Kalem was concerned that it might again lose its primary screenwriter and leading lady or perhaps Marion had already spoken with Olcott, because, as Gauntier recalled,

> Then without warning—and it those days of the pictures almost everything came without warning—I was summoned to the office.
>
> "When can you and Olcott start for Ireland?" demanded Marion.
>
> "Tomorrow, if necessary," I replied without hesitation.
>
> "Good. The *Baltic* sails on Saturday. Better see Mr. Lindsey, the passenger agent, and engage passage for yourself, Olcott and Hollister."[5]

Director/leading man Sidney Olcott, cameraman George K. Hollister, screenwriter/leading lady Gene Gauntier, and Gauntier's mother left New York on August 6, heading for Queenstown (now Cobh). While on board, Gauntier wrote the scripts for *The Lad from Old Ireland* and *An Irish Honeymoon*. The latter was to be shot not only in Ireland, but also on board ship and in New York upon the company's return. *An Irish Honeymoon* featured only Gauntier and Olcott in the roles of Aileen and Terry, and its scenes were filmed around those for *The Lad from Old Ireland*. Upon arrival, the company booked accommodation at Cork's Victoria Hotel, but before shooting could commence on *The Lad from Old Ireland*, Gauntier and Olcott had to seek out old costumes in Cork's old clothing market, purchasing baggy, homespun trousers, hobnailed boots, a corduroy coat and cap for the latter; and a fully-gathered skirt, an elbow-sleeved, coarse cotton "ballyshirt," and a plaid shawl for the leading lady. Exterior scenes were shot on a jaunting care ride outside of Cork.

From Cork and its environs, the company moved to Killarney to film scenic shots for *An Irish Honeymoon* at Kate Kearney's Cottage, the Gap of Dunloe, and Ross Castle. Finally, the group headed for Dublin and the Glencairn home of Richard Croker (1841–1922), the former head of Tammany Hall in New York, and manager of Democratic politics there from 1886–1902. The uncooperative Croker, who was now living the life of a country gentleman, was persuaded to be filmed, greeting Olcott and Gauntier as they stepped from their automobile and welcoming them into his home.

To conclude *An Irish Honeymoon*, footage was shot of tourist attractions in London. Also in London, Gauntier hastily put together the screenplay for *The Little Spreewald Maiden*, whose sole purpose was to get her, Olcott, and Hollister to Germany for the operatic debut of her sister.

Olcott and Hollister returned first to the United States and New York in September, followed two weeks later by Gauntier, whose ship, the *Manitou*, docked in Boston. No sooner did she reach New York than she was in make-up and acting in an interior set modeled after the cottage near Cork. The

Rory O'More (1912), with Jack Clark in the dock.

dying grandmother, played in Ireland by a Cork woman, was "doubled" in New York by Mrs. Thomas Santley, with a frilled cap hiding most of her face. Once *The Lad from Old Ireland* was completed, interior shots for the other two films were quickly made. As Gauntier wrote,

> In a little more than two months from the day we had sailed from New York, the three pictures were finished. We had traveled over six thousand miles and had filmed scenes in four countries and on the high seas.[6]

When *The Lad from Old Ireland* was released on November 23, 1910, Kalem quite rightly advertised it as "the first drama ever made on two continents." The trade paper the *Film Index* (November 5, 1910) noted "the linking together of the old and new world. In each picture the scenes shift to and from America and Ireland . . . the first instance in the making of the photoplay in which anything of this character has been attempted."

Those first Irish films were relatively well received by the trade press. "Its chief interest lies in the scenery," commented the *Moving Picture World*

(December 3, 1910) of *The Lad from Old Ireland*. "Probably most audiences will enjoy it, and of course the Irish lad will make the Irish portion of any audience hilarious." *An Irish Honeymoon* was not released until the spring of 1911. At that time, it was hailed by the *Moving Picture World* (March 25, 1911) as "a series of excellent pictures, showing what Ireland is like in its most picturesque portions. . . . This photography has been admirably done, the viewpoints having been selected by an artist of ability."

The following year, Kalem decided to repeat the Irish exercise, but on a far grander scale. Once the filming season in Florida was completed, the company arranged transportation on the *Baltic*, leaving New York on June 3, 1911.[7] The company now included not only Olcott, Gauntier, and Hollister, but also Hollister's wife, Alice, who would take occasional acting assignments, actor Jack Clark (who was later to marry Gauntier and was accompanied on the trip by his mother, who took on a number of character roles)[8], J. P. McGowan and George Melford, who were to work as both actors and general assistants, actor Arthur Donaldson, actress Agnes Mapes (a friend of Gauntier, specially engaged for this trip), and scenic artist and set builder Allen Farnham. Prior to leaving for Ireland, Gauntier completed screenplays for *Rory O'More*, *The Colleen Bawn*, and *Arrah-Na-Pogue*. For the first time in print, the company is identified as "The O'Kalems."[9] The epithet was also becoming familiar beyond the film community to the public at large, as evidenced by the title of one of the Kalem films from this visit, the half-reel, or split-reel, travelogue, *The O'Kalems Visit to Killarney*, released on January 5, 1912.

The company arrived in Ireland on June 10, 1911, and set out for Killarney. From there, the O'Kalems moved on to the village of Beaufort, where an outdoor studio was to be built and the company housed in the self-styled Beaufort Hotel, run by Patrick O'Sullivan. The "hotel" was a two-story building with eight bedrooms, a kitchen, and a parlor. There were no bathrooms. The men built a shower for themselves at the rear of the hotel, while the women used a local swimming hole. It is not clear if Olcott and Gauntier had come across Beaufort on the 1910 visit to Ireland or whether happenstance took them there for the first time in the summer of 1911. According to Patrick Sullivan's daughter, Annie, Olcott did not care for Killarney and determined to find a more pleasant spot to stay and film. He stumbled upon Beaufort while touring the district by jaunting car. The residents had never seen a motion picture, but after discovering that they were familiar with magic lantern entertainments, Olcott explained that "films are just like magic lantern slides, but they move."

Allen Farnham, who did not consider himself an actor, built an open-air stage behind the O'Sullivan home, and supervised the construction of sets for various interior scenes. Props were generally borrowed from family homes in Beaufort. After filming a number of general scenic shots, including market day in Killarney, the O'Kalems began work on their first 1911 production *Rory O'More*, with Jack Clark in the title role of the seventeenth-century rebel, based on the 1837 novel, later dramatized, by Samuel Lover (1797–1868).[10] On November 5, 1911, *Rory O'More* was the inaugural film in a series of Sunday performances at Dublin's Volta Electric Theatre, managed by James Joyce.

Rory O'More was followed by Kalem's first three-reel production, Dion Boucicault's *The Colleen Bawn*.[11] The play was probably Boucicault's finest work, first presented at the Adelphia Theatre in London in 1860; Boucicault himself, while renowned as an Irish-born playwright, preferred the pleasures of life in London and New York.

Released in the US on October 16, 1911, *The Colleen Bawn* featured Gauntier in the title role, with Jack Clark as Myles na Coppaleen, Sidney Olcott as Danny Mann, Arthur Donaldson as Father Tom, and the entire company in supporting roles. The locations described by the dramatist were all utilized in the film, including the Colleen Bawn Rock, the Gap of Dunloe, the ruins of the Colleen's home on Muckross Head, and Danny Mann's Cottage. It was the subject of a fulsome two-page review in the *Moving Picture World*, which noted,

> The pictured story follows very closely the drama of Boucicault, with the exception that in a number of instances the picture portrays events to which the dialogue merely alludes. In these instances the picture tells the story with greater clearness. Then, too, the scope of the camera picture is at all times greater than the stage picture. The events follow each other through the three reels in such close and logical sequences that the absence of the dialogue is scarcely noticeable.[12]

The second Boucicault adaptation and the second three-reel production was *Arrah-Na-Pogue*, with a cast again headed by Gauntier and Olcott, and with Agnes Mapes taking on the prominent part of Fanny Power, which is, in reality, more the central role than that of the title character. "There is not a dull moment in the entire three reels of this subject," reported the *Moving Picture World* (November 18, 1911), "and there are many situations that are intensely gripping. For sustained action it is the best three-reel subject we

The Colleen Bawn (1912), with (from left to right) Mrs. Clark, Gene Gauntier, Jack Clark, and Sidney Olcott.

have seen up-to-date." *Arrah-Na-Pogue* is important in film history in that, in all probability, it is the first American film to boast an original musical score. Kalem engaged Walter Cleveland Simon to write a complete piano score with a four-piece orchestration.[13] Simon continued to compose for the motion picture through 1919, working on thirteen Kalem films in 1912, but no further Irish productions.

Aside from filming in Beaufort, the O'Kalems visited Howth, where they filmed the drama *The Fishermaid of Ballydavid*, released on November 17, 1911, and a half-reel scenic subject, *Among the Irish Fisher Folk*, released on November 29, 1911.[14]

In all, Gene Gauntier claims that the O'Kalems made seventeen films during their eighteen-week stay in Ireland. The exact number is open to question, but, aside from the above, definitely produced at this time are: *The Franciscan Friars of Killarney*, released on November 29, 1911, on a double reel with *Among the Irish Fisher Folk*; *The O'Kalems Visit to Killarney*, released on January 5, 1912; *The O'Neill*, released on January 12, 1912; *His Mother*, released on January 26, 1912; *Far from Erin's Eye*, released on February 14, 1912; and *You Remember Ellen*, released on March 4, 1912.

Life for the O'Kalems in Beaufort was simple, and dispatches home were filled with stories of the O'Sullivans with Brandy, the dog, one of the most favored members of the family. Many nights, the group would sit around the peat fire, while Annie O'Sullivan played the accordion and Jack Clark took out his violin.[15]

What must have been difficult, and about which there is no written documentation, is the technical aspect of filming, processing, and editing on location at this time. It seems doubtful that Ireland had any film laboratories, and, thus, the company must have been forced to ship the footage for processing to London, which would have taken an estimated two days. In all probability, the O'Kalems would have had no means of projecting a positive image, and one must assume that the processed negative alone was returned to Beaufort, where it could be checked using a magnifying glass and rewind arms. An argument might be made that the film was not processed until the company returned to New York, but this is extremely unlikely and in regard to some titles patently untrue. It is not recommended that shot footage sit for weeks awaiting processing; without refrigeration, which was obviously not available in Beaufort, the images fade and contrast changes. Further, if there was any problem with the film, there would be no way to reshoot once the O'Kalems were back in the United States.

It is very obvious that some Kalem Irish films, such as *Rory O'More*, were released in the United States prior to the company's return. This raises further unanswered questions as to how much of the processed film was shipped directly to the United States and whether Sidney Olcott and Gene Gauntier were involved in the editing of the films or was that task undertaken by the New York office? None of the trade paper stories on the return of the O'Kalems to the United States make any reference to their bringing processed film back with them. Did the O'Kalems make copies of the scripts and forward them to New York with the processed film to ease the editing problem? We know that the script for *Rory O'More* was written prior to Gauntier's departure for Ireland, and, obviously, she could have taken one copy with her and left one with the New York office. Who wrote the captions (or intertitles) for the films, which must have been shot in the United States? Gene Gauntier claims to have been involved in the editing and captioning of all the films she wrote, and, if this is true, then, arguably, the editing, or at least some basic assembly of the footage, took place in Beaufort.

The O'Kalems spent four months in Ireland, returning to New York on the *Cedric*, which arrived on October 6, 1911. (They narrowly missed the 1911 railroad strike, catching the last train out of Dublin.) Arthur Donaldson stayed on in Europe to appear on stage in Stockholm.[16] Some interior scenes for the Irish productions were shot by the company in New York, and then

Olcott, Gauntier, and the others moved on to Jacksonville, Florida, to begin the winter filmmaking season there.

Upon his return from Ireland, Olcott had threatened to resign from Kalem, and the company had gone so far as to offer his position to Gauntier. However, Olcott reconsidered and signed a new contract, and his leading lady/screenwriter was given a pay raise. No sooner had the couple left for the winter in Florida than they were asked to return to New York. Kalem had decided to send them again abroad, not to Ireland, but to Madeira, Gibraltar, Italy, Egypt, and, most importantly, Palestine. Embarking on the *Adriatic* on December 2, 1911, were much the same group as before: Olcott and Gauntier, George K. Hollister and his wife, Alice, Jack Clark, Robert Vignola, J. P. McGowan, and Allen Farnham. They were no longer the O'Kalems but the El Kalems, the screen's peripatetic players. This trip, more than any other, was to prove the company's claim that "the Kalem lens is turned upon all parts of the world."[17] The work of the El Kalems, which culminated in the making of feature-length *From the Manger to the Cross*, is outside the scope of this book. However, in terms of Kalem's history, it is of preeminent importance in that *From the Manger to the Cross* is one of the earliest, if not the first, American feature film, and this third trip placed the company at the apex of American production. As the *Moving Picture World* commented,

> Encouraged by the success of its two expeditions to Ireland for the purpose of taking pictures upon Irish soil, the Kalem Company has undertaken a campaign in foreign countries that makes the Irish affair look like a mere Sunday school picnic and which will, if successful, place the promoters at the very top of the list of motion picture makers of the world in point of enterprise.[18]

One cannot mention *From the Manger to the Cross* without reference to British actor R. Henderson Bland, who plays the adult Christ and is the first actor to play the character on American screens. Sidney Olcott engaged Bland for the part over the telephone because he liked the sound of his voice, no matter that the film was silent!

Too few of the Kalem Irish productions are available for re-evaluation, but based upon what does survive, along with other non-Irish Kalem films, it is very obvious that the company understood how to use natural settings to advantage. The emphasis is on the "look" of the scene rather than innovative directing or editorial techniques, and certainly not superior acting.

The Kalem films are clearly not on a par with the D. W. Griffith-directed Biograph shorts of the same period, nor are they as good, or entertaining, as the films from what was the country's leading producer of the day, the Vitagraph Company of America. Just as Olcott comes third in the triumvirate of Irish-American silent film directors, behind Rex Ingram and Herbert Brenon, so does Kalem come third in the top three of American producers of the 1909–13 period. However, based on his visionary use of outdoor settings and natural lighting, Sidney Olcott is deserving of the title, referencing America's leading playwright and producers, "The [David] Belasco of the Open Air."

From Palestine, the company moved on to Austria, Germany, and England, where it made at least one film, *The Poacher's Pardon*, released in September 1912, and starring J. P. McGowan as the gamekeeper and Jack J. Clark as the poacher, and, finally, Ireland. It was a joyful return to Beaufort, as McGowan wrote,

> After months, in arid countries, among foreign-speaking people, with only an occasional mail to connect us with the outside world, we could appreciate this garden spot of Ireland and the cool breeze that swept down through the Gap and fanned our cheeks seemed to re-echo the welcome that we had found irresistible.[19]

Frank Marion had contacted the widow of Dion Boucicault (1820–90) and offered her $500 for the rights to *Con the Shaughran*. He also located Joseph Murphy, and offered to purchase the rights from him to *The Kerry Gow* and *Shaun Rhue*. Despite their age—both Murphy plays had been touring the United States for thirty years—Kalem had no doubts as to their value. Emmett Campbell Hall wrote a script for a two-reel production of *Shaun Rhue*, which Marion pointed out to Olcott contained "very little of the original plot . . . I think we will give it a different name with a subtitle 'Based on Joe Murphy's famous Irish play *Shaun Rhue*.'"[20]

The Kerry Gow is typical stage melodrama involving a villain who holds the mortgage on the cottage of the beautiful daughter's father and his attempts to steal her from the hero. Reviewing Kalem's three-reel adaptation, released on November 18, 1912, in the *Moving Picture World* (November 9, 1912), W. Stephen Bush prophesized, "Now that the Kalems have gone to Ireland and have brought back with them the true atmosphere and every real characteristic of the Irish soil and the Irish heart there will be a tremendous revival of *The Kerry Gow* all over the country."

The Shaughraun, originally written to show off the talents of its actor-playwright, was also produced in three reels. Here, Olcott replaces Dion Boucicault in the title role. "He did wonders with his eyes and his face generally," wrote Bush in the *Moving Picture World* (December 14, 1912). "The shaughraun's good humor, his indestructible optimism and resourcefulness were brought out with great artistic skill."

Other productions filmed during this visit are:[21] *The Mayor from Ireland*, released on November 30, 1912; *Conway, the Kerry Dancer*, released on December 9, 1912;[22] *Ireland the Oppressed*, released on December 14, 1912; *The O'Neill*, released on January 12, 1913; *Lady Peggy's Escape*, released on February 8, 1913; and *The Belle of North Wales*, released on February 12, 1913.[23]

While the O'Kalems were in Beaufort, Ireland was also visited, albeit briefly, by another US producer, the Vitagraph Company of America. With his director, Larry Trimble, rotund and avuncular comedian John Bunny had come to England to shoot footage for *Pickwick Papers* and

The Mayor from Ireland (1912), with J. P. McGowan and Gene Gauntier.

other productions. Bunny was born in New York, but his father came from Cornwall and his mother from County Clare, Ireland. For *Pickwick Papers*, a supporting cast of British players was hired, and when the three-reel production was released beginning February 28, 1913, Hugh Hoffman in the *Moving Picture World* (February 15, 1913) wrote that "Mr. Bunny as Pickwick needs hardly to be described. Nature endowed him for the part, and one who cannot imagine him as Pickwick must have imagination poorly developed indeed." While shooting *Bunny at the Derby*, released on October 29, 1912, his fans became so enthusiastic that a near riot broke out.

Bunny took time out to visit Ireland, making two one-reel comedies there, *Michael McShane, Matchmaker*, released on November 6, 1912, and *The Blarney Stone*, released on March 28, 1913, while Larry Trimble filmed a couple of travelogues in Cork and Dublin. Bunny visited the Rotunda Theatre in Dublin, where he praised its Irish Ladies Orchestra, commenting that "an orchestra composed of women is an undeniable asset to every hall in the world."

Bunny's return to the United States and Vitagraph was greeted with great enthusiasm. Less responsive was the Kalem management. When the O'Kalems returned to the United States on the *Adriatic* on October 12, 1912, they were in high spirits. They had been away for almost a year, and based on the tremendous success of *From the Manger to the Cross*, both Olcott and Gauntier expected pay raises and encouragement to produce further feature-length films. They received neither. Kalem never made another feature, and informed Olcott that economic conditions forced it to renew his contract at $150, rather than the previous $200 a week. At the end of 1912, both Olcott and Gauntier said goodbye to Kalem and the O'Kalems. The company did make one last "Irish" film, *The Octoroon*, released on December 1, 1913, and again based on a Dion Boucicault play, but it was directed by Kenean Buel and shot in Florida.[24] Kalem continued production through 1916, but it seemed to have lost its way along with the ability to move forward.

The O'Kalems were no more, but the annual visits to Ireland did not entirely cease. In December 1912, Gene Gauntier announced the creation of the Gene Gauntier Feature Players Company, releasing its productions through Warner's Features.[25] The company, consisting of its star, along with Sidney Olcott, Jack Clark, and Allen Farnham, set up headquarters in Jacksonville, Florida. However, following in the O'Kalem tradition, the group set sail for Ireland on the *Adriatic* on August 14, 1913; the "Gee Gees" had become the "O'Gees." The stay in Beaufort was shorter than in previous years, in part because of poor weather conditions, but the company did film two productions there, *For Ireland's Sake*, released on January 12, 1914, and *Come Back to Erin*, released in March 1914.

Both were three-reel productions, with the first involving an Irish peasant lad, played by Jack Clark, sentenced to be hanged by the British, but saved by a sympathetic priest, played by Sidney Olcott, and escaping to America with his new wife, played by Gene Gauntier. "*For Ireland's Sake* is a good picture," reported the *Moving Picture World* (January 31, 1914). *Come Back to Erin* was shot in both Beaufort and New York, and concerned Peggy, an peasant girl, played by Gene Gauntier, accused of stealing a diamond tiara, and saved by the village blacksmith, played by Jack Clark.

While the Gene Gauntier Feature Players Company remained extant until the spring of 1915, when Gauntier and Clark joined Universal, Sidney Olcott left the organization in January 1914, and formed his own company, Sid Olcott International Features.[26] With his leading lady and future wife Valentine Grant (1881–1949), Olcott returned to Beaufort for a last time in the summer of 1914.[27] He and Grant left for London on the *Adriatic* on June 11 of that year, accompanied by cinematographer Hal Young, scenario editor and publicist Fred Gunning, and a group of actors, including Pat O'Malley.[28] In Ireland, they filmed *The Irish in America* and *Bold Emmett, Ireland's Martyr*, both released the following year by the Lubin Company.

Olcott spoke of building a permanent studio in Beaufort, noting that the Irish were natural actors and that the mild Kerry climate was perfect for year-round filming. The advent of World War I put an end to his plans, and the director never returned. In fact, he arrived in New York on the *Adriatic* on August 29, 1914, after the outbreak of hostilities.

A number of O'Kalem productions were reissued in 1914 by Kalem. Noting that *The Lad from Old Ireland* was first released in 1910, the *Moving Picture World* (August 15, 1914) reported it "was considered one of the best of those days and worthy of a reproduction and presentation now." *Rory O'More* was reissued in September 1914 as a result, or so it was reported, of numerous requests. It was obviously not coincidental that these reissues were concurrent with publicity relating to the Sidney Olcott-Valentine Grant visit to Ireland. Following the 1916 Easter Rebellion in Dublin, *The O'Neill* was reissued with the new title of *The Irish Rebel*.

The Colleen Bawn was reissued in February 1914, and as a publicity stunt Kalem shipped several tons of Irish soil on the *Megantic* from Killarney to New York. The soil was portioned out into trays, four feet square and one inch deep, and these were distributed with the film. Thus, patrons attending screenings had the unique opportunity actually to stand on Irish soil.

In his seminal work, *The Rise of the American Film*, Lewis Jacobs claims that because Sidney Olcott would sometimes choose controversial subjects dealing with Irish rebellion "these provoked much disturbance in the home office, and Kalem wanted to recall Olcott."[29] There is absolutely no evidence to support this assertion. Nor is there any proof that Olcott's Irish films found disfavor with the British authorities. They were well received by the British trade paper, the *Bioscope*. In fact, the only Olcott production of this period which did arouse controversy in both England and Ireland was *From the Manger to the Cross*.[30] In Beaufort, there was strong displeasure with the film in that the Virgin Mary was portrayed by a divorced woman, namely Gene Gauntier.

When *The O'Neill* was released in the United Kingdom on February 25, 1912, the *Bioscope* described the plot, involving an Irish patriot who takes to highway robbery to raise money for the cause of Irish freedom, as "picturesque, romantic and altogether delightful." Olcott may have been a patriotic Irish-American, but he was certainly not averse to working in England. After completion of his last film in the United States, *The Claw*, in 1927, he moved to Britain with the announced plan to direct *The Ringer* for British Lion at Elstree, receiving the extremely high salary of 450 pounds a week, for a ten-week period. Ultimately, he never made a film there, not because of any anti-English sentiment but because he rejected the production as not the "super-film" he was hired to make.

There was a contentious aspect to the first Kalem visit to Ireland, but it involved American and not British politics. As already noted, the company filmed Richard Croker at his home outside of Dublin, where he was living the life of an Irish gentleman. Croker had been active in Tammany Hall politics in New York, eventually controlling the Democratic organization. He was notorious for taking bribes from the owners of brothels, saloons, and gambling dens, and for manipulating the 1897 election of his candidate, Robert A. Van Wyck, as the first major of five-borough New York. Croker was ridiculed by Mark Twain in an October 1901 speech in which he lifted remarks from Edmund Burke's oration in the British House of Commons, advocating the impeachment of Warren Hastings of the India Company. Twain substituted New York for England, Tammany for India, and Croker for Hastings.

Croker left America for England, where in 1907 his horse Orby won the Epsom Derby. Shunned by British society, he moved to Ireland, where he died in 1922. Despite Croker's scandalous and corrupt political life, he was very much admired by Irish-Americans, as the Kalem Company realized. To most Irish-Americans, Croker was one of their own. That admiration continued through to his funeral, which was attended by Arthur Griffith, president of Dail Eireann, the Lord Mayor of Dublin, Michael Collins, and the British Under-Secretary to the Lord Lieutenant. Croker's infamy extended far beyond his death, and in a gossip piece about the Kalem Company in the *Los Angeles Times* in 1932 the only discussion of its Irish ventures is a passing reference to the footage of Richard Croker.[31]

If Sidney Olcott and company may not have fallen foul of the British authorities on that first trip to Ireland, the second year they did experience animosity from the local Roman Catholic Church. While filming *Rory O'More*, there were rumors that the parish priest had forbidden the Beaufort villagers to work on the production. When the Catholic members of the company, Robert Vignola, Alice Hollister, Jack Clark, and his mother, attended services that Sunday, they heard the priest deliver a sermon against "those tramp photographers" and urge his parishioners to drive the O'Kalems out of Beaufort. The next day, Olcott visited the bishop in Killarney, and possibly the American consul in Queenstown, and (depending upon whose story is to be believed), the priest was either dismissed from the parish or forced to apologize. It later transpired that the priest had made his comments after being approached by local traders whose businesses were hurt as tourists went off to watch the filming instead of patronizing their stores.[32]

For whatever reasons, Sidney Olcott's career ended with the coming of sound. When his wife, Valentine Grant, died on March 12, 1949, the former director moved in with his old Kalem companion, Robert Vignola. A few weeks before Christmas, Olcott wrote out his Christmas cards and parceled up pieces of Val's jewelry to be sent to those he thought his wife would wish to have them. On December 16, Olcott told Vignola that he felt ill, and went to his room. A few hours later, he died.

Shortly before Christmas, 1949, Annie O'Sullivan received two letters from America. The first was from Vignola, telling her of Olcott's death. The other was from Sidney Olcott, containing his wife's gold bracelet. He had never forgotten Beaufort.

CHAPTER THREE

The American-Anglo-Irish

HE AMERICAN-ANGLO-IRISH CONNECTION DID NOT CEASE WITH THE end of Sidney Olcott's visits to what was to become the Republic of Ireland decades later. In 1920, the British fan magazine *Picture Plays* had extolled the virtues of Killarney as a new Los Angeles for filmmakers:

> The day that Ireland is "discovered" will be a red-letter day for the British film, for it will give to us what we have lacked too long—a great film centre which will supply all the needs, both of scenery and climate of all the films we can produce.[1]

While Ireland was part of Britain, there was no interest in this new filmmaking El Dorado, and very little after the formation of the Irish Free State and the Republic of Ireland.

Politically, the most important and influential of American filmmakers to visit Ireland while it was still part of Britain was Walter Macnamara. Born in County Waterford, Ireland, in 1876, Macnamara was educated in Wales and came to the United States in 1911. His early career included work as a war correspondent in South Africa, a novelist, a comedian, and an actor. According to the *Moving Picture World* (November 8, 1913), he was also one of the first vice presidents of the Gaelic League and one of the founders of the Irish Club in London.

He entered the film industry at Universal and wrote the screenplay for its 1913 production of *Traffic in Souls*, which has claim to fame thanks to the technical expertise of its director, but is, in reality, little more than a tawdry melodrama dealing with white slavery. The theme of the film provides a clear indication of Macnamara's character. He was an opportunist. In January 1914, he formed his own company, and a month later, he sailed for London, where he began filming—at the Ec-ko Studios at Kew Bridge—a political feature titled *Ireland a Nation*. The film was intended as a complete history of the Irish nation from 1798 through 1914. Exteriors were filmed in Ireland by Macnamara, who was arrested on arrival for importing arms, which he insisted were merely being used as "props." Between filming, Macnamara was busy rallying citizens to the nationalist cause. In an interview with George Blaisdell in the *Moving Picture World* (August 29, 1914), Macnamara discussed the filming in strong nationalist terms:

> Did I have any difficulties finding locations? Yes, in one instance, certainly, when I tried to find a mud hut and failed. Parnell wiped those out. I did, though, get some wonderful backgrounds, as I think you will agree when you see the picture. Here is a fort built by Oliver Cromwell. To this day no real son of the old sod passes it without spitting—that's the only way he can adequately express his feelings for the builder. I have tried to get absolute accuracy in my backgrounds—authentic locations—and I think I have succeeded.
>
> Were obstacles placed in my path in the making of *Ireland a Nation*? Yes, indeed, by the soldiers. Sometimes we would start to make a scene with not a soul in sight. It seemed sometimes that in two minutes soldiers would come from everywhere and demand to see a permit. Think of having a permit to take the side of a mountain! Of course, the picture was revolutionary in character, and the military tried in every way to handicap us. That's why we were five months over there. The people? They couldn't do enough for us. The Nationalist Party gave us unofficial sanction.

Ireland a Nation received its world premiere at New York's Forty-fourth Street Theatre on September 22, 1914. The critics were not too impressed. *Variety* (October 10, 1914) noted, "The producer has overlooked scores of opportunities to make the picture effective. The whole is not too well produced and the acting cast, numbering sixteen, discloses but one capable actor in the person of Barney Magee." The *Moving Picture World* (October 3, 1914) commented, "The production covers a vast amount of ground for a five-reel subject, and if it is to be criticized for anything it is the constant shifting of the interest from one character to another." The critics notwithstanding, *Ireland a Nation* proved tremendously popular with Irish-American audiences, who were what counted, and helped raise both moral and financial support for the cause of Irish independence. If *Ireland a Nation* is considered a British film, then it has the distinction of being the first to be reviewed by the *New York Times*—on September 24, 1914—when it was pronounced "a well-photographed and interesting movie drama."

The film's Irish premiere was somewhat delayed because the first prints shipped from New York to Europe were on board the *Lusitania*, which was sunk by a German submarine off the Irish coast on May 7, 1915. It is more than a little ironic that while Irish nationalists supported Germany during World War I, it was a German torpedo that prevented Ireland's seeing a film aimed at promoting the nationalist cause.

Ireland a Nation eventually opened in Dublin at the Rotunda on January 8, 1917, less than six months after the execution of the sixteenth leader of the Easter Week rising. Two days later, the management of the Rotunda was ordered to halt the screenings, despite the film's being approved for exhibition by both the British Board of Film Censors and the Military Censor of Dublin. The reason given for the ban was that audiences cheered at the suggestion that "England's difficulty was Ireland's opportunity" and at the murder of an English soldier by an Irish rebel. Bookings for the film outside of the Irish capital were canceled.

The film reappeared in 1920, when the *New York Dramatic Mirror* (November 6, 1920) reported it was playing at the Valencia Theatre, San Francisco. "The picture is said to have been smuggled out of Ireland after the cast was jailed by Scotland Yard detectives," reported the paper, quite erroneously. The 1920 reissue print included contemporary newsreel footage of Eamon De Valera and Arthur Griffith, founder of Sinn Féin. Its distributor was the Gaelic Amusement Company. Long considered a "lost" film; the reissue version was rediscovered by this writer in the early 1970s. The re-edited version was screened in Dublin in late January/early February 1922 for one week, but failed to garner much interest outside of the city.

Walter Macnamara had long vanished from view. In late 1915/early 1916, he did write and direct a minor feature titled *The Heart of New York*, a social drama concerned with the underprivileged in society and political corruption. His last known employment was with Mack Sennett's Keystone Company in 1917; perhaps not surprisingly, Sennett, though born in Canada, was of Irish extraction.

There were three major American directors of the silent era who were born in British-Ireland. One of whom generally considered himself Irish, at least in public. One had an extensive career in both Britain and the United States, and used his British birth to aid in his hiring as part of Britain's quota

William Desmond Taylor.

system. The third is generally not discussed in terms of the quality of his work, but rather the manner of his leaving this world and becoming arguably the first major Hollywood scandal.

William Desmond Taylor was born William Cunningham Deane-Tanner in Carlow, County Cork, in 1869. His family was upper middle class and very much Anglo-Irish. An actor on both stage (from the age of eighteen) and screen, Taylor became a film director in 1914. He was not particularly accomplished, as Irish film historians like to claim, but he was competent and responsible for some major Paramount features of the late 1910s, including *Tom Sawyer* (1917, with Jack Pickford), *Johanna Enlists* (1918, with

Mary Pickford), *Anne of Green Gables* (1919, with Mary Miles Minter), and *Huckleberry Finn* (1920, with Lewis Sargent in the title role).

Under normal circumstances, Taylor would be only a footnote in film history, a minor director of relatively minor interest. But his biggest claim to fame is not through his work as a director but that he had the misfortunate (as far as his life was concerned) and the good fortune (as far as his lasting notoriety is concerned) to have been murdered, and that murder is one of the great unsolved mysteries of Hollywood. Books have been devoted to the subject, with much discussion as to whether it was Mrs. Charlotte Shelby, the mother of actress Mary Miles Minter, with whom Taylor was romantically involved, who committed the deed, or was it a drug dealer or a gay pickup or anyone else living in Hollywood at that time. Taylor's death on February 1, 1922, has generated a minor business in Internet research and gossip, aimed primarily at the film-buff market. It also, coupled with other scandals of the period, and more importantly, led to the appointment of Will Hays as head of the newly formed Motion Picture Producers and Distributors Association, an organization which within a decade was to become to all extents and purposes the Hollywood censor.

Born Reginald Ingram Montgomery Hitchcock in Dublin, Rex Ingram (1893–1950) is generally considered to be Ireland's greatest native-born director. A colorful character with a penchant for dwarfs, the deformed, and the Arab world, Rex Ingram's films display no evidence of his Irish background nor his upbringing as the son of a Church of Ireland minister. He left Ireland in 1911 and never returned. His career as a director lasted from 1916 through 1932, and included the discovery of the two leading matinee idols of the silent era, Rudolph Valentino and Ramon Novarro. Ingram directed the former in what is arguably the star's greatest film, *The Four Horsemen of the Apocalypse* (1921), a film in which Valentino's co-star was Ingram's wife, Alice Terry, a brunette who always wore a blonde wig on screen.

Rex Ingram spent the most creative years of his career—in the 1920s—working not in Hollywood but at the Victorine Studios in Nice, where he made a series of films for Metro-Goldwyn (he would never allow the detestable Louis B. Mayer's name on his productions). Indirectly, Ingram ended his film career in 1932 in Britain in that his last film, *Baroud*, was produced by Gaumont-British but shot in North Africa. Ingram co-directs with Alice Terry and also plays the leading character, the dashing André Duval, with an Irish accent and a handsome if slightly aging face. Playing opposite Ingram is his longtime mistress, Rosita Garcia. *Baroud* was released in America as *Love in Morocco*, opening at New York's Mayfair Theatre on March 17, 1933.

Rex Ingram in the uniform of the Royal Flying Corps.

In Los Angeles, it opened at the Filmarte, double-billed with a Russian feature film. Reviews were lukewarm, with Andre Sennwald in the *New York Times* (March 20, 1933) noting that Ingram "plays with shy reticence," and that "the picture is flooded with picturesque types."

Variety (March 21, 1933) was not as kind, writing of "a dull story, badly handled and acted. . . . It is all Ingram. He retains his looks, but what he's actually done is to make a good old-fashioned Western and transpose it to Morocco."

Born in Kingstown (now Dun Laoghaire), just outside of Dublin, in 1880, Herbert Brenon was educated in London, where his father was a drama

Baroud/Love in Morocco (1932), with Rex Ingram and Rosita Garcia.

critic, and he had the advantage of British citizenship, assuring that when he did return to Britain in the 1930s he would be classified as a British director for quota purposes. At the age of sixteen, Brenon came to the United States with his family; he worked as an office boy in Pittsburgh and later held a similar position with a vaudeville agent in New York. His stage experience dates from 1897, beginning as an extra, then a call boy, and eventually as an assistant stage manager. He met his wife, Helen Oberg, in Minneapolis, while working as a director with the Dick Ferris stock company, and the couple was married in 1904, remaining together until his death.

Brenon entered the film industry as a screenwriter at a reported $75 a week with Carl Laemmle's IMP Company (later to become Universal) in 1910, and within six months was promoted to director. Brenon returned to the British Isles in May 1913, when he was sent by the studio to film a spy drama, *Across the Atlantic*, starring King Baggot. The film included footage of the Derby horse race and also featured British aviator Claude Grahame-White (notorious in America for having flown his bi-plane over Washington, D.C., and landing near the White House in October 1910).

While it seems somewhat improbable, Brenon was so taken with a stage production in London based on Sir Walter Scott's novel *Ivanhoe* that he decided to produce a three-reel film of the drama, for which he received permission from the studio. Brenon's version of *Ivanhoe* was filmed on location at Chepstow Castle in Wales, with locals serving as extras. King Baggot starred in the title role, with Leah Baird as Rebecca of York, Brenon as Isaac of York, and Brenon's wife as Elgitha. Filming took place in June and July 1913, and the film was released in September of that same year. Once filming on *Ivanhoe* was completed, Brenon and company moved on to Paris and Berlin to make further films—including the four-reel *Absinthe*—and then returned to America in October. Brenon and leading man Baggot did not get along, in large part because Baggot really wanted to be a director and not an actor, and after *Absinthe*, the latter was replaced by William Shea.

These early European productions gave Brenon a reputation as one of America's leading directors, and he was assigned direction of the Annette Kellermann vehicle *Neptune's Daughter* (1914) in Bermuda, with himself as the villain Roador the Wolf, also for Carl Laemmle. From Laemmle's company, he moved on to independent production and then joined the William Fox Company, filming a number of Theda Bara features as well as *A Daughter of the Gods* (1916), again with Kellermann, and on location in Jamaica. William Fox was far from happy at the film's reported cost and lengthy shooting schedule, and, as a result, Brenon again became an independent producer with the Nazimova antiwar drama *War Brides* (1916) and *The Fall of the Romanoffs* (1918).

Brenon brought over the great British actor Sir Johnston Forbes Robertson to America and starred him as the Stranger in Jerome K. Jerome's *The Passing of the Third Floor Back*.[2] To Brenon, Forbes Robertson was "the embodiment of our Saviour as The Stranger." He was paid $50,000, Brenon claimed, to appear in a film that was a major flop, and which has disappeared not only as a physical entity but also in terms of major written documentation (there is no *Variety* review). Brenon, however, had no regrets, noting, "He like all great artists was easy to direct. One guided him—not lead him, through the intricacies of the new medium."[3] Brenon made *The Passing of the Third Floor Back* at his studio in New York and it was completed in December 1917 for release early in 1918.

In the meantime, Brenon was invited by the British government to make a propaganda film initially identified only as the "British National War Film" and subsequently titled *The Invasion of Britain* or *Victory and Peace*. Edward Elgar was to compose the score and the script was by novelist Hall Caine, who was perhaps the most ardent supporter of Brenon as director. It has been reported that the latter shot the production on location in Chester beginning in October 1917 and finishing in June 1918, but, in reality, Brenon was involved with *The Passing of the Third Floor Back*[4] through until late 1917, and did not come to Britain until February 1918. A fire at the offices of the London Film Company destroyed most of the negative in June 1918, and no sooner had Brenon completed re-filming over a four-month period than the armistice was declared and the project abandoned. It has been strongly suggested that the British government was embarrassed by the production's anti-German theme and ordered its destruction. Up to that time, and much later, it was certainly the most expensive film that never was. Of the production, Helena Millais recalled,

> I played a part which [musical comedy star] Jose Collins couldn't play in a film written by Hall Caine for the Government. Sir William Jury seemed to be the important man at the back of the film. Herbert Brenon was the producer and it had an all-star cast. It was supposed to portray what would have happened here if we had been invaded like Belgium. My part was that of a work girl who refused to work for the enemy and who set the women against them. She was arrested and put in a cattle truck with others, from which she escaped and was shot.
>
> Marie Lohr played a sort of Nurse Cavell. Ellen Terry played a grandmother, saying goodbye to her grandson. She was a dear and rehearsed over and over again and cried real tears every time. We took some lovely scenes at Chirk Castle, a lovely place on the Welsh border; most of it was taken at Chester.[5]

Herbert Brenon returned to the United States, and became an American citizen. No sooner done than he returned to Europe to direct films with Marie Doro in London and Paris and an additional feature in Sicily. He had some pungent remarks on European filmmaking upon his eventual return:

> I found the English fearfully handicapped by undramatic phlegmatic temperament and bad photographic climate. The French, unambitious, are willing to make pictures exactly as they did ten years ago. The Italians have ideal surroundings and, racially, are camera actors at birth. But they lack a sufficiently large audience to be able to afford expensive productions. . . . Germany is our one serious contender. They have every reason to try to expand, are master technicians, and are wise enough to see beyond their own boundaries. They are going to make, and are making, pictures intended for the world market.[6]

Despite being away from Hollywood, Brenon was still regarded as one of the industry's finest directors, as evidenced by a long-term contract with Famous Players-Lasky in 1923, which led to his making some of his greatest works: *The Spanish Dancer* (1923), *Peter Pan* (1924), *A Kiss for Cinderella* (1926), *Dancing Mothers* (1926), *Beau Geste* (1926), and *The Great Gatsby* (1926). He had wanted to direct the screen adaptation of Warwick Deeping's novel *Sorrell and Son*, concerning the relationship between a World War I British officer and his son. Famous Players-Lasky was uninterested in the story, and Brenon produced it independently, filming many location scenes in England, including excellent sequences on a moving open-top London bus and a punt on the River Thames with Nils Asther and Mary Nolan. Starring is H. B. Warner, clinging to the "remnants of gentility," giving a beautiful performance opposite Alice Joyce as the wife he should have had.

Brenon always regarded *Sorrell and Son* as his favorite film. It is unfortunate that he did not have the opportunity to make the British sound version, filmed in 1933 by producer Herbert Wilcox and director Jack Raymond, with H. B. Warner reprising his original role.

After *Sorrell and Son*, Brenon's career went into decline, although his first talkie, *Lummox*, based on the Fannie Hurst novel, is not unworthy of his talent. In December 1931, it was reported that he was relieved of direction of the Joel McCrea/Dolores Del Rio vehicle, *Bird of Paradise*, and replaced by King Vidor. There were rumors that he was to come over to Britain and to Elstree, but nothing came of the notion.[7] It was not until 1935 that Brenon embarked on a major new career as a British director, making a total of eleven films there through 1939.[8] He obviously did not move permanently to Britain but commuted on a frequent basis. Of his British films, the two most important are *Royal Cavalcade* (1935) and *The Housemaster* (1938). The first, on which Brenon is one of several directors, is a historic and all-star review of the reign of King George V, at the time of his Silver Jubilee, with

Herbert Brenon and Mary Nolan en route to England on the SS *Majestic* to film location scenes for *Sorrell and Son* (1927).

appearances by Marie Lohr, Alice Lloyd (playing sister Marie), Sir Seymour Hicks, Matheson Lang, George Robey, Lady Astor, and many others.

The Housemaster is based on the 1936 Ian Hay play, which was to open on Broadway concurrent with the film's US release, and boasts a distinguished cast headed by Otto Kruger, Diana Churchill, and Phillips Holmes. Kynaston Reeves reprises his role of the headmaster, the Reverend Edmund Ovington from the stage production. It was a role that Reeves was to play in one form or another throughout his career. Somewhat akin to the later *Goodbye, Mr.*

Chips, and with perhaps a slight hint of a more civilized version of Lindsay Anderson's *If*, the story concerns a housemaster at a British public school who is understanding of the problems of his boys but is harassed by the new headmaster with new ideas of discipline. *Variety* (February 9, 1938) hailed it as "a money-maker," noting, "Thing that strikes the spectator is the well-knit progression of the tale, undoubtedly due to the handling of the picture by a well-seasoned Hollywood director."

When the film opened in New York at the Little Carnegie Playhouse, Frank Nugent in the *New York Times* (April 10, 1939) was equally enthusiastic, praising the performances of Otto Kruger and Kynaston Reeves, and writing, "A more serene little comedy would be hard to find and possibly would not be worth the bother, for its charm arises principally from its rarity." Playwright Ian Hay was also pleased, writing to Brenon: "What I particularly admired was the skill with which you brought out the real theme of the story, which is the clash of wills between the headmaster and the housemaster . . . your touch was sure all through."[9]

Herbert Brenon ended his career, both in Britain and elsewhere, with *The Flying Squad*, based on a play and British *Daily Mail* serialization by Edgar Wallace, and starring Sebastian Shaw and Phyllis Brooks. It was released in May 1940, long after Britain had declared war on Germany, and months after Brenon had returned to the United States. He died in Los Angeles in June 1958. In America, Brenon had a cottage at Malibu named the Peter Pan Cottage, and in England, he similarly named his home in the Surrey village of Elstead, Peter Pan Cottage.

Brenon is a major directorial figure of the silent era and of British cinema in the 1930s, but he was also a controversial one. He himself noted, "I have a pretty bad reputation for Intolerance."[10] He also had a reputation as an anti-Semite, openly making anti-Semitic comments at the studio in the 1920s, and as late as 1951, he wrote of Samuel Goldwyn, "the type of JEW I abhor, crude, coarse, ignorant."[11]

In a 1918 article in *Photoplay*, it was maintained that "the Irish dominate the production side of the motion picture business."[12] The claim is more than a little spurious in that the majority of the actors and actresses named in the piece were not actually born in Ireland. In reality, only five had been born in what was then part of Britain, and is now the Irish Republic; three were brothers, Matt, Owen, and Pat Moore, and there were also William Desmond, who claimed to be "the veteran of a thousand films," and Creighton Hale, a pleasant if undemonstrative leading man who had worked with everyone from Pearl White to D. W. Griffith.

Greer Garson and Ian Hunter help Dame May Whitty and Ben Webster celebrate their fiftieth wedding anniversary (July 1942).

Actors and others born after 1922 in Southern Ireland can rightly claim to be Irish and not British. Those born in Northern Ireland, the province of Ulster, have the choice to be either British or Irish. Greer Garson was, at one time, the most famous British star from Northern Ireland, but, in reality, she was born in London, in 1904, although her family came from Northern Ireland. In retrospect, it seems almost unthinkable that an actress so representative of British fortitude, British common sense, British ideals, and the British way of life at its most upper middle class could have been born anywhere but in a part of Britain in which nationality could be an issue. (For the record, she did actually play an Irish maid in the 1945 long-forgotten MGM production of *The Valley of Decision*.)

Garson began her acting career with the Birmingham Repertory Company in January 1932, with her first appearance on stage being in Elmer Rice's *Street Scene*. In the fall of 1936, she was screen tested by Douglas

Fairbanks, Jr., for the female lead in *Jump for Glory*, but she was under contract at the time to producer Noel Coward, appearing in London's West End in *Mademoiselle*, and he refused to release her. A year later, in September 1937, MGM's Louis B. Mayer, on a visit to London, saw Garson, gave her a screen test, and signed her to a seven-year contract. She was no sooner settled in Los Angeles than MGM decided she should return to Britain in 1938 for her first film, *Goodbye, Mr. Chips*, playing the doomed wife of the title character.

Back at Culver City and MGM, she was cast as the female lead in *Remember?* (1939), with Robert Taylor and Lew Ayres, and *Pride and Prejudice* (1940), replacing Vivien Leigh in the role of Elizabeth Bennet opposite Laurence Olivier as Darcy. Greer Garson played opposite Walter Pidgeon in *Blossoms in the Dust* (1941), and was reunited with him for her most famous screen role, the title character in *Mrs. Miniver*, which began filming in November 1941. As Mrs. Miniver, Garson exemplified for Americans how British womanhood was fighting and winning the war, even if the film was not always popular with British audiences, with its Americanized view of a British society ruled by class. One fan, however, was the wife of King George VI, later to become the Queen Mother, who told Garson, "You made us feel more brave than we actually were by your performance."[13]

A far more hostile response came from the leftist-leaning newspaper, the *Sunday Pictorial*, which described the film as being

> full of ghastly caricatures meant to represent the workers of Britain, while at the other end of the social scale, the Minivers themselves are portrayed as the backbone of the country—the comfortable, easy-going middle class. A few years ago you may remember how this class saved Britain from disaster by putting [prime minister] Baldwin into power and applauding Munich. . . . While Mrs. Miniver and her ilk drifted uselessly around village flower shows and vicarage tea parties, nine out of every ten men in Jarrow [in the economically depressed north of England] were out of work . . . and now we are asked to applaud this useless baggage resurrected from the Court Page of *The Times* to represent a nation at war while the woman who created *Mrs. Miniver* [author Jan Struther] announces that she plans to wait out the rest of the war in America.[14]

For her work in *Mrs. Miniver*, Garson received the Academy Award for Best Actress, and excelled herself at the awards ceremony on March 4, 1943, by speaking for five-and-a-half minutes and comparing herself to Alice in Wonderland.

Greer Garson remained popular in America, becoming a citizen in 1951. Her contract with MGM ended in March 1954, but she continued on screen, notably as Eleanor Roosevelt, opposite Ralph Bellamy as FDR, in *Sunrise at Campobello* (1960). In 1949, she had married a Texas millionaire, and in 1996, she died in Texas, a state it sometimes seems that has few values, either British or American.

Marsha Hunt played Garson's sister in two films, *Blossoms in the Dust* and *Pride and Prejudice*, and she recalls the actress as very professional on the set but also very impersonal. There was no suggestion of friendship outside of the studio. Many years later, after Garson had married her Texan, the two women met again, and Hunt notes how Garson had changed. She was far more outgoing, relaxed, and, basically, down-to-earth. Samantha Eggar points out that America could change the attitude of an English actor. One might be very English and withdrawn, but after a time in the United States, one adjusted and one's attitude and response changed drastically. As she points out, that is one good aspect of coming to work in the American film industry.[15]

Kenneth Branagh became an international star with *Henry V*, which he directed and scripted (with a little help from Shakespeare) and in which he also starred. His co-star, playing Katherine, was his then-wife Emma Thompson. Together, as one writer has noted, they became the "Most Famous theatrical couple in England since Laurence Olivier and Vivien Leigh."[16]

Born in a Protestant working-class area of Belfast in 1960, Branagh studied at the Royal Academy of Dramatic Art, made his West End debut opposite Rupert Everett in *Another Country* in 1982, and consolidated his reputation as a great Shakespearian actor with a 1992–93 appearance as Hamlet at London's National Theatre. Those were heady days for Branagh, and since then he has perhaps remained a star but never achieved again the greatness of his early performances. He is and sounds very English, but as he once noted, "I feel Irish. I don't think you can take Belfast out of the boy."[17]

And then there is Daniel Day-Lewis, whose background is *very* English, but who is so determinedly Irish that he would abhor the label of Anglo-Irish. He was born in the "posh" London neighborhood of Kensington, on April 29, 1957, the son of Cecil Day-Lewis, who was to serve as Britain's Poet Laureate, and Jill Balcon, the daughter of the most prominent of British-born film producers, Sir Michael Balcon. Actress Anna Lee once recalled

Daniel Day-Lewis.

for me that because of her friendship with Jill Balcon, she would sometimes bathe the infant Daniel. "Had I known what he was going to become, I would have drowned him," she proclaimed.

Educated at public schools (in the British sense of the term), Day-Lewis enrolled with the National Youth Theatre in 1973 and went on to work in repertory with the Bristol Old Vic for a year. His first film appearance was as a racist South African bully in Richard Attenborough's bio-picture *Gandhi* (1981). He was ship's officer Fryer in *Mutiny on the Bounty* (1984), and then came to fame as Johnny, the gay lover of Gordon Warneckee's Omar in Hanif Kureshi's *My Beautiful Laundrette* (1985). The director, Stephen Frears, had also considered him for the role of the gay novelist Joe Orton in his screen adaptation of *Prick Up Your Ears*.

In 1989, Daniel Day-Lewis abandoned Britain, largely because of what Mrs. Thatcher had done to the country, and applied for an Irish passport on the basis of his father's being born in the Irish province of County Laois. As his biographer has it, Ireland represented "another country, a romantic alternative home."[18]

Also in 1989, Day-Lewis became Irish on screen, playing physically handicapped Christy Brown in *My Left Foot*. The role gave him his first Academy Award for Best Actor, and led to his proclaiming his nationality very pointedly at the March 26, 1990, awards ceremony with the words, "You have provided me with the makings of one hell of a weekend in Dublin." Ironically, immediately before Christy Brown, Day-Lewis had appeared as *Hamlet* at London's National Theatre.

There were other films, including, of course, *Lincoln* (2012), for which he was again honored with an Academy Award, and which, thanks to his playing an American historical icon, gave him the status of a modern American icon. However, it was *In the Name of the Father* (1994), as Gerry Conlan, one of the so-called Guildford Four, imprisoned by the British as an IRA terrorist but released and exonerated after serving fifteen years for a crime that he did not commit, that gave Day-Lewis the opportunity to move still further away from his biological homeland and closer to his adopted one.

Somewhat in the tradition of Day-Lewis is Michael Fassbender, born in Germany, but with a mother from Northern Ireland. He was brought up in Southern Ireland, and so rightly does not belong here, although his role as IRA hunger striker Bobby Sands in *Hunger* (2008) is in the Daniel Day-Lewis tradition. However, unlike, Day-Lewis, Fassbender makes his home in London.

Although not directly a worker in the film industry, film critic Alexander Walker is certainly deserving of acknowledgment as someone born (in 1930) and educated in Northern Ireland. He was resolutely British, and, indeed, it would be difficult to identify his Irish background except that he was outspoken in his condemnation of IRA terrorists. Walker was immensely influential as the film critic for London's *Evening Standard* from 1960–2003, when he died, and also as the author of a number of preeminent film books on individuals such as Stanley Kubrick and Elizabeth Taylor, and the British cinema in general. He is famous also for being physically attacked, with a rolled up copy of the *Evening Standard*, on a 1971 BBC television program by director Ken Russell, whom the critic despised. He was as self-important as many a Hollywood star, and this writer recalls his once visiting the Margaret Herrick Library of the Academy of Motion Picture Arts and Sciences, and when asked to produce a photo identification, responding, "Just look on the back covers of my books." In a way, it might be written that Walker's description of the Andy Warhol film *Heat* serves as a description of himself: "stoked with self-importance. In a word, overheated."

Florence Turner.

CHAPTER FOUR

American Silent Stars to the Rescue of British Cinema in the 1910s and 1920s

AS PREVIOUSLY NOTED, VITAGRAPH WAS THE SECOND MAJOR AMERICAN film producer to make the journey to the United Kingdom, although the visit was in no way as extended as that by Kalem. That 1912 excursion was headed by director Larry Trimble, and it may well be that he suggested to the company's leading lady, Florence Turner, that she expand her horizons and embark on an extensive visit to Britain, the imminent outbreak of World War I notwithstanding. Space was rented at the Walton-on-Thames Studio of Cecil Hepworth, and the new entity made use of Hepworth's stock company, as well as hiring a young leading man named Henry Edwards, who was later closely to be associated with Hepworth.

Florence Turner had been the first star of the Vitagraph Company of America, joining the concern in 1907; she is arguably the country's first film star (although that honor should perhaps go to or at least be shared with Florence Lawrence). The actress left Vitagraph in 1913 to embark on a major vaudeville tour, and then announced that she would move to England, with her director Larry Trimble, Jean, the Vitagraph Dog (which Trimble owned), and Vitagraph actors Tom Powers and James Morrison. The plan was not only to make films in Britain, but also tour British music halls. It was a sudden and very unexpected move and somewhat inexplicable in that neither Turner nor Trimble had any known British connections. The only possible explanation can be the immense popularity of Vitagraph films in Europe in general and in Britain in particular.

Ultimately, Turner, Trimble, and Jean traveled to Britain, Powers came later, and Morrison did not make the journey. Florence Turner made her British stage debut, at the London Pavilion, on May 26, 1913. With the formation of her new film company, Turner Films, Trimble became head of production and Henry Edwards was chosen as Turner's leading man. As Trimble explained it,

> We located in England because three years ago the power of large combines in this country left slight opportunity for an independent producer with small capital. Miss Turner's popularity in Vitagraph pictures was our great asset in appealing directly to British exhibitors, who, as you know, were buying in the open market. But the extent of Miss Turner's fame on the other side none of us realized until the night of her first personal appearance in the London Pavilion. I never saw such a demonstration for any player. She was forced to remain on the stage six minutes beyond the allotted time, and even then the audience was not content.[1]

After the London appearance, Turner, accompanied by Trimble, toured the British Isles, appearing at 160 venues over a six-week period.

In all, Florence Turner was to star in some thirty or so productions in England, both features and short subjects. Among the films was the two-reel *Rose of Surrey*, released in September 1913, which the British trade paper the *Bioscope* described as "one of the most charming English film comedies ever produced," and *Far From the Madding Crowd*, released in February 1916, and the last in a series of six Turner British productions released in the United States by Mutual. Turner's comedic skills were highlighted in *Florence Turner Impersonates Film Favorites*, in which, as the title suggests, she appears as a reported thirty-two popular film stars, including Broncho Billy Anderson, Mabel Normand, and even Sarah Bernhardt in the final scene from *Queen Elizabeth*. The film was released in America in November 1915 by MinA (an acronym for "Made in America").

The most important of Turner's British films is *My Old Dutch*, which Universal released in America in November 1915, and based on Albert Chevalier's popular music-hall song, concerning a couple, Joe and Sal, growing old together. Trimble directed and Chevalier co-starred and co-wrote the script. As Trimble explained it, *My Old Dutch* best exemplified the filmmaking aims of Turner and Trimble, in that "it contains . . . a universal appeal, something striking deep in human nature, not dependent upon race or prejudice and comprehensible to both old and young. The theme in this instance is idyllic love."[2]

Contemporary critics would appear to have agreed. The *Moving Picture World* (November 13, 1915) wrote, "*My Old Dutch* is a rare picture, great in its simplicity, strong in its appeal, and splendidly played by its two principles. It is wholesome. It is a story that might have come from between the covers of a Dickens—with its sunshine and shade, its quaint types, its life." "The worst that can be said of it," commented *Variety* (July 23, 1915), "is that Albert Chevaliar looks too old in the early portion and Florence Turner too young in the later section." (In 1926, Trimble was to direct another version of the film, in America, with May McAvoy replacing Florence Turner.)

Some of Turner's films were directed by Henry Edwards, and Larry Trimble made some films without her, including, all released in 1916, *Caste*, with Sir John Hare and Peggy Hyland, soon to journey to America, *Sally in Our Alley*, and *A Place in the Sun*, starring Reginald Owen. Tom Powers appeared in a handful of films, most notably as *Barnaby Rudge*, a Cecil Hepworth production, co-starring Henry Edwards and Chrissie White, and released in March 1915.

One of the Turner films directed by Henry Edwards, who also co-stars, is *East Is East*, released in February 1917 but shot in the summer of 1916, in which the second female lead is taken by Edith Evans long before she had become famous on stage. The film, which survives, was released in America by Mutual but dismissed by *Variety* (November 10, 1916) as "totally unsuited for American audiences," because of the Cockney phrases and slang used in the subtitles and its essentially English atmosphere. Evans had appeared earlier in another Turner film, *A Welsh Singer*, released in December 1915, again with Edwards directing and co-starring.

Wartime conditions in Britain, coupled with the difficulty of releasing the films in America, forced Turner and Trimble to return to the United States, Trimble in August 1916 and Turner in November of the same year. While she had been gone, the American film industry had changed and Turner was no longer the star she once had been. She was perhaps a little too homely, a little too ordinary-looking to be a big name anymore. Eventually, in 1922, she returned to Britain. Joyously, she told the British trade paper *Motion Picture Studio* (April 15, 1922),

> So here I am again, glad, and, oh most happy to be in the country where its people have always made me so heartily welcome, and hoping never to leave it again. I can only say most sincerely that coming back to Great Britain has just meant coming home to me.

Sadly, the British film industry had also changed. It was in a massive economic slump. There was no market for British films, and no market for

Florence Turner. She made some stage appearances in British music halls, giving impersonations of various stars. Of the half-dozen films in which she appeared, only two have any minor importance, *The Old Wive's Tale* (1921), based on the Arnold Bennett novel and co-starring Fay Compton, and *Sally Bishop* (1923), based on the play by E. Temple Thurston and starring Marie Doro.

By 1924, Florence Turner was basically stranded in Britain, without work and without funds. It was Marion Davies who paid for Turner and her mother's return to the United States, and gave her a small part in her next vehicle, *Janice Meredith*.[3] That small role was emblematic of what the future held. The parts got smaller and smaller until, by the 1930s, Turner was nothing more than a Hollywood extra. She died in August 1946, after retiring to the Motion Picture Country House in Woodland Hills, California, where she lived reliant on the financial support of others in the film industry,

There is another American production company with an indirect link to British cinema and that is Edison. It may not have been by design, but several former employees of the company came to Britain in the 1910s and 1920s and established prominent careers there. The biggest star, although such a designation is somewhat relative, was Gertrude McCoy, who was to be seen in sixteen British feature films, released between 1919 and 1926. The most prominent was her last British film, *Nelson*, released in September 1926, in which she appears as Lady Hamilton opposite Cedric Hardwicke in the title role, and which is directed by Walter Summers, a director deserving of reevaluation. Three of the films—*The Usurer* (1919), *The Auction Mart* (1920), and *Burnt In* (1920)—were directed by Scottish-born Duncan McRae, whom McCoy married in 1919 and who died in 1931. Gertrude McCoy died in 1967 in the state of Georgia, where she was born seventy-seven years earlier.

Edison leading lady Edna Flugrath was the lesser-known of three acting sisters, and unlike the other two, Viola Dana and Shirley Mason, she retained the family name. She starred in some nine British films, released in 1914 through 1916, and a further six British films released in 1920 and 1921, with the most prominent being an adaptation of H. G. Wells's *Kipps*, with George K. Arthur in the title role, shot in London and on the south coast at Folkestone. The *Bioscope* (January 27, 1921) hailed it as a "faithful and entertaining version of H. G. Wells' novel." Arthur became a star thanks to his appearance here and went on to work in Hollywood, most notably opposite Karl Dane in a series of MGM comedies of the late 1920s, and was later a producer and distributor of short subjects. It was George K. Arthur who financed Josef von Sternberg's first film, *The Salvation Hunters* (1925),

Edna Flugrath.

in which he also appeared, and in 1956 he received an Academy Award for Best Short Subject—Two Reels for *The Bespoke Overcoat*.

The most prominent of Flugrath's British films it would seem was not a feature, but the two-reel *England's Menace*, released in June 1914. Here, she plays Lady Betty Talbot, daughter of the prime minister's secretary, identifies the butler as a spy and thwarts a German invasion of Britain. The film opened at New York's Million Dollar Strand Theatre on August 29, 1914, and created "a sensation" according to the *Moving Picture World* (September 12, 1914).

Flugrath was often criticized for playing roles for which she was too old, although such fault-finding would seem to be somewhat unfair in that she was still only in her twenties. In view of her casting, it is not totally without surprise that one discovers her films were directed by her future husband, Harold Shaw, with whom she had first worked at Edison. Initially, Shaw did

George Loane Tucker.

his "bit" for the war effort by joining the Twickenham Volunteers in April 1915, and Flugrath was reported as thinking "England a beautiful country and has been happy there,"[4] but eventually, as the war dragged on, the couple left England and moved to South Africa. Here they were married (in Johannesburg) in January 1917, and Shaw made *Die Voortrekkers* (released in Britain as *Winning a Continent*) also in 1917. Except for *Kipps*, the return to England did not generate any memorable films for either party.

The Flugrath-Shaw films were produced by the London Film Company, located in Twickenham on the outskirts of London, and founded in 1913. If nothing else, London had a perhaps unrealistic view of the importance of American filmmakers. Aside from Flugrath and Shaw, who was hired as "general director" in May 1913, it also employed George Loane Tucker, Jane Gail, and Bannister Merwin. The latter was a busy screenwriter with more than 140 films to his credit, some forty or more of which he also directed—and he was another refugee from Edison, remaining in London until his death in February 1922. One of Merwin's last films, which he both directed and adapted for the screen from the play by Sir Arthur Wing Pinero is *The Magistrate*, produced by G. B. Samuelson in 1921.

Jane Gail is best remembered today for her performance as one of the two female leads in the 1913 "white slavery" exploitation film, *Traffic in Souls*. She came to Britain in 1914, and made eight feature films and a large number of short subjects there through into 1915. The most prominent of her roles is as Princess Flavia in *The Prisoner of Zenda* (which was not shown in the United States) and *Rupert of Hentzau*, both released in 1915. The director of these and other feature-length films is George Loane Tucker, who was also responsible for *Traffic in Souls*. Despite their work together, Gail and Tucker were not married, and, in fact, the latter married British actress Elizabeth Risdon in 1916.[5] As did Gail, Tucker returned to America, along with his new wife. George Loane Tucker died in 1921, two years after making his most famous film, *The Miracle Man*, in which Lon Chaney demonstrates his gift for makeup and physically challenged roles. Unlike his American contemporaries in Britain, Tucker is associated with films that have not only commercial titles but also familiar ones, including Hall Caine's *The Christian* (1915) and *The Manxman* (1917), both starring Elizabeth Risdon, and *Arsène Lupin* (1916).[6] As Rachael Low has pointed out, it is curious that three prominent males associated with the London Film Company—Merwin, Shaw, and Tucker—all died in the 1920s and all at young ages.

One other link between Edison and Britain is worth recording. The subject was not an actor but Harry Furniss (1854–1925), one of the country's leading illustrators, associated with the humor magazine *Punch* from 1880–94. Rather like J. Stuart Blackton, Furniss gave illustrated lectures utilizing his cartoons, and in 1912, he came to the United States. He joined the Edison Company and produced a number of animated shorts and series, including *War Cartoons* and *Peace and Pencillings* (both 1914).

The two most prominent American "names" to appear in British films of the 1910s did so because they happened to be appearing—separately—on the London stage. In 1914, Thomas Meighan, who was as much a stage actor as a later screen star, made his film debut in a two-reel short, *Dandy Donovan, the Gentleman Cracksman*, in which he plays a jewel

Malvina Longfellow.

thief, accidentally kissed by Gladys Cooper to the anger of her husband, Owen Nares. Obviously nothing more than a one-act play transferred to the screen, it must have been quite an impressive film with three stars of equal prominence. American vaudeville star Cecelia Loftus appeared in a 1917 British film, *Diana of Dobson's*, playing the title role.

Malvina Longfellow had a brief career on the New York stage after studying at the American Academy of Dramatic Arts, but her main career—in film from 1919 onwards—was in Britain, a result of her marrying a British army officer. She starred in more than a dozen features, including *Adam Bede* (1919) and *The Wandering Jew* (1923). In 1922, she was selected by E. O. Hoppé, who was a connoisseur of this sort of thing, as one of the most beautiful women in the world. Longfellow was dark-haired and statuesque, and she made a perfect Lady Hamilton in two British films, *Nelson* (1918) and *The Romance of Lady Hamilton* (1919). There was even talk in 1921 that Ernst

Lubitsch wanted her to play Lady Hamilton opposite Reinhold Schunzel in a German film on the life of Nelson. Longfellow's career ended in 1924, except for a supporting role in a 1929 British Instructional Films adaptation of Baroness Orczy's novel, *The Celestial City*. She never returned to America and died in London in November 1962.

Marie Doro was an exquisite American beauty of stage and screen, whose greatest performance was perhaps not a female one but as Oliver Twist at first on the stage in 1912 and then on screen in 1916. She starred in two British films from 1919, *A Sinless Sinner* and *Twelve-Ten*, directed by Herbert Brenon, both for British & Colonial. She returned to America but became disillusioned with life here, and moved back to Europe, appearing in one last British film, *Sally Bishop*, in 1923.

In the 1920s, there were a number of American actors making brief trips to Britain for a single appearance on screen. In 1922, ingénue Constance Binney starred in the first screen adaptation of Clemence Dane's play *A Bill of Divorcement*. Also in 1922, a somewhat lesser ingénue, Ann Forest, starred for Famous Players-Lasky British, under the direction of John S. Robertson, in *Perpetua*. Seena Owen, who had been D. W. Griffith's Princess Beloved in *Intolerance* had the lead in Ideal's last film, *The Great Well* (1924). In association with a German company and in the Berlin studios of Ufa, Herbert Wilcox directed Lionel Barrymore in his epic *Decameron Nights*, released in the autumn of 1924. Later, in 1927, Herbert Wilcox directed Pauline Frederick in a screen adaptation of Edward Knoblock's play *Mumsie*, with Herbert Marshall as second lead. Tallulah Bankhead spent most of the 1920s starring on the London stage, and it was no great effort for her to find the time for at least one British film, an adaptation of Sir Arthur Wing Pinero's play *His House in Order*, released in 1928.

Making the journey for starring roles in a couple of British films of the 1920s there was Jane Novak,[7] directed by Graham Cutts, in *The Blackguard*, filmed in Berlin, and *The Prude's Fall*, with the latter also featuring American leading lady Julanne Johnstone. Both films were shot in 1923 but not released until 1925. Wanda Hawley's years as a Paramount leading lady were over when she also came to Britain in 1923 to star in *Fires of Fate* and *Lights o' London*. The serial star Charles "Hutch" Hutchinson was brought over to England by Ideal in 1923 to star in two short features, *Hurricane Hutch in Many Adventures* and *Hutch Stirs 'Em Up*. Despite the latter title, he failed to stir the audience. Catherine Calvert was never much of a star in America, and it is no surprise that she ended her career with three 1923 films in Britain, *The Indian Love Lyrics*, *Out to Win*, and *The Green*

Caravan. Japanese star Sessue Hayakawa and his wife, Tsuru Aoki, had been appearing in American films of the 1910s and early 1920s, and, of course, Hayakawa was later to have a leading role in David Lean's *The Bridge on the River Kwai* (1957); they made two silent films in Britain, for Stoll, in 1923 or 1924, *The Great Prince Shan* and *Sen Yan's Devotion*. Alice Joyce added more than a touch of class—as well as her own elegance and underplaying—to two British films some years apart. In 1924, she was seen in *The Passionate Adventure*, directed by Graham Cutts, and co-starring Clive Brook and American Marjorie Daw. It was one of the better British films of the 1920s and the first from Gainsborough Pictures. Joyce returned in 1928 to star opposite Jameson Thomas in *The Rising Generation*. (Marjorie Daw and Clive Brook had also starred in *Human Desires*, but it did not receive a release until 1925, two years after it was shot.)

Producer Michael Balcon had visited Los Angeles to try and arrange distribution for his films with Myron Selznick, whom he brought back to England with him. There, Selznick met Marjorie Daw and Alice Joyce. As a result, Daw and Selznick married and the latter formed the Joyce-Selznick Agency with Alice Joyce's brother, Frank.

Thanks to a brief engagement on the American stage, Juliette Compton received offers of work in London's West End and from that made the obvious transition to films. Virtually her entire screen career in the 1920s was in British films from 1924 onwards, including *Her Redemption* (1924), *Bulldog Drummond's Third Round* (1925), *Nell Gwynne* (1926), *The Chinese Bungalow* (1926), and *The Triumph of the Scarlet Pimpernel* (1928), in all of which she appears as a sultry-looking beauty with the eyes of a seductress. Returning to the United States, Compton was a busy supporting player in Hollywood, her years in England providing her with a British accent where needed, as in her last screen appearance in *Lady Hamilton/That Hamilton Woman* (1941).

Brooklyn-born Josephine Earle had found fame with the Vitagraph Company, also from Brooklyn, and in 1917, she accepted an engagement in London in *The Lilac Domino*, which made "an agreeable impression," according to the *New York Times* (March 31, 1918). A year later, she met a Canadian Air Force captain in Britain, and the couple was married in September 1918. It was perhaps the marriage that kept Earle in England and persuaded her to embark on a film career, which lasted from 1920 through 1923 and included seven starring roles in feature productions as well as second female lead in the most important of her films, *Woman to Woman*, in 1923. She went with her husband to Canada in 1921, but the visit and the marriage ended later that year. Earle alternated film roles with appearances on stage and in

Juliette Compton, star of British films of the 1920s, ends her career as Lady Spencer in *Lady Hamilton/ That Hamilton Woman* (1941).

cabaret. She made two sound films in 1929, appearing in supporting roles in *Unto Each Other* and *Raise the Roof*, both released in 1930. In later years, Earle moved with her second husband to Stratford upon Avon, where she died in April 1961.

Evelyn Brent had been on screen since 1914, initially as an extra and then as a second female lead. She came to Britain in June 1920 to appear on stage, as an American chorus girl, in the comedy *The Ruined Lady*. As a result of publicity from the play, she was quickly asked to star in one British film after another, along with three in the Netherlands and one in Spain. They were not major productions, although three—*Sonia/The Woman Who Came Back* (1921), *Married to a Mormon* (1922), and *The Experiment* (1922)—featured Clive Brook as her leading man. *Married to a Mormon* is the sequel to the strongly anti-Church of Jesus Christ of Latter Day Saints production, *Trapped by the Mormons* (1922), which deals with the influx of Mormon missionaries into Britain and the fear that they planned to enslave decent British girls and ship them back to Salt Lake City and polygamous lives. Thanks to her British career, when Brent returned to America, as a result of a slump in British filmmaking, she was hailed as a leading lady and future roles were prominent ones.

"The Americans have left us with very few stories to tell," complained Alfred Hitchcock to the London *Evening News* (November 16, 1927). Well, if you can't beat them, join them, and more than a decade before he actually did journey over to America, Hitchcock brought American stars over for his first films. Or perhaps they were simply forced upon him. For the first, *The Pleasure Garden* (1925), he had two Hollywood leading ladies, Virginia Valli and Carmelita Geraghty, neither of whom can be described as stars. In fact, the two British leading men, Miles Mander and John Stuart, were certainly of equal, if not superior, talent, and had both gained recognition for their work throughout Europe. Nita Naldi, famous as a Hollywood vamp and for little else, appeared in Hitchcock's second film as director, *The Mountain Eagle* (1926). He was not pleased with her performance; as he told François Truffaut, "She had fingernails out to there. Ridiculous!"[8]

If asked to select the one American actor who contributed the most to British silent films, the name of Carlyle Blackwell might not come immediately to mind. On screen in America since 1910, he typified the older British leading men, slightly graying around the temples and with a digni fied, somewhat harried appearance. And like many of his colleagues, he obviously had a high opinion of his body, insistently showing off his bare chest in *She* (1925), despite its not being a particularly attractive sight.

Blackwell made the journey to Europe in 1922, with the intention of working in British, French, and German films. He was to remain in Britain, on and off, for some fourteen years, working not only as an actor but also a producer and director. Blackwell's first European film was made neither in Britain, France, or Germany, but in the Netherlands. Released in November 1922, *Bulldog Drummond* was made by Hollandia Company and directed by American Oscar Apfel, who had co-directed *The Squaw Man* with Cecil B. DeMille. (Apfel directed a second Dutch film, *The Lion's Mouse*, released in April 1923.) Blackwell's first British screen appearance was in *The Beloved*

Carlyle Blackwell.

Vagabond (1923), directed by Fred Leroy Granville, whose career began as a cinematographer and who had been active in Hollywood in the 1910s.

Blackwell had the lead opposite Lady Diana Manners in J. Stuart Blackton's Prizma Color production of *The Virgin Queen* (1923) and opposite Betty Blythe in an adaptation of H. Rider Haggard's *She*, shot in Berlin in 1925. Also in 1925, Blackwell met the diamond millionairess Leah Barnato, whom he married in July 1926 and whose wealth was undoubtedly beneficial to her husband's career. Barnato was Blackwell's second wife, and she was followed by three others.

In July 1926, Blackwell and Michael Balcon established Piccadilly Pictures, with themselves as joint managing directors, and their first two productions together were Alfred Hitchcock's *The Lodger* and Graham Cutts's *The Triumph of the Rat*. Cutts also directed Blackwell at Piccadilly in *The Rolling Road* (1927), in which the leading lady was Flora Le Breton, a petite British ingénue who had limited success in pursuing a film career in America.

Blackwell returned to the United States in October 1927, but within a year he was back, starring opposite Benita Hume in *The Wrecker* (1929), filmed in Berlin, and playing opposite Madeleine Carroll in *The Crooked Billet* (1930). Despite or because of its theme song, "Are You Really Mine?", the critic in the *New York Times* (August 13, 1929) dismissed *The Wrecker* as "a childish melodrama, in its direction and acting." For Piccadilly, Blackwell produced, directed, and starred in two 1930 releases, *Bedrock* and *Beyond the Stars*. Blackwell's was a formidable British career and one deserving of more recognition and certainly one as important as his American career, which was not revived after his return to this country in 1931.

On screen in America from the mid-1910s, Bryant Washburn was somewhat similar to Carlyle Blackwell in that he was never in the top rank of Hollywood leading men but was always busy. Both were distinguished rather than overly handsome leading men. In 1921, Washburn came to Britain to star in and produce *The Road to London*, in which his leading lady was Joan Morgan, daughter of director Sidney Morgan, who had recently played the title role in *Little Dorrit* (1920). She recalled,

> At this time the American star, Bryant Washburn, had come to make a film in England and was looking for a leading lady. We heard of this, but never for a moment thought of it in relation to me. He came to the trade show of *Little Dorrit* and afterwards asked to see me. I looked in those days exceptionally young for my age—small, socks, shoulder-length hair. He gasped: "Is this the girl?" But he chose me! He was a wonderful person. They dressed and photographed me beautifully and at the end offered me a five-year contract. And this is where the happiness ends; my father would not let me go.[9]

The storyline was simple: a visiting American helps a young English socialite avoid an arranged marriage to a viscount by escaping with her in a stolen car through the English countryside. The film was short—only five reels—but crammed with shots of London landmarks and locations in

Surrey along the River Thames (including Windsor). At its New York release by Associated Exhibitors/Pathé in the summer of 1920, *Variety* (August 5, 1921) could not find enough good things to write about the film, describing it as "a fine sincere effort, adequately and expertly registered on the screen. And also a distinct relief from the problem and sex play." The *Los Angeles Times* (September 15, 1921) noted that *The Road to London* was "of much delightfully nonsensical and beautiful pictorial stuff."

Bryant Washburn had returned to New York in early November 1920. He was not exactly enthusiastic about British production techniques, commenting, "In their equipment the English are ten years behind us, but they were most generous in co-operating with us while we were abroad—even the city officials and the police department."[10] *The Road to London* opened at the New York Hippodrome on September 15, 1921, running for only three days, and then Washburn embarked on a cross-country tour, promoting the production.

In the spring of 1917, D. W. Griffith was invited to make a World War I propaganda film for the British, which became *Hearts of the World*. He came to London, along with Lillian and Dorothy Gish, Robert Harron, and cinematographer Billy Bitzer, and some scenes were shot in Britain, on Salisbury Plain and in the Cotswold village of Stanton. It was in Stanton that Noel Coward made his screen debut, playing a "bit" part under Griffith's direction. While in Britain, Griffith also shot footage of members of the aristocracy which he utilized in *The Great Love*. Samuel Goldwyn's 1922 release, *Sherlock Holmes*, features a number of exterior scenes shot in London with John Barrymore. The film was released in Britain as *Moriarty*, apparently to avoid confusion between this superior Hollywood production and lesser British Sherlock Holmes films. From Hollywood, Richard Dix and Mae Busch came over to London and the Isle of Man in 1923 to shoot exterior scenes for *The Christian*, based on the Hall Caine novel and play. There were rumors that the couple was to return in 1934 for a remake, but nothing came of the project and by then certainly Busch was past her prime as a leading lady. *If Winter Comes* (1923) and *Sorrell and Son* (1928) were two other Hollywood productions that made use of British locations, and Thomas Meighan returned to the British Isles to film *Irish Luck* for Paramount on location in what was now the Irish Free State.

There were four prominent American stars who came to Britain in the 1920s: Mae Marsh, Betty Compson, Betty Blythe, and Dorothy Gish. Two men were largely responsible, together and separately, for the success of the films these American actresses made in England, and they are Herbert

Wilcox and Graham Cutts, who had formed their own production company, Wilcox-Graham, in 1921. The two men were the best British cinema had to offer at that time—young, energetic, talented, and innovative. Both were directors, although at the start of their partnership Wilcox was serving as producer.

The two had something else in common. They were both tremendous admirers of D. W. Griffith, and when sufficient financing became available (after two initial productions), it is not surprising that Cutts and Wilcox should have decided to hire a star associated with Griffith. They didn't pick Lillian Gish, but they did choose Mae Marsh—an actress whom Cutts idolized,[11]—and certainly the greatest dramatic star that Griffith nurtured and who gives two of the finest performances ever in silent films with her work in Griffith's *The Birth of a Nation* (1915) and *Intolerance* (1916). The reality also was that while Gish was expanding her career and her stardom, Marsh was already in something of a decline, appearing in films definitely inferior to anything that either Griffith or Gish were making in the late 1910s and early 1920s.

Woman to Woman (1923), with Betty Compson and Marie Ault.

Marsh was paid between 750 and 1,000 pounds a week to star in two films, *Flames of Passion*, released in November 1922, and *Paddy-the-Next-Best-Thing*, released in January 1923. The actress was obviously immensely popular in Britain, and, as Wilcox recalled, "there must have been thirty to forty thousand people at Waterloo Station to meet this little wisp of a girl."[12]

Both films secured American release, with Wilcox and Cutts actually traveling to America to help promote *Paddy-the-Next-Best-Thing*, which boasted a finale shot in Prizma Color. Of the two, only *Tides of Passion* was reviewed by Mordaunt Hall in the *New York Times* (August 20, 1925), at its opening at the Rialto Theatre; he found it "a very sad affair." Marsh returned to America and to Griffith, appearing in his 1923 production of *The White Rose*, for which the director brought over British star, Ivor Novello.

Both Novello and Marsh were reunited in 1925 in Britain by Graham Cutts, when he directed the two stars in *The Rat*, which Novello had written initially as a film script while working on *The White Rose*. It was actress Constance Collier who persuaded him to rewrite it as a stage play, his first as author and actor-manager. *The Rat* opened in Brighton in January 1924 and transferred successfully to London's West End in June of that year.

There may be faults with the film in terms of its being a romantic melodrama set in Paris with Novello as a somewhat effeminate-looking criminal and Marsh as his long-suffering love interest, but the direction and the camerawork (by Hal Young) is brilliant, with Cutts as much as possible using fluid camera movement in lieu of editing cuts. *The Rat* was Mae Marsh's last silent film and was perhaps intended as her farewell to the screen, with her becoming a mother and a housewife. She could not have made a better choice to end her career had that actually signaled the close of her work on screen.

Immediately after directing Marsh, Cutts was again hired to direct an American star—Betty Compson—in *Woman to Woman*. The film was the first from a new production company, Balcoln-Saville-Freedman, headed by Michael Balcon, Victor Saville, and John Freedman. Based on a 1921 stage play by Michael Morton, *Woman to Woman* was an adult drama concerning a shell-shocked soldier with no memory of a wartime romance. Compson was paid 1,000 pounds a week for her work. The film is no longer extant, but supposedly one scene required the presence of four Nubian slaves, two of whom were played by Victor McLaglen and his brother.

Despite its popularity as film material in England, the first version of *Woman to Woman* was not well received by the *New York Times* (April 1, 1924) at its New York opening at the Rivoli Theatre. Both Clive Brook and

Graham Cutts were criticized, and of Betty Compson, the anonymous reviewer wrote,

> while her work in this picture is far better than any of the other players, it is not enough to make up for the poor direction and rather worn-out theme. . . . Summed up, this picture has too much agony and too little real action.

Woman to Woman was released in November 1923, and immediately upon completion, Cutts, Compson, leading man Brook, and others were reunited for *The White Shadow*, which was advertised in the trade papers as having "the same Star, Producer, Author, Hero, Cameraman, Scenic Artist, Staff, Studio, Renting Company as *Woman to Woman*."[13] Despite the promotion, when it was released in February 1924, *The White Shadow* was not particularly successful.

Betty Compson reprised her role in *Woman to Woman* in a 1929 sound version, directed by Victor Saville, and filmed at the Tiffany-Stahl Studios in Hollywood, with Michael Balcon producing. It ran for two weeks at New York's Globe Theatre, beginning on November 11, 1929. There was yet a third version of *Woman to Woman*, released in November 1946, starring Joyce Howard and American leading man Douglass Montgomery.

Betty Blythe was known for her exotic roles in Hollywood, particularly as the title character in *The Queen of Sheba* (1921). In 1923, she starred for Graham-Wilcox in *Chu Chin Chow*, with Herbert Wilcox taking over the directorial reins from Graham Cutts, and filming at the Ufa Studios in Berlin. Neither the film nor the cast was particularly memorable. The same might be written of the second Blythe-Wilcox production, *Southern Love*,[14] also filmed in 1923 for 1924 release. Betty Blythe was back in Germany in 1925 to star in a British film adaptation of *She*, produced by G. B. Samuelson. The actress was promised but did not receive 2,000 pounds a week for her work.

Chu Chin Chow opened in New York at the Piccadilly Theatre, and Mordaunt Hall in the *New York Times* (February 11, 1925) wrote, "Here we have a carefully made picture, with imposing settings and pleasing costumes, which often drags in the unfolding of the tale."

In 1926, another D. W. Griffith leading lady, Dorothy Gish, came to England at Herbert Wilcox's invitation to play the title role in *Nell Gwynne*. She accompanied her husband, James Rennie, who was appearing on the London stage in *The Great Gatsby* and who so impressed Wilcox that he gave him a role in his 1933 production of *The Little Damozel*. *Nell Gwynne*

Betty Blythe en route to England to star in *Chu Chin Chow* (1923).

was an instantaneous success and is arguably the best film that Dorothy Gish ever made. As critic George Jean Nathan commented, "It took a British director and an English-made film to reveal how sexy Dorothy Gish can be." And "sexy" she is, displaying much of her very appealing body and obviously enjoying every minute of her seduction by King Charles I (played by Randle Ayrton). *Photoplay* warned, "Just for the grown-ups."

Nell Gwynne received a gala premiere at New York's Ritz-Carlton on January 25, 1926, and proved, as *Motion Picture News* (February 6, 1926) noted that the British could make a film with "class." The critic for the *New York Times* (July 19, 1926) hailed the film as a "smoothly developed and charming presentation," concluding,

> Whatever may be the shortcomings of English motion picture producers, if they can put together other pictures as simply and with as much dramatic effect as the story of Nell Gwynne they should have no difficulty obtaining a showing for them anywhere.

Dorothy Gish in *Nell Gwynne* (1926).

Herbert Wilcox directed the final three Dorothy Gish films made in England. Producer J. D. Williams of British National Pictures, based at Elstree, announced he had

> signed a contract with Famous Players-Lasky Company by which that concern agrees to reimburse the entire outlay of the next three films by National Pictures, give the films a world-wide distribution and pay the British company a percentage of the gross receipts as a royalty.

It was evidence not only of Gish's continuing box-office appeal, but also that Wilcox had become a British director worthy of special attention.

The first production, *London*, was released in January 1927, and based on a story by Thomas Burke, who had provided the story material for *Broken Blossoms*, starring Dorothy's sister, Lillian. Despite a lavish premiere at New York's Rivoli Theatre on October 24, 1926, *Variety* (October 27, 1926) complained that the film was "weak," and audiences received it with indifference. *London* was followed by *Madame Pompadour*, released in Britain in April 1928, and with Hollywood leading man Antonio Moreno, playing opposite Dorothy Gish. *Madame Pompadour* opened at New York's Paramount Theatre on July 31, 1927, to less than ecstatic reviews. It should have been as impressive as *Nell Gwynne*, but it is not thanks to a weak story and antiquated direction which seems to overemphasize the costume drama and ignore the human touches. The final film of the trio was *Tip Toes*, based on the 1925 musical by Guy Bolton, Fred Thompson, and George and Ira Gershwin, of primary interest because of the presence of Will Rogers in the cast. Dorothy Gish returned to Britain and to Herbert Wilcox in 1930 to star in *Wolves*, with a cast including Charles Laughton. Wilcox produced, with Albert de Courville, from the musical and revue stage, directing. *Wolves* was the first all-talkie to be made by British & Dominions, and Wilcox always claimed, probably incorrectly, that it was Britain's first talkie.

Indeed, some years earlier there had been sound films in Britain thanks to American sound-on-film pioneer Lee DeForest, who had made sound shorts for New York presentation in 1923, and a year later began production in Britain, at the DeForest Phonofilm Studios in the South London suburb of Clapham. The first film, in 1924, was the two-reeler, *Love's Old Sweet Song*, starring American actress Una Merkel. A number of talkie short subjects were made from 1925 onwards, starring a number of prominent British performers, including Billy Bennett, Dorothy Boyd, Mary Clare, George Robey, Arthur Roberts, Jameson Thomas, and Robb Wilton.

The company was acquired in August 1928 by British Talking Pictures, Ltd., which formed British Sound Film Productions, Ltd., a month later to continue production.

The importation of American stars (and that phrase is used somewhat loosely) made a lot of sense in view of what appealed to British moviegoers and what would not. As a prominent London film critic wrote in 1927:

> The plain truth about the British film situation is that the bulk of our picturegoers are Americanized to an extent that makes them regard the British film as a foreign film, and an interesting but more frequently irritating interlude in their favorite entertainment. They go to see American

stars. They have been brought up on American publicity. They talk America, think America, and dream America. We have several million people, mostly women, who, to all intent and purpose, are temporarily American citizens."[15]

During a parliamentary debate on the British cinema in the late 1920s, one politician commented that it was "not good that Britishers should be compelled to imbibe the ideas . . . of foreigners." Another complained that "the theatres are booked up with masses of American rubbish."[16] In the decade to follow, it would not merely be "rubbish" produced in America on British cinema screens, but also, and perhaps more insidiously, a major and often undetected American invasion of British cinema by "rubbish" American players and directors making British films. The only positive aspect of the "rubbish" invasion was that the ideas put forward were quite definitely and often quite unfortunately British in content. Any attempt at Americanization of the product itself was decidedly unhealthy and amateurish.

The coming of sound in the late 1920s should have boded well for British cinema. Unlike filmmakers in France, Germany, and Italy, the British did not have to concern themselves with production in a foreign language. British producers could compete in both America and Britain without the need for dubbing. Unfortunately, the British cinema did not take into account the need not merely for a single language but, more importantly, a need for quality and sophistication.

CHAPTER FIVE

American Cinematographers of the 1920s and 1930s in Britain

THE FIRST MAJOR INVASION OF BRITAIN BY AMERICAN CINEMATOGRAPHERS began, to all intents and purposes, in 1919 when Famous Players-Lasky[1] decided to establish a British film studio on Poole Street in the London suburb of Islington. The first two productions, *The Call of Youth* and *The Great Day*, were both shot in 1920 by Hal Young.[2] The director was Hugh Ford, whose American career had begun in 1913 but was now at an end; the screenplay for *The Call of Youth* was by American Eve Unsell, who may not actually have traveled to England to accomplish the work.[3] Nine further features were filmed at Islington prior to the closing of the studio in 1924.

Roy Overbaugh photographed two of those Famous Players-Lasky British features, *Perpetua* and *Spanish Jade*, both released in 1922, before being brought back to the United States by the company. Overbaugh returned to England in the late 1920s to photograph Harry Lauder in *Hunting Tower* (1928) and Jack Buchanan in *Confetti* (1927). His most important work at that time, however, was with producer-director Herbert Wilcox, for whom he photographed Dorothy Gish in her three starring 1928 vehicles, *Madame Pompadour*, *Nell Gwynne*, and *Tip Toes*. While not belittling Gish's performances, much of the credit for their success outside of the United Kingdom belongs, as critic Iris Barry noted at the time, to the "able American cameraman."[4]

Another American cinematographer working at the Islington studios was Arthur C. Miller, who photographed *Three Live Ghosts* and *The Man from Home*—both released in 1922—for American director George Fitzmaurice. Miller utilized a concealed camera to film candid scenes for the former on the streets of London. Here, for the first time Miller met Alfred Hitchcock, who worked as a prop boy at Islington. Hitchcock, for whom Miller was to film *Lifeboat* in 1944, did not make a very good impression on Miller, but it was script girl Alma Reville of whom Miller spoke glowingly in later years, and of Reville's then-fiancé, assistant director Leslie Hiscott.

Although born in France, René Guissart had gained a considerable reputation in the 1910s for his photography on American films, particularly those of director Maurice Tourneur. After completing work on *The Lying Truth* for writer-director Marion Fairfax in 1922, Guissart was called to England by Harley Knoles to film a silent version of the Balfe opera, *The Bohemian Girl*, a somewhat tepid melodrama which was not helped by the presence of a coterie of British stage performers, including Gladys Cooper, Ivor Novello, Constance Collier, and C. Aubrey Smith, all of whom were later to go to the United States for careers on screen of varying length and variable quality. Guissart was to work later for Knoles on the 1927 British features, *Land of Hope and Glory* and *The White Sheik*.

It may well be that when an American star visited Britain in the 1920s she would expect better lighting than British cinematographers could provide, or perhaps even the stars demanded a top-rate cinematographer. Certainly, Guissart was called upon to photograph American stars Betty Blythe in *Chu Chin Chow* (1923) and *Southern Love* (1924), Mae Marsh in *Flames of Passion* (1922) and *Paddy-the-Next-Best-Thing* (1923), and Syd Chaplin in *A Little Bit of Fluff* (1928, released in the US as *Skirts*). Guissart's American career is also the reason why American-born director Tim Whelan should ask for Guissart as his cameraman on *Adam's Apple* (1928), starring Monty Banks, an Italian-born comedian who worked in Hollywood in the 1920s and was later to marry Gracie Fields. Certainly, it is interesting and profitable to compare the "look" of a British silent feature with an American star, photographed by an American, with that of a similar feature photographed by a British cinematographer. Evelyn Brent in the 1922 production of *Trapped by the Mormons* could not have been more poorly photographed than by British Theodore Thurmwood (whose name alone is enough to severely limit one's confidence). Meanwhile, British actress Madeleine Carroll, photographed by René Guissart in *The American Prisoner* (1929), is positively luminescent, and it is easy to see why she was signed up by a major Hollywood studio a few years later.

Guissart's British career did not end with the coming of sound. In 1929 at Elstree, he photographed Jameson Thomas in *The Hate Ship*, and in 1930, also at Elstree, he photographed Madeleine Carroll again, along with Brian

Aherne, in *The "W" Plan*, Lillian Rich in *High Seas*, and Betty Balfour, who had been Syd Chaplin's leading lady in *A Little Bit of Fluff*, in *Raise the Roof* and *The Brat*.[5] In 1937, Jack Buchanan invited Guissart to return to England from France, where he was now working, not as a cinematographer but as a director of *Sweet Devil*, which starred Bobby Howes, and was released early the following year.

Also arriving in Britain at approximately the same time as René Guissart was American cinematographer Nick Musuraca, brought over by J. Stuart Blackton, whose career by the early 1920s was at a creative low point. With Musuraca, Blackton filmed three features in England: *The Glorious Adventure* (1922), *A Gypsy Cavalier* (1922), and *The Virgin Queen* (1923).

Although they lacked a certain artistry, all three are important. The first is the only major feature to be filmed in Prizma Color, a two-color process, the forerunner to Cinecolor, invented by William Van Doren Kelley. Kelley provided his own cameraman, British-born William T. Crespinel, to work with Musuraca on the production, which was set around the time

Nick Musuraca, J. Stuart Blackton, and William T. Crespinel filming *The Glorious Adventure* (1921).

of the Great Fire of London, and which began filming at the Stoll Studios in Cricklewood in July 1921. The film has another claim to fame in that it brought Victor McLaglen to the public's attention, and Blackton took the actor back to Hollywood with him.

The son of a clergyman and born in the very English community of Tunbridge Wells in Kent, McLaglen gained a reputation in American films for his portrayal of Irish and to a lesser extent Scottish hard-drinking characters. With the one exception of *While Paris Sleeps* in 1932, McLaglen never used his natural speaking voice on screen, which identified his true nationality.

Both *The Glorious Adventure* and *The Virgin Queen* starred the British society beauty, Lady Diana Manners, whose looks were not, unfortunately, matched by her acting ability. *The Virgin Queen*, as its title suggests, was a drama concerning the life of Queen Elizabeth I, written by historian Harry Pirie Gordon, and filmed entirely on location at Beaulieu Castle and Abbey, the ancestral home of Lord Montagu, on the edge of the New Forest. Blackton's daughter Marian, who plays a major role in the film, recalled,

> We did not use a single studio set during the entire production. Instead we took our cameras and equipment directly into the castle and the abbey. For daytime shots we combined artificial light with sunlight and the effects achieved were superb. Much of the credit for the spectacular camera effects that distinguish this otherwise mediocre motion picture belongs to Nick Musuraca, our cameraman, and to our staff of expert technicians, many of them my father's American helpers from way back.[6]

While Lady Diana was vacationing between pictures, Blackton starred French boxing champion Georges Carpentier in *A Gypsy Cavalier*, which is notable for a climactic rescue involving a coach containing heroine Flora Le Breton, trapped in rising flood water. The camerawork of Musuraca is exemplary, but the film as a whole is lackluster, and poorly directed and edited.

In the mid-1930s, British cinematographer Henry Harris urged that British film producers save themselves by "ceasing to feebly copy the big American successes, by forgetting to make their films 'camera conscious.' Let us only copy the one thing that has made American pictures great—telling the story . . . their belief in the emotions. Let us go back to our traditions, to Shakespeare, Dickens, to drama, to telling our story sincerely, whole-heartedly, enthusiastically."

One American cinematographer working in Britain in the 1920s whose work possesses many of the characteristics for which Harris pleads, but which is also very sophisticated, is Hal Young. An Australian who began his career in the United States, working chiefly for Famous Players-Lasky, Young photographed a dozen British feature films of the 1920s, ranging from rural dramas such as *Fox Farm* (1922) to the self-assured productions of Graham Cutts.

Interestingly, Henry Harris told me that he was originally to have photographed *Fox Farm*, but had a disagreement with director-star Guy Newall, and was replaced by Young. Newall is rather good as the fatalistic owner of Fox Farm who is blinded at the end of reel three. Young's camera never intrudes. It records the drama with emotion and simplicity. Little wonder that one trade paper, the *Kinematograph Weekly*, commented, "Pictures of this excellence show what strides the British industry is making."

Hal Young's best British work is with Graham Cutts: *The Prude's Fall* (1925), *The Rat* (1925), *The Sea Urchin* (1926), and *The Triumph of the Rat* (1926). "Masterpiece" is perhaps too strong a word to use, but the definitive Hal Young-Graham Cutts feature is, unquestionably, *The Rat*, starring Ivor Novello as a Parisian Apache who has taken up with a society lady seeking adventure, played by Isabel Jeans, but who is loved and cared for by a street waif, played by Mae Marsh. The romantic melodramatics of the storyline are dated, but the fluid camerawork which follows the characters as they move around the scene and negates the use of editing is quite astonishingly fresh. Credit for the camerawork was given at the time to Cutts, whom the *Bioscope* (May 7, 1925) wrote, "is using a new device of his own design in photographing *The Rat*. This eliminates jumping from long-shots to close-ups, and will enable the artist to play continuous scenes without a break in a semi-close shot. This will not only be more agreeable to the eyes of the spectator, but will give the artists better scope for their acting." Young photographed the sequel, *The Triumph of the Rat*, but the third and last film in the series, *The Return of the Rat* (1929), was, interestingly, photographed by Roy Overbaugh.

The same camera technique in *The Rat* is also present in *The Sea Urchin*, which contains three separate stories, becoming one at the climax, when the relationship of the various characters becomes clear. It is obviously influenced by *Intolerance*, and Herbert Wilcox once told me that D. W. Griffith was Cutts's idol, and that the director always yearned to be praised as "the British D. W. Griffith." Sadly, because he used Alfred Hitchcock as

Broken Blossoms (1936), with Dolly Haas and Emlyn Williams, poor substitutes for Lillian Gish and Richard Barthelmess in D. W. Griffith's original version.

an assistant director on some of his films, but not those under discussion here, obsessed academics have claimed, quite ridiculously, that the credit for Cutts's films belongs to the former, with one academic even suggesting that Cutts, one of Britain's top directors of the 1920s, is nothing more than a "hack."[7]

Hal Young returned to Britain in 1936, working in tandem but uncredited with Curt Courant (who had fled Nazi Germany and was quickly establishing himself in Britain) on the sound remake of *Broken Blossoms*. The film was to have been directed by D. W. Griffith, who actually came to London and the Twickenham Studios where it was shot, but, if truth be told, he quickly found himself incapable of the task, and was replaced by Hans Brahm, who soon thereafter left for Hollywood, where he changed his name to John Brahm and enjoyed a successful career. It was American Bernard Vorhaus, who was involved in the production, who was assigned by the producer to tell Griffith that he was not to direct the remake; as he recalled, he did the sad deed "with a minimum of humiliation."[8]

David Kesson, whose career as a cinematographer lasted only a decade, from 1920–30, first came to Britain in 1924 to shoot exterior scenes at Stonehenge for *Tess of the d'Urbervilles* (1924) and in Scotland for *The Sporting Venus* (1925), in company with the films' star Blanche Sweet and director-husband Marshall Neilan. While in England, the trio shot some

Blanche Sweet as Lady Glyde learns the secret of *The Woman in White* (1929) from Irene Rooke as Mrs. Catherwick.

location scenes for a proposed screen adaptation of *Return of the Soldier*, the Rebecca West novel, rights to which were owned by Sweet. "I loved it," she recalled, "and I'm afraid I talked the book into being a film. Well we did make a few exteriors, and would have to go back and finish them. And we talked many times with Rebecca West, but we never finished the film. We didn't want to finish it with MGM, and, I don't know, everyone was suing everyone else, and it was very unpleasant. So we never did finish making the picture."[9]

In 1928, Kesson returned to England to shoot *The Bondman* for Herbert Wilcox. At the same time, Blanche Sweet was in Paris awaiting a divorce from Marshall Neilan, and she was persuaded to come over and join Kesson in filming the Wilkie Collins novel, *Woman in White*. Recalled Blanche, "When Herbert wired me and offered me this film I thought it would be nice. I'd made so many scenes and things for American films there that it was like a second home to me. We had a pleasant time making the film because I admired Herbert as a director, and he had arranged for Dave to be the photographer." Kesson photographed two final films in England for Wilcox; one is *Splinters*, released in the winter of 1929, and starring comedian Sydney Howard in the first of three films in the "Splinters" series, all mediocre and all destined for low-class British consumption only; the other is *Loves of Robert Burns*, released in the spring of 1930, starring tenor Joseph

Hislop in the title role and with Kesson's location shots in Scotland its only redeeming feature.

Kesson had worked as second cameraman to Charles Rosher on *My Best Girl* (1927), and Rosher was to end the decade working in England. He photographed E. A. Dupont's primitive multilingual talkie of the Titanic disaster, *Atlantic* (1929) as well as a second Dupont feature, *Two Worlds* (1930), two atrocious 1930 features, *Knowing Men* and *The Price of Things*, directed by novelist Elinor Glyn who had earlier made a name for herself in Hollywood, naming Clara Bow as "the It Girl," the embodiment of sex appeal, and *The Vagabond Queen* (1930), starring Betty Balfour, supported by legendary British stage actor Ernest Thesiger, whose greatest fame to cinematic fame is as Dr. Pretorius in *The Bride of Frankenstein* (1935). Rosher, who had enjoyed a long association in Hollywood with Mary Pickford, was described by the British press as "Pickford's right-hand man," and, because he was actually born in London, he was identified as having "British ways and American looks."[10]

Rosher returned to England in 1936 to photograph Alexander Korda's prestige production of *Men Are Not Gods*. He retired to Portugal, and I can recall his coming to London on a number of visits in the late 1960s. He was always very amenable and happy to talk with young film enthusiasts such as myself, often over a couple of coffee at the Mayfair Hotel. What was somewhat distressing was Rosher's extreme right-wing attitudes, particularly toward African Americans, whom he regarded as a danger to the country and the principal reason for his no longer living in the United States.

Writing to E. B. Derr of Pathé, on December 27, 1929, American film historian and industry commentator Terry Ramsaye commented, "May I, at this time, observe that I consider all British picture makers lousy—and, that the art of photography is practically unknown in Great Britain as far as the motion picture is concerned?" While there might be some justification for Ramsaye's comment, it can be easily refuted by pointing to the work of a distinguished group of American cinematographers at work in Britain in the 1920s. They were to a certain extent pioneers, and they paved the way for a new influx of American cinematographers in the next decade.

Almost a dozen American cinematographers found employment in the British film industry in the 1930s. Some came over to work on prestigious productions with international appeal, while others certainly give one the impression, in retrospect, that they were little more than journeyman cameramen picking up work wherever they could. Three Americans worked on a large number of British productions during the decade. Phil Tannura has credit on at least twenty-two, Glen McWilliams on nineteen, and Charles Van Enger on fourteen. Most of them are unworthy of attention, and would have held little interest outside of the United Kingdom. Only Glen McWilliams can boast of a distinguished list of titles, including two Paul Robeson features—*King Solomon's Mines* (1937) and *The Proud Valley* (1940)—as well as seven Jessie Matthews vehicles, *Waltzes from Vienna* (1934), *Evergreen* (1934), *First a Girl* (1935), *It's Love Again* (1936), *Head over Heels* (1937), *Gangway* (1937), and *Sailing Along* (1938). Matthews remembered MacWilliams as "tall, bespectacled and serious-looking," and historian Rachael Low points out that McWilliams was second only to director Victor Saville "in the creation of Jessie the film star, for he changed her makeup and lit her to stress her large, wistful eyes."[11]

Phil Tannura has a career that stretches back to Edison. It began on the East Coast of America, but in the 1930s, it was centered on England. As he recalled,

> I had nine-and-a-half good, nice years over there. And there was only one person in all that nine-and-a-half years I was there that I had difficulty with, and he was so anti-American that I had to stay away from him. A fellow by the name of [Phil] Samuel. He was a man that never learned the business. He was the production manager of Gaumont-British, and he had it in for Americans in the worst way.

Tannura experienced no antagonism from British cinematographers, who became his friends, with two of his assistants, Jack Hildyard and Geoffrey Unsworth, becoming major names in their own right. Tannura found that he could make demands of the studios that British cameramen could not, obtaining up-to-date lighting equipment and introducing back-projection.

He became a personal cameraman to Tom Walls, a character comedian and also director who produced his own films for Gaumont British and later Max Schach:

> He wanted me because he'd had trouble with another cameraman, and he didn't like the way he'd say, "We do it this way in Hollywood." You never do that in a foreign country. You just keep your mouth shut and do what they ask you to do, and if it's wrong, you tell them so in a nice way.
>
> I never saw a man like him. He would never study his dialogue. He would look at his dialogue, read it through once, and then go right through

> two pages. He was really marvelous. I would go out to fights with him, go out nights. It was quite a life with him. Really a nice man. [The films] I thought were really funny. Ben Travers wrote all the dialogue. And [leading lady] Yvonne Arnaud was so funny with the dialogue they gave her. The situations, that's what made the thing funny. Nobody tried to be funny—that's the object of good comedy.[12]

If nothing else, the Tannura-Walls partnership illustrates that American filmmakers found employment and pleasure with British filmmakers whose reputations might not stretch across the Atlantic and whose performances might not suggest any transatlantic appeal.

Of the films that Tannura photographed between 1932 and 1939, very few are memorable.[13] *Men of Tomorrow*, released in October 1932, is of interest in that the director is the Viennese-born Leontine Sagan, who made only one other film, the lesbian-themed *Maedchen in Uniform* (1931). The most prominent of Tannura's films is *Dinner at the Ritz*, starring Annabella, Paul Lukas, and David Niven. Viewing it at New York's Roxy Theatre, Frank S. Nugent in the *New York Times* (December 4, 1937) wrote that it "deserves at least your polite attention—by which we mean that you should not yawn at all. . . . it moves with old world decorum and occasional touches of gout."

Some observers might wonder why Ernest Palmer does not make the list here. By my count, he has credit on at least twenty-nine British films of the 1930s. But the problem is that the prolific Ernest Palmer shooting British films is not the Ernest Palmer filming American ones. The latter received three Academy Award nominations as well as one Oscar for *Blood and Sand* (1941), and was active from the 1910s through 1960. The British Ernest Palmer, sometimes identified with the initials H. E., was active from the 1930s through 1959 and never made it to Hollywood. Unfortunately for British cinema, he had neither the capability nor the creativity of his American namesake.

Memphis-born John Boyle had a busy career from 1915 onwards until his death in Hollywood in 1959. In Britain, between 1935 and 1937, he worked on seven films, all with prominent stars, including *Midshipman Easy* with Margaret Lockwood (1935), *Queen of Hearts* with Gracie Fields (1936), *Laburnum Grove* with Edmund Gwenn (1936), *Land without Music*, with Richard Tauber (1936), and *Jericho* with Paul Robeson (1937).

Harry Stradling did not have much of a career in Hollywood prior to coming to France in the early 1930s and then in 1937 moving on to England where he was responsible for the cinematography of a number of British

films with international appeal. Stradling had been associated with Jacques Feyder in France, and when Alexander Korda hired the latter to direct Marlene Dietrich in *Knight without Armour* (1937), Stradling was the natural choice as cinematographer. Korda used Stradling on three further films, *The Divorce of Lady X* (1938), *The Lion Has Wings* (1939), and *Over the Moon* (1939), all starring Merle Oberon. Of *The Divorce of Lady X*, Frank S. Nugent wrote in the *New York Times* (April 1, 1938) that "the lines are bright and the color most attractive." Stradling was obviously a favored cameraman of Victor Saville, working for him on *Dark Journey* (1937), *Action for Slander* (1937), *South Riding* (1938), and *Pygmalion* (1938), which Saville produced but did not direct. Two of Stradling's most prominent films of the period are *Pygmalion* (1938), starring Leslie Howard, and *Jamaica Inn* (1939), Alfred Hitchcock's last film in England prior to his contract in Hollywood with David O. Selznick. With the outbreak of World War II, Stradling returned to Hollywood, where he and Hitchcock were reunited on *Mr. and Mrs. Smith* and *Suspicion*, both released in 1941.

Over the Moon (1939), with Rex Harrison and Merle Oberon, photographed by Harry Stradling.

Harry Stradling received many Academy Award nominations and two Oscars, both for films set in England, *The Picture of Dorian Gray* (1945) and *My Fair Lady* (1964). As the last indicates, he is the only individual to photograph two films, one in Britain and one in the United States, with the same literary source.

Harold (Hal) Rosson's career dates back to before 1910, and he is best remembered as the cinematographer of *The Wizard of Oz* (1939) and for his brief marriage to Jean Harlow, whom he also photographed. His career in England lasted somewhat longer than his marriage to Harlow and includes five major productions, all of which enjoyed success in the United States and the first three of which were produced by Alexander Korda: *The Scarlet Pimpernel* (1934), starring Leslie Howard in the title role; *The Ghost Goes West* (1935), starring Robert Donat; *The Man Who Could Work Miracles* (1936), with Roland Young, returning to his native England in an H. G. Wells screen adaptation; *As You Like It* (1936), produced and directed by Paul Czinner, with his wife Elizabeth Bergner starring opposite Laurence Olivier; and *A Yank at Oxford* (1938), with two Americans, Robert Taylor and Lionel Barrymore, and two British leading ladies, Maureen O'Sullivan and Vivien Leigh.

Chinese-American cinematographer James Wong Howe had been active in Hollywood from the late 1910s, graduating from laboratory assistant to clapper boy to cameraman. In 1936, he was brought to England by Alexander Korda to work on two films, released in 1937, that he was producing with Erich Pommer for newly formed Pendennis, shooting at Korda-owned Denham Studios. The first was the historical drama *Fire over England*, directed by American William K. Howard,[14] and starring Flora Robson as Queen Elizabeth I. She was joined by Leslie Banks, Raymond Massey, along with Laurence Olivier and Vivien Leigh, who were making their first appearance together on screen. Its international success was assured both by the quality of the cast and the quality of the production. The second film, *Farewell Again*, also starred Flora Robson and Leslie Banks, but it failed to achieve similar success. For his final British film, also shot at Denham, Howe worked for producer Robert T. Kane on the 20th Century-Fox release, *Under the Red Robe*, starring Conrad Veidt, Annabella, and Raymond Massey, and directed by the Swedish Victor Seastrom. Collaborating on the cinematography was Frenchman Georges Périnal, who was active in the British film industry from the 1930s through the 1950s. In many respects, both *Fire over England* and *Under the Red Robe* typifies the internationality of British filmmaking in the 1930s.

Flora Robson, as Queen Elizabeth, shares a moment of humor with cinematographer James Wong Howe on the set of *Fire over England* (1937). Director William K. Howard stands next to Robson.

Howe's female companion, Sanora Babb, whom he had met in 1934, followed him to Europe and the two were married in Paris. However, because of American anti-miscegenation laws, the couple could not reveal their matrimonial status, and the two remarried in Mexico in the late 1940s, by which time Howe had become an American citizen. The marriage survived despite Babb's later being accused of Communist sympathies in the 1950s.

Lee Garmes had entered the American film industry in the mid-1910s and within a decade was one of Hollywood's more prominent cinematographers. He worked with writers Ben Hecht and Charles MacArthur in the mid-1930s on three independent productions on which Garmes had the credit of associate director: *Crime without Passion* (1934), *Once in a Blue Moon* (1935), and *The Scoundrel* (1935), with the last arguably offering Noel Coward the best role in his entire film career. Two years later, in 1937, Garmes came to England, photographing Elizabeth Bergner under the direction of her husband, Paul Czinner, in *Dreaming Lips*, which the British loved and Americans hated, and, surprisingly, co-directing with Jack

Buchanan *The Sky's the Limit*, which *Variety* (November 17, 1937) hailed as "probably the best film in which Jack Buchanan ever appeared."

Garmes's career arc from cinematographer to director reminds one somewhat of the careers of British cameramen Ronald Neame and Guy Green, who were promoted to director, first in the United Kingdom and then continued in the same capacity in Hollywood. A different type of career arc is exemplified by Gilbert Taylor, who worked as an assistant and camera operator on British films of the 1930s and ended his career as cinematographer on major American-sponsored films shot in Britain, including Hitchcock's *Frenzy* (1972), Richard Donner's *The Omen* (1976), and *Star Wars* (1977). Gilbert's visual style for that first *Star Wars* set the tone for the rest of the productions in the series. It was Gilbert's proud claim that he never actually made a film in Hollywood.

CHAPTER SIX

The 1930s and the Golden Age of the Hollywood Has-beens

MORE AMERICAN "STARS" WERE WORKING IN BRITISH FILMS IN THE 1930s than probably in any other period of its history at least until relatively modern times. Some actors came to Europe while in the midst of a contractual dispute with their respective studios. Occasionally, an actor was actually sent to England by the studio, and equally occasionally, some major stars were brought over by a British producer anxious for a "star" name to guarantee a semi-major US release—for example, Sylvia Sidney in Alfred Hitchcock's *Sabotage* (1936)[1] and Robert Young in another Hitchcock film from 1936, *Secret Agent*. Edmund Lowe starred in two prominent British films, *Seven Sinners* (1936)[2] and *The Squeaker* (1937), for which producer Alexander Korda hired American William K. Howard[3] to direct and Miklos Rosza to compose the score. Korda always understood the value of an American star, as with his choice of Miriam Hopkins for his 1936 production of *Men Are Not Gods*.

And for all the American "stars" who did come over, there were quite a few who announced plans to star in British films of the 1930s, but never actually made it. Most notable in their number are James Cagney, Jean Harlow, and Barbara Stanwyck.

A number of leading players came over for one film, and often from a modern perspective the lack of immediate name recognition seems puzzling. For a circus picture, *Red Wagon*, Wardour Films hired Hollywood players, Charles Bickford, the Mexican-born Raquel Torres, the Norwegian-born Greta Nissen, and Don Alvarado, American-born but with an English father. The film was not a success on its initial 1933 release and again failed to garner an audience when reissued and cut in length in 1936.

Why bring over William Gargan to co-star as the "love interest" opposite Cicely Courtneidge in *Things Are Looking Up* (1935)? He is hardly star material and even he seems unlikely to be attracted to an over-the-top performer such as Cicely Courtneidge. And did the presence of character comedian Skeets Gallagher in *Mr. Satan* (1938), opposite Chili Bouchier, add anything to the production?

Courtneidge attracted more than one inappropriate American as her leading man. In *Everybody Dance* (1936), she is directed by American Charles "Chuck" Reisner, who perhaps took the assignment because of the opportunity it offered his son, Charles Reisner, Jr., to be the co-star. The latter is much too young for Courtneidge, and she is much too grotesque for him.

Secret Agent (1938), with Robert Young and Madeleine Carroll.

Almost 100 American actors and actresses received starring billing, although it must be admitted that a fair number of those are probably unworthy of denomination as "stars," being more featured or supporting players at home in Hollywood. In reality, few were still "stars" in their native land but had come to England as their career faded or, in some cases, had just about ended. It was a dispiriting decline from top of the bill in America to starring in British films, which often constituted bottom-of-the-bill fare, as far as American audiences were concerned. As the distinguished British director Anthony Asquith once commented, "In Hollywood there was a popular saying: 'When an actor is finished he can either go over the hill to the poorhouse or over the seas into British movies'. . . . And indeed we were flooded."[4] Certainly, the productions in which they appeared in the United Kingdom might generally be mediocre in comparison to their American output, with some not even receiving a release in the United States as even the second half on a double bill, but they did constitute work, decent money, and the opportunity for a free European vacation. By the spring of 1933, it was reported that "the trek to London is assuming astounding proportions."[5]

Even at the time, there was recognition that the use of American talent could be financially detrimental to a British production. As *Motion Picture Daily* editor Maurice Kann wrote in 1937,

> Salaries beyond the Hollywood level, which is ridiculously high, have been dangled temptingly before the eyes of available talent. *De Luxe* travelling accommodations from Hollywood to New York, and from New York to London, at the expense of the British studios, have been furnished.

Peter Noble has written: "And so the false boom began—an extraordinary combination of 'new' companies and 'old actors.' From the Continent and from Hollywood came a constant stream of actors, writers, directors and technicians, some of them first-class, but many of them distinctly second-rate."[6] These "phony" personalities were even the subject of two novels of the period: Eric Siepmann's *Waterloo in Wardour Street* (Chatto and Windus, 1936) and Jeffrey Dell's *Nobody Ordered Wolves* (Heineman, 1939).

Typical of former American silent players on the downward slope is Conway Tearle, the American son of a British father, whose stage career began when he was a teenager and who had made his London stage debut in 1901. In American silent films, he had been a leading man to major stars, including Mary Pickford, Pola Negri,[7] and Corinne Griffith, but by the early 1930s, his screen career was basically over, in part perhaps because he was past fifty, an age that might suggest that his leading ladies craved a father figure rather than a juvenile. In 1931, Tearle came to England to star in a film titled *Captivation*. It did anything but captivate, and the review from *Variety* (June 2, 1931) exemplifies the response of many to British films hoping for American interest thanks to an American star:

> Even the British film industry, in its distinguished record of misapplied talent and over-applied incompetence, has seldom evolved anything quite so dreary as this futile frolic in the Mediterranean. . . . Having stuck six reels this reviewer walked. Conway Tearle looked like a guy who regretted signing the contract.

Tearle made no more British films. And who can blame him? But there were other former Hollywood leading men of the silent era who emulated Tearle with a one-trip, one-film visit to England: Don Alvarado (actually two films), Francis X. Bushman, Alexander D'Arcy, Conrad Nagel, Rod La Rocque, and James Rennie.[8] When American Charles Farrell came over to England to star in *Falling in Love* (1934), it must have caused considerable confusion to fans of the Dublin-born British Charles Farrell, who appeared in more than fifty films from 1931 through into the 1970s. Ricardo Cortez was cast opposite American leading lady Sally Eilers in *Talk of the Devil*, released in December 1936; the direction, story, and script were handled by Carol Reed, early in his career, and the film—the last produced by British & Dominions—was good enough to garner a United Artists release. Richard Arlen also starred in only one British production *The Great Barrier/Silent Barriers* (1937), but it had wide international appeal (thanks to location filming in Canada and South Africa) and good reviews, concerned with the building of the Canadian Pacific Railway, and it also features American character actor J. Farrell MacDonald. On the distaff side with one film each are Olive Borden, who took second billing to comedian Gene Gerrard in *Leave It to Me* (1933) and Corinne Griffith in *Lily Christine* (1932)[9].

Richard Dix enjoyed a career both in silent and sound films, and in 1935, when he came to England to shoot *The Tunnel/Transatlantic Tunnel*, he was still a prominent leading man. The film, directed by Maurice Elvey is a sci-fi drama involving Dix as a man obsessed with the notion of building a tunnel between England and the United States. Despite the presence briefly of George Arliss as the British prime minister and Walter Huston as the American president (described as "courtesy appearances"), and American leading ladies Madge Evans and Helen Vinson, the production is not as good as it should have been—perhaps due to Elvey's usual uninspired direction. However, *Variety* (October 30, 1935) was most enthusiastic, describing it as "a big picture, and will be big b.o." *Film Weekly* (March 14, 1936) described it as "on the whole a worth-while piece of imaginative entertainment."

Richard Barthelmess had been a major Hollywood silent star, working with D. W. Griffith and starring in the classic *Tol'able David* (1921), but by the 1930s, alcohol abuse and a weight problem, not to mention aging, had all affected the actor's career and starring potential. It was time for a visit—not to the gym or the clinic—but to England, where Barthelmess was starred in *The Spy of Napoleon*, released September 1936, a costume drama produced by Julius Hagen, one of the worst of British producers. The film was mediocre, with the British critic of *Variety* (September 23, 1936) writing, "If the casting of Richard Barthelmess was intended to strengthen the film, it was a gamble that has not succeeded, for his performance is colorless." Happily, the actor did enjoy one last role of some significance three years later, in the American *Only Angels Have Wings* (1939).

Another Griffith leading man, Neil Hamilton, just kept on working, regardless of the quality of his later films, in the United States, and eventually enjoyed renewed fame as Police Commissioner Gordon in television's *Batman* series. Hamilton had a busy couple of years in Britain in 1936 and 1937, starring in five films: *Southern Roses, You Must Get Married, Early in Life* (all released in 1936), *Secret Lives*, and *Mr. Stringfellow Says "No"* (released in 1937).

Unquestionably, the best of the bunch is *Secret Lives*, which is also one of the most artistic British films of the 1930s—probably because of the non-British talent involved. A drama of one woman's forced involvement in World War I by spying for the French, *Secret Lives* has a strong pacifist leaning, with stylized direction and cinematography by Edmond Gréville and Otto Heller. It also has a remarkable performance by its star, the German Brigitte Horney, who was at one time compared to Dietrich and performs a very Dietrich-type number here. The ending is sudden, abrupt, and depressing, with the leading character's being driven off to be executed, starkly at odds with just about any British film from this period.

(Czech-born Otto Heller worked on many major British films in later years. He is also responsible for the invention of "soundless rain," which involves the creation of illusory rain shot while held in special apparatus. The concept was first used in the 1948 film *Bond Street*, and may have been used in some American productions.)

Esther Ralston had been a Paramount contract leading lady of the 1920s, but by the early 1930s her career was in decline. As early as June 1929, she had placed an advertisement in the British trade paper, the *Bioscope*, advising of her availability following cancellation of her Paramount contract.[10] Ralston was playing vaudeville and this led to an invitation to perform on stage in England, most importantly at the London Palladium in the spring of 1932. Her success there led to Michael Balcon's offering her the pivotal,

Dance Band (1935), with Charles "Buddy" Rogers.

but somewhat small, role of the American movie star in his latest production, *Rome Express.* "Miss Ralston is one of the few film stars who really look and behave the part," commented *Film Weekly.*[11] The film's prominent cast, including Conrad Veidt and Cedric Hardwicke, along with superb, sophisticated direction by Walter Forde, helped it achieve great success both in Britain and in the United States, where it was released in a somewhat truncated form by Universal. Following *Rome Express*, Ralston appeared in a second Balcon production, *After the Ball*, released in November 1932, in which her leading man was Basil Rathbone. After a brief provincial music-hall tour, she returned to Hollywood.

Probably the best film in which Ralston appeared in the 1920s was the first screen adaptation of *Peter Pan* (1925), playing Mrs. Darling, and with Mary Brian as daughter Wendy. Like Ralston, Brian's career was in decline in the 1930s, and, as with Ralston, she had taken to appearing on stage in vaudeville. As a result, Brian was invited by André Charlot to come to London in April of 1935, and appear in his latest stage revue, *Stop—. . . Go!*, which featured prominent and sophisticated female impersonator Douglas

Byng, who used only minimal female attire and was very popular with nightclub audiences. While appearing on stage at night, Brian followed many of her British colleagues in working during the day at one of the suburban London film studios.

Her first film, *Two's Company*, released in April 1936, was directed by Tim Whelan, and had American character comedian Ned Sparks in a supporting role, serving as a perfect foil to British character-comedian Gordon Harker. In reality, *Two's Company* was not Mary Brian's first production to be designated as British. In 1929, she had appeared opposite James Kirkwood, under Marshall Neilan's direction, in *Black Waters* at the Sono Art-World Wide Studios in Hollywood. While shot in the United States, the film's producer was Herbert Wilcox and it was identified as a British & Dominions production.

For her second film actually shot in England, Mary Brian was teamed with Charles "Buddy" Rogers, with whom she had co-starred in Hollywood in Paramount's 1928 production of *Varsity*. The two were close friends and worked well together in *Once in a Million*, released in March 1936. Rogers worked in two other British films, *Dance Band*, released in June 1935, and *Let's Make a Night of It*, released in June 1937. The latter featured six dance bands, including, of course, one led by Rogers. His co-star in both was June Clyde, an American-born singer, dancer and actress, who had come to England with her husband, director Thornton Freeland. She continued to work on screen, both in England and Hollywood, through into the late 1950s.

Mary Brian had pretty much decided to abandon film work while appearing on stage in London. As she remembered, "The fogs that they had would come up so often in the evening. And I had to get back from working in the studio and do the show at night. And sometimes it was a pretty close call. And I had to get into costume and make-up."[12] What persuaded her to make one final British film was her leading man, Cary Grant, the British-born actor who had been placed under contract to Paramount (Brian's home studio) in 1932 and played opposite its top stars, Marlene Dietrich and Mae West. Grant saw the offer of the film role as an opportunity to return to England to visit his family, in particular his ailing father, who was to die during production. The film, *The Amazing Quest of Ernest Bliss*,[13] released in August 1936, is not a major one in terms of either the careers of its stars or British cinema, but it did lead to a close relationship between the two actors, culminating in their engagement: "It just progressed I guess. We had cars that took me to the theatre, and we decided we should go in the same car. And we had a lot of time to talk, and we liked each other. And it just evolved. Sunday would be the only time we had off, and we went exploring London. And there were a lot of parties and things in London."[14]

While in London, Cary Grant also met up with Virginia Cherrill, to whom he been briefly married for a few months between 1934 and 1935. She had enjoyed early fame as Chaplin's leading lady in *City Lights* (1931), which led to a contract with Fox. The relationship with the studio was almost as short as with Grant. Cherrill came to England and starred in three films, *Money Mad*, released in September 1934, *Late Extra*, released in November 1935, and *Troubled Waters*, released in February 1936. The last two were produced by Fox, and perhaps were a conclusion of the Hollywood contract; both were directed by Albert Parker and both co-starred James Mason, whom Cherrill disliked, and Alastair Sim (although the storylines and characters are very dissimilar). The English films marked the end of Cherrill's film career, but she remained in Britain through the war, hobnobbing with and marrying into the minor aristocracy. Parker and Mason remained firm friends, with the latter reporting in 1947 that Parker's "previous opinion of Hollywood remains unaltered. 'These heels & bastards,' he foams."[15]

Sally O'Neil was Irish-American from New Jersey—the family name was Noonan—and she had enjoyed moderate success in silent films during the mid-1920s but little in talkies. She came to England to star in the title role of *Kathleen Mavourneen*, a dramatization of the song released early in 1938 in both Britain and the United States (where the title was shortened to "Kathleen"). The film also featured Sara Allgood, a perennial and genuine Irish character actress in British films from the late 1920s onward. She came to America in the 1940s, where she had far greater success than O'Neil, giving a superb performance as a Welsh, rather than Irish, matriarch in John Ford's *How Green Was My Valley* (1941) and working there until her death in 1950.

It was not only silent players who made the ignominious trip to England. There were some from the early talkie period whose careers were equally in decline. Bernice Claire had been in films since 1930, in which year she showed off her attractive singing voice and somewhat lackluster personality in *No, No, Nanette*. By 1935, she was starring in her last feature-length production, *Two Hearts in Harmony*, a somewhat lesser operetta than *No, No, Nanette*, directed at Nettlefold Studios on the River Thames at Walton by American William Beaudine. Unlike her sister, Loretta Young, Sally Blane was a small-time actress on screen, and her one British film—*Crime on the*

Hill, released in December 1933—can have seemed little different to the actress. Even here, she had to take second billing to another actress, a British one.

Surprisingly, few Hollywood actors on the way up made the trip to England. Perhaps a visit there signaled a rapid decline in the climb to success. One exception is Philip Reed, who was already playing second leads in Hollywood when he came to the Argyle-British Studios at Welwyn Garden City to appear in support of Binkie Stuart, Britain's answer to Shirley Temple, in *My Irish Molly*, released in December 1938. One of a series of ill-advised films made by producer John Argyle to showcase the dubious singing and dancing talents of moppet Binkie Stuart, *My Irish Molly* is entertaining only in that there is something affectionately crude and unsophisticated about the production. Reed plays an American writer who comes to Ireland for atmosphere, and there meets Miss Molly, involved in a guardianship dispute, and, more importantly, Maureen Fitzsimmons in what is apparently her only screen appearance under her real name, before she became Maureen O'Hara and went on to a celebrated Hollywood career.

Brought over in 1938 for a starring role in *We're Going to Be Rich*, Brian Donlevy was paired with arguably Britain's biggest film star, Gracie Fields, and was joined in the cast by Victor McLaglen. It was thought that Donlevy would help the film in the United States, but as Rachael Low writes, Gracie Fields's "humour was strictly for local consumption and teaming her with American stars in an unfamiliar format dismayed her British fans without attracting an American following."[16]

Why would a brilliant character actor like Edward Everett Horton, whose humor often relied on his interplaying with the star (most notably Fred Astaire), decide to leave Hollywood for trips to Britain? The answer lies in the description of his Hollywood roles. They were always in support of the star. In Britain, he was the star and yet, at the same time, the characterizations were remarkably close to those he had created in the United States. "I enjoyed all my British films," he told a writer,[17] and why would he not? They were quickly made with little effort on anyone's part, least of all the directors who relied on Horton's innate sense of performance and timing. Horton brought to British films his worried look and nervous manner, and as *Film Weekly* (July 7, 1933) aptly described it, "Hollywood subtlety."[18] The first two of Horton's films, *Soldiers of the King/The Woman in Command* (1933) and *It's a Boy* (1933) were produced by Michael Balcon. The last two, *The Private Secretary* (1935) and *The Man in the Mirror* (1936), were produced by Julius

Hagen, a man wary of any unnecessary expense, who probably spent the bulk of the budget on his star's salary and, with *The Man in the Mirror*, also the salary of American leading lady Genevieve Tobin.

Davina Craig was a British character actress generally cast as a maid, and Hagen would have parts written into his films for her in the belief that servant girls with perpetual colds were box office. Here was an actress who might be described as nasally challenged. Apropos of which, she recalled of Edward Everett Horton in *The Private Secretary* that he was "a dear old auntie. He had a little shawl around his shoulders. He used to point up to the sky and say, 'There's old man pneumonia up there waiting for me.'"[19]

With a facility equal to that of Horton for milking the maximum of farce from a situation with the minimum of effort is Eric Blore, a British-born actor whose Hollywood career was not quite as lengthy as that of Horton but did include more appearances opposite Fred Astaire. Blore returned to England in 1939 to play the character most associated with him in *A Gentleman's Gentleman*. The type of gentleman that both Horton and Blore might have had to cope with is exemplified by rotund, often exasperated Eugene Pallette, another major Hollywood character actor. He also came to England to play a typical role in Alexander Korda's 1935 production of *The Ghost Goes West*. Graham Greene wrote in the *Spectator* (December 27, 1935) that Pallette as the American millionaire who purchased a haunted Scottish castle "gave the finest performance of his career."

It should not, of course, be assumed that the only non-British stars finding employment in the country's film industry were those whose careers were in decline or sometimes rapid freefall. Just as there were major European stars active on British sound stages—such as Elizabeth Bergner, Brigitte Helm, Fritz Kortner, and Conrad Veidt, etc.—so, also, were major American stars making the trip to England, although often the casual observer must wonder why they bothered and what the incentive was, beyond an all-expenses-paid vacation.

Constance Bennett and Douglass Montgomery were brought over by Gaumont-British in 1936 to co-star in *Everything Is Thunder*, whose storyline involves the latter's escape from a German prisoner-of-war camp during World War I and being helped by a Berlin prostitute played by Bennett. "Story, production and direction will not hold it up," reported *Variety* (November 25, 1936). The British fan magazine, *Film Weekly* (August 15, 1936), agreed, describing the film as "a moderate, rather artificial thriller." It was not terribly impressed by either American star, commenting, "Constance Bennett gives a highly competent, quite artificial performance

as the street girl—the sort of person she has played so often before. She and Montgomery both overact badly at times; but they do their best, and in two scenes almost succeed, in the difficult job of making the love at first sight seem credible." The direction was the work of multitalented Milton Rosmer, who began his career in Britain as a child actor on stage and alternated screen acting and directing without making his mark in either. Montgomery stayed on in the UK to star in one other film, *Tropical Trouble*, a very minor effort, released in the autumn of 1936.

Wynne Gibson excels as the prostitute lead in one of the stories in Paramount's 1932 production of *If I Had a Million*, but generally—while busy in Hollywood—her performances were limited to "B" pictures. Little wonder, therefore, that in 1935 she should have come to England to play the lead opposite Fritz Kortner in *The Crouching Beast*. Here, in a screen adaptation of a novel by popular mystery writer Valentine Williams, Gibson is an American newspaperwoman involved in spy activities in wartime Turkey.

Soldiers of the King (1933), with Cicely Courtneidge and Edward Everett Horton.

Love from a Stranger (1937), with Ann Harding (at right).

Suave, debonair, and American, Adolphe Menjou might have made his European debut in French films, being fluent in the language and often assumed to be French. Instead, he came to England in 1932 to star in two films, *Two White Arms* (released in the US as *Wives Beware*) and *Diamond Cut Diamond*, a title so dull that it could only have been conceived by the British, and not surprisingly the film was released in the US as *Blame the Woman*. The former is best known today for a title song performed disastrously by Menjou, proving that he could never have starred in a musical. At the time, it was also noted for its naïve dialogue, at which British audiences openly laughed. Both films are directed by Fred Niblo, who had directed some of the biggest stars at MGM in the 1920s as well as *Ben-Hur* (1926). His career had basically ended with the coming of sound and after these two British ventures, he retired.

Menjou enjoyed the London trip in that it gave him the opportunity to purchase some custom-made clothing. He returned in 1936 on his honeymoon with actress Verree Teasdale, and took the opportunity not to star in another British film but to order four suits. The actor was back in England in 1943, entertaining American troops stationed there.

Agatha Christie's short story "Philomel Cottage" had been adapted for the stage by Frank Vosper, who also starred, as *Love from a Stranger*. Gertrude Lawrence had been Vosper's leading lady, but for the British screen version, released in the UK in January 1937, Ann Harding was brought over from Hollywood to play opposite Basil Rathbone in the melodrama of a modern-day Bluebeard and his eighth wife. Directing was American Rowland V. Lee, who had earlier worked in England in 1932, supervising production of *The Sign of the Four* and directing *That Night in London* (released in the US as *Over Night*). Other Americans were involved in the production, with the cinematography in the capable hands of Phil Tannura and the script by Frances Marion, who was in England at the time working on *Knight without Armour*.

Love from a Stranger had a gala opening at the London Pavilion, and according to the *Hollywood Reporter* (January 6, 1937) "qualifies for a spot in the top rank of British production." The film was released in the US by United Artists, and opened at New York's Rivoli Theatre. Writing in the *New York Times* (April 19, 1937), Frank Nugent commented, "If you feel like taking it seriously it is a tense and moving melodrama; if you want to laugh at it you can."

George Raft is the most famous of classic Hollywood screen gangsters. While he did visit the United Kingdom in 1966, the following year he was denied entry because of his involvement with gambling interests. Raft's closest gangster impersonator in Hollywood was Jack La Rue, who took over the role originally intended for the former, opposite Miriam Hopkins, in *The Story of Temple Drake* (1933). It was the biggest production in which La Rue was to star. Certainly, it is superior to the two British films in which La Rue starred, both released in 1939, *Murder in Soho* (released in the US as *Murder in the Night*) and *The Gang's All Here* (released in the US as *The Amazing Mr. Forrest*). The latter boasts a superior cast, headed by Jack Buchanan, who also produced, along with Googie Withers, Edward Everett Horton, and Otto Kruger.

La Rue's leading lady in *The Story of Temple Drake*, Miriam Hopkins, starred in one British film, *Men Are Not Gods*, produced by Alexander Korda, with a story and direction by Walter Reisch, who was to enjoy a substantial Hollywood career, editing by William Hornbeck, cinematography by Charles Rosher, and costumes by René Hubert (who worked on a number of British films prior to coming to Hollywood with Korda). Noah Beery, the less familiar brother of Wallace Beery, was generally cast in villainous roles, thanks to his build and facial features. Shortly after admitting he was "flat broke" in March 1935, Beery signed a $2,500-a-week contract with Gaumont-British and sailed for England. He made two films with the company, *King of the Damned* (1935), with Conrad Veidt in the title role, and *Strangers on a Honeymoon* (1936). He appears to have stayed on in England through early 1937, appearing in a further seven films, none of any real merit and none in which he played the leading role. Billed above Noah Beery in *Our Fighting Navy* (1938) are English-born H. B. Warner and American juvenile Richard Cromwell (in his only British film).

Like La Rue and Beery, Edward G. Robinson was generally cast in villainous roles, but unlike the other two he was a major star and Hollywood celebrity. On loanout from Warner Bros. to Columbia Pictures, he was sent to England to star in *Thunder in the City*, playing an American salesman learning how the British sell cars in a dignified manner. Also assigned to the 1936 production, released early the following year, was Russian-born director Marion Gering and composer Miklos Rosza. Supposedly, Robinson asked his friend Robert Sherwood to help improve the script for a film which was very superficial but enhanced by first-rate character performances by Nigel Bruce and Constance Collier. Robinson welcomed the European trip as an opportunity to visit commercial art galleries in London and Paris and purchase a number of paintings to add to his impressive and growing collection.

Producer Alex Esway noted that

> the release of Atlantic Films' first production *Thunder in the City* was undertaken and guaranteed by Columbia before active production began. Without such a step it would have been impossible to employ artists of the importance of Edward G. Robinson, Luli Deste, Nigel Bruce or Constance Collier. Nor would it have been practical to finance a production of this weight without a previous guarantee of an American release.
>
> For this reason American stars are the life-blood of the British industry today. But their importation does not only benefit the foreign release, but is equally invaluable for the domestic market.
>
> So evident has this become that while in the past years, England has been content with stars who were finished in Hollywood, today British producers will only sign headliners.[20]

In the early 1930s, Fay Wray had got into something of a rut, appearing in one horror film after another, most notably *King Kong* (1933). The chance for some variant roles came in 1935 from the United Kingdom. "When I was

offered these films in England," she recalled, "I just leapt at the chance because now I thought I would break away from this thing that seems to have happened to me with these horror films." However, as she also recalled, "I was a little surprised and a little bit shocked when I got to England to find that everyone wasn't Ronald Colman. Things didn't run as smoothly as they did in the American films."[21] Her first production, *Bulldog Jack*, released in April 1935, was directed by Walter Forde and she and he did not get along. Forde dismissed her as a typical arrogant Hollywood star and was outraged at her late arrival on the set. Wray disliked Forde's dictatorial manner. She was far happier on her second film, *The Clairvoyant*, which had "an interesting story and concept," along with a major leading man, Claude Rains, and a mediocre but friendly director, Maurice Elvey.

Wray's last two films, *Come Out of the Pantry*, released in November 1935, and *When Knights Were Bold*, released in February 1936, teamed her with the popular Jack Buchanan, and featured songs by the American composers Maurice Sigler, Al Goodhart, and Al Hoffman.[22] This American trio is responsible for the delightful "I'm in a Dancing Mood" and the iconic

Strangers on a Honeymoon (1936), with Noah Beery and Constance Cummings.

"Everything Stops for Tea," introduced by Buchanan in *Come Out of the Pantry*. Reviewing the production, *Film Weekly* (April 25, 1936) noted that "Fay Wray has little to do that calls for the exertion of her acting ability, but she is beautifully poised, utterly competent, and makes Buchanan a charming partner." Who could ask for more?

The English trip was not a particularly happy one for Wray in that her husband, John Monk Saunders, who provided the original story idea for *A Yank at Oxford* in 1938, was involved in a couple of extramarital affairs and also attempted suicide.

Gaumont-British brought over Walter Huston to add gravitas to its production of *Rhodes of Africa*, released in the spring of 1936 and directed by Berthold Viertel. The latter explained, "Huston is not at all like Rhodes in looks or figure. Yet he is well suited for the part because, being a Canadian, he has a genuine feeling for the Colonial life—and Rhodes's whole life was devoted to colonizing Africa."[23] It was not Huston who was the problem but rather, as Graham Greene noted, that the film is "sober, worthy, humourless," unrolling in "eleven well-bred reels."[24] Huston's son, John, provided the story for the 1935 British production, *Death Drives Through*, but it is unlikely that the film required his actual presence at the studio or either in the country.

One of Huston's greatest American films, in which he turns in a sensitive and moving performance, is *Dodsworth* (1936), wherein his overbearing wife is played by the statuesque and regal Ruth Chatterton. She had received two Academy Award nominations and been a major star on stage and screen when she came to London in May 1937 to play the lead on stage in Somerset Maugham's *The Constant Wife*. The play enjoyed only a brief run, but it led to two British film appearances, in *The Rat* (1937) and *A Royal Divorce* (1938), which was picked up for distribution by Paramount. While Chatterton continued as a celebrity in a number of fields, these two British films ended her screen career.

Otto Kruger was the consummate and "durable actor who mastered the art of portraying complex, almost amiable villains," according to *Time* magazine (September 16, 1974). He was a frequent visitor to Britain in the 1930s, not always playing villains on screen in some six films between 1936 and 1939, three of them—*Living Dangerously* (1936), *The Housemaster* (1938) and *Black Eyes* (1939)—directed by Herbert Brenon. He also found time to make his television debut on the BBC's new service. Kruger enjoyed alternating English and Hollywood assignments. He told *Good Housekeeping* (September 1956) that he always liked the "tar-and-fish smells" of the London docks.

Joining Kruger in *The Housemaster* was American juvenile Phillips Holmes, who also worked in another Herbert Brenon production, *The Dominant Sex* (1937), and a third British film, directed by American Bernard Vorhaus, *Ten Minute Alibi* (1935). In all probability, his pro-British stance drove him to join the Royal Canadian Air Force at the outbreak of World War II, resulting in his death in a midair collision in August 1942.

Marriage to a British national could sometimes result in a British film career for an American leading lady. The most obvious example is the perky and effervescent Zelma O'Neal who introduced the "Varsity Drag" in the 1927 stage production of *Good News* and sang "Button Up Your Overcoat" with Jack Haley in both the stage (1929) and film (1930) versions of *Follow Thru*. In 1928, she married the elegant and well-spoken British actor Anthony Bushell, whose career had commenced on stage but who made his mark as the cowardly Hibbert in the 1930 screen adaptation of R. C. Sheriff's *Journey's End*. O'Neal returned to England with Bushell and starred in six films there, none of which gave opportunity for her unique talent as a singer and comedic dancer, and the best of which is probably the 1934 version of the stage hit, *Mr. Cinders*.[25] The actress complained that she was not given the opportunity to co-star with her husband, and that British producers did not include enough close-ups.[26] O'Neal returned to America following her 1935 divorce from Bushell but her career basically ended with her British sojourn.[27]

There would have been little point in bringing the ethereal and difficult-to-cast Helen Chandler to Britain had it not been for her impending 1935 marriage to British actor Bramwell Fletcher, whose career was primarily in the United States. Initially, Chandler worked for Anthony Asquith in an Austrian-British co-production on the life of composer Franz Schubert, titled *The Unfinished Symphony*, and released in the UK in August 1934 and in the United States in May of the following year. Her first "true" British film was *Radio Parade of 1935*, released in December 1934, followed by *It's a Bet*, released in February 1935. The films were succeeded by a leading role in George Abbott's stage production of the comedy *Boy Meets Girl* in the summer of 1936, and, later, by a 1940 divorce from Fletcher.

Two of the screen's greatest comedians were British-born. Charlie Chaplin ended his career, through no fault or decision of his own, in England with *A King in New York* (1957), which not even the presence of some great British character players could save. However, the South London neighborhood where he spent his formative years was not far from his memory while he was producing his own films in Hollywood. Here, as studio sets, he recreated

Anthony Bushell and Zelma O'Neal in 1932.

the streets, homes, and buildings that he remembered from his childhood. Stan Laurel was born in Ulverston in the north of England, and with his rotund American partner, Oliver Hardy, he made some of the finest and most entertaining of American silent and sound comedies. The couple was dearly loved in Britain, and played extensively there on stage on tour in 1932, 1947, 1952, and 1953–54. On the first tour, some 35,000 fans gathered in Laurel's home county of Lancashire to sing "Will You No Come Back Again" to them. Obviously, a contract with American producer Hal Roach prevented the couple from working in British cinema in the 1930s, but why, at the end of their career in the 1950s, were they not approached to star in a British film rather than the abysmal French/Italian co-production, *Atoll K.* (1951)?

Just as that last film is sad, so is the couple's final departure on June 3, 1954, from the United Kingdom, not on a major ocean liner but on a merchant ship, traveling from Hull to Vancouver and stopping en route in Los Angeles to drop off Laurel and Hardy.

Laurel and Hardy foil Jimmy Finlayson, with his unique double take and slow burn, was Scottish-born, and while he began his career in the United States and appeared almost exclusively on stage and then on screen there, he did return to Britain in the early 1930s to star in three films, all produced by Irving Asher (more on whom later): *Strictly in Confidence*, released in August 1933, *Trouble in Store*, released in January 1934, and *What Happened to Harkness*, released in August 1934. The last was directed by Milton Rosmer. The first two are of more interest in that they are the only feature films directed by Clyde Cook, an Australian-born comedian who, like Finlayson, was always a reliable and instantly recognizable supporting player in both silent and sound films.

Another lesser American comedian who came to Britain and actually starred in one feature film—in Hollywood his roles were always in support in features, with only comedy shorts providing him with starring material—was Edgar Kennedy. Famous for his exasperated facial expression, the "slow burn," Kennedy is featured in *Hey! Hey! U.S.A.*, which stars Will Hay, a comedian best remembered for his schoolteacher roles in which he displays exasperation on a scale that Kennedy cannot possibly emulate with his facial contortion. The film, released in September 1938, is set on an ocean liner and involves Chicago gangsters. Cut to one hour, *Variety* (October 5, 1938) thought it might serve well as the second half on a double feature.

After filing for bankruptcy in the United States, Buster Keaton journeyed to Paris in 1934 to star in *Le Roi des Champs Elysées*. From Paris, he moved on to London, where he starred, with Mexican-born Lupita Tovar as his leading lady, in *The Invader*, for which he also provided the story and gags, both with credit. Adrian Brunel directed and, by all accounts, had a difficult time with Keaton's alcoholism. Perhaps that is why the film is so shoddy and was so unsuccessful on its American release a year later as *An Old Spanish Custom*. The film is primarily of interest in that it was remade by Keaton and Columbia in 1939 as a two-reeler, titled *Pest from the West*, and is often considered one of the comedian's best sound shorts.

Like Keaton, Harry Langdon's American career was in major decline by the 1930s. Indeed, it was barely surviving. Initially, Langdon came to Britain in the spring of 1937, not as a performer but as a director, an occupation at which he had proved himself very unreliable in the late 1920s.

Nevertheless, Fox British did hire him to oversee production of an extremely minor comedy, *Wise Guys*, starring Charlie Naughton and Jimmy Gold, two lesser members of the "Crazy Gang" group of stage and screen comedians. He was back in England the following year—his wife, Mabel, had relatives there—and was approached by Morgan Productions, based at Elstree, to accept a cameo role in *Mad about Money*, which featured Americans Lupe Velez (born in Mexico),[28] Wallace Ford, and Ben Lyon. Langdon's part seems almost an afterthought, although his role as a theatrical backer who gets drunk, falls asleep, and dreams of taking off by rocket to the stars leads to an incredibly awful musical number, "Dustin' the Stars" (directed by Len Lye). Aside from the Hollywood leading players, *Mad about Money* also claims a principal American director, Melville Brown, and an American dance director, Larry Ceballos, who is obviously having an off day. Brown also directed *Head Office* (1936) in England, and died in January 1938, shortly after returning to the US after making *Mad about Money* (which was released in the US under the uninspired title of *He Married an Actress*). Lupe Velez was also seen in the British films, *The Morals of Marcus* (1935) and *Gypsy Melody* (1936).

Some British films of the 1930s featured Americans who were not generally recognized as having film careers but were popular in other media, most notably vaudeville. There was also one opera singer, Marguerite Namara, a lyric soprano from a wealthy Ohio family, who certainly helped, with her aspirations to become prominent both in the United States and Europe. She had starred opposite Rudolph Valentino in a 1920 feature film, *Stolen Moments*, at a time when her fame was bigger than his. She made her second film and her most important at Elstree Studios and on location in Spain in 1931. An adaptation of Bizet's opera *Carmen*, *Gipsy Blood* has a score conducted by Malcolm Sargent, but little else to recommend it to a general audience, which is perhaps why Madame Namara always referred to it as "The Bloody Gypsy."

A major star of the musical theatre, who had actually made her debut with the Metropolitan Opera, was New York-born Mary Ellis, who came to London in 1930 after her 1929 marriage to British actor Basil Sydney. Despite later divorcing him, happily Ellis stayed on in Britain, starring on stage in three of composer Ivor Novello's greatest hits, *Glamorous Night* (1935),[29] *The Dancing Years* (1939), and *Arc de Triomphe* (1943). Ellis starred in the 1937 screen adaptation of *Glamorous Night*, which failed to live up to expectations, despite Ellis having two leading men closely associated with American cinema, Otto Kruger and Canadian Victor Jory. She had earlier starred in *Bella Donna* (1934), again with two leading men who enjoyed success in Hollywood, Conrad Veidt and Cedric Hardwicke, and had three later and minor screen roles in the British productions of *The Astonished Heart* (1949), *The Magic Box* (1951), and *The Three Worlds of Gulliver* (1960).

Long-legged comedienne, dancer, and singer Charlotte Greenwood made her London stage debut at the Theatre Royal, Drury Lane, in 1932 in *Wild Violets*, an operetta boasting a score by Robert Stoltz but little else. During part of its 291-performance run, Greenwood spent her days at Shepherd's Bush Studios filming *Orders Is Orders* (released in the summer of 1933) under the direction of Walter Forde. Playing opposite Greenwood and helping with the on-screen dialogue is American character actor James Gleason, making his only British film appearance. *Orders Is Orders*, with its storyline involving a Hollywood film company trying to shoot on a British army base, features Ray Milland and Cedric Hardwicke, both destined for Hollywood careers, and the brilliant Scottish actor Finlay Currie attempting a somewhat uneasy American accent as he seems to do in an awful lot of British films of the 1930s.[30] Singer-pianist Harry Richman was in England during 1937. He appeared at a royal command performance, telling the king and queen, "May God bless you and keep you. I wish I could afford it." He also appears as the principal guest star in *Kicking the Moon Around*,[31] a vehicle for Bert Ambrose and His Orchestra, which went into production at Pinewood Studios in November of 1937, again with Walter Forde directing. It is of primary importance for the appearance of Maureen O'Hara in a small part prior to a major Hollywood career. Top billed in *Kicking the Moon Around* is Ambrose's vocalist Evelyn Dall, billed as the "Original British Blonde Bombshell," who appeared in some eight British films between 1936 and 1944; although generally assumed to be British, she was actually born in the Bronx.

Sophie Tucker was a frequent visitor to the UK from 1922 through 1965. She made only a handful of films in the United States and only one, her second, in England. Released in the summer of 1934, *Gay Love* stars Sophie Tucker, playing herself, and despite the modern meaning of the title, it must be recorded that here she does not sing the highly suggestive "I Picked a Pansy in the Garden of Love." Tucker, however, does provide some heterosexual innuendo with "My Extraordinary Man." Equally popular in the UK was "nut" comedian Will Mahoney, whose performance piece involved his dancing on a xylophone. Like Tucker, he starred in one British film *Said O'Reily to McNab*, directed in 1937 by American William Beaudine; Mahoney plays an Irish conman opposite Will Fyffe as the Scottish equivalent.

Adding immeasurably to *Gay Love*, as well as so many other British films of the 1930s, is brilliant comedienne Florence Desmond, who on screen and on record provided devastatingly accurate impersonations of Hollywood stars as varied as Janet Gaynor and Greta Garbo. She made only a couple of American films, but in one, the Will Rogers vehicle, *Mr. Skitch*, she is at her best, making a flustered ZaSu Pitts even more flustered as she impersonates her voice and her gestures. Pitts was to bring her fluttery hand gestures, dithering, and easily excitable style to the British film, *Wanted*, released early in 1937, but less so to *Merry Comes to Town*, released later that same year.

Jimmy Durante was starring at the London Palladium when he made his British film debut in *Land without Music*, released in April 1937. The original comic lead, Jonah J. Whistler, was Eugene Pallette, but as director Walter Forde recalled, he walked out on his first day at the studio. Forde got on well with Durante, but admitted the production was "a very poor film because of casting." The problem was Richard Tauber, a great tenor but a rotund and unattractive-looking individual. "Tauber, he was a fine singer but cast him as the lead, as the lover!" laughed Forde.[32]

The most popular of American entertainers, as opposed to actors, who came to Britain in the 1930s was Arthur Tracy, whose sentimental delivery of sentimental songs, such as his theme song "Marta," "Trees," and "It's My Mother's Birthday Today," had been perfected on radio, where he was billed as "The Street Singer." While his performances are generally greeted with derision by modern audiences, there is no question that Tracy took himself very seriously. As Margaret Lockwood, his leading lady in the 1937 British film, *The Street Singer*, recalled for me, he would sit for hours in his dressing room, listening to his own recordings with tears of emotion in his eyes.[33]

Tracy came to Britain in 1935 for a seven-week music-hall tour and remained for six years, starring in five films: *Flirtation* (1935), *Limelight* (1935), *The Street Singer* (1937), *Command Performance* (1937), and *Follow Your Star* (1938). His style seemed to suit the mood of British audiences if not British critics; James Agate wrote that *Limelight* was "a syrupy concatenation to win all British hearts."[34] Well into the 1980s, Tracy still had a British fan club, and his recordings continue to be available there. In fact, his singing style is very similar to that of the British entertainer Cavan O'Connor, who began his career as a mystery singer on the BBC in the early 1930s, billed as "The Vagabond Lover."

Along with performers, there were also American directors and other creative individuals working at British studios, where they joined the ranks of a considerable number of non-British participants. In fact, James Agate sarcastically commented in regard to one 1935 release from a company with the stoutly patriotic name of British & Dominions Film Corporation: "That *Escape Me Never* is a thoroughly British film is proved by the fact that among the technical staff occur names like Andrejiev, Strassner, and Allgeir, the principal actress is the German Miss [Elizabeth] Bergner, and the producer is the German, Dr. Paul Czinner." Similarly, it was somewhat unfortunate that when Corinne Griffith attempted to demonstrate her support for British films by singling out three from 1932, *Under the Greenwood Tree*, *The Calendar*, and *These Charming People*, she didn't take into account that the first two were directed by Americans (Harry Lachman and T. Hayes Hunter) and the third by Swiss-born Louis Mercanton.

While the evidence of the poor quality of most British films of the period would deny the claim, it was suggested that American directors were brought over because they made box-office films, whereas their British counterparts were more concerned with "art." In an unsigned article in *Film Weekly*, one critic wrote,

> British films will never win through until our directors abandon the out-of-date technique of [E. A.] Dupont and the pyrotechnics of Pudovkin and come down to earth. In other words, until our directors either de-bunk themselves or are de-bunked.[35]

Some American directors were in England only briefly. The most famous, of course, is Josef von Sternberg, brought over by Alexander Korda to direct Charles Laughton in the abortive *I Claudius*. The project was abandoned early in 1937, and created such bitterness between Korda and Laughton that the latter formed his own production company, Mayflower Pictures Corp., with German producer Erich Pommer.[36] After completing *Man of Aran* (which some might argue is as much an Irish film as an English one) for Michael Balcon early in 1934, documentary filmmaker Robert Flaherty was hired by Korda to go to India and film *Elephant Boy*; Flaherty went way over budget and was briefly replaced by another American, Monta Bell, before Korda's brother, Zoltan Korda, completed the project for February 1937 release. Also working for Korda was the distinguished production designer William Cameron Menzies, who directed a stylized version of H. G. Wells's *Things to Come*, released in February 1936, and starring Raymond Massey and Ralph Richardson, and served as associate producer on *The Thief of Bagdad* (1940). Menzies also found time in 1938 to direct *Four Dark Hours* for Robert T. Kane and 20th Century-Fox, but despite an original story by

Graham Greene and judicious use of the London locations, the film was not released until 1940, and then under the title of *The Green Cockatoo.*

Prolific American director Allan Dwan, who had been active since 1911, made three films in England. As he recalled, he used to visit Carlsbad, Germany, each year to take the waters and lose some weight. On his way back, he stopped in London and was asked if he would like to direct a film there. It was *Her First Affaire*, released in 1932, and marking one of the first appearances of Ida Lupino. "I liked it, and stayed to make three," said Dwan. The others were *Counsel's Opinion* and *I Spy* (both released in 1933). "I enjoyed the change of working in England, not the pictures themselves. . . . I stayed there during the worst part of the Depression."[37] Like many of Dwan's films, his British trio is far from memorable, although *Counsel's Opinion* was remade a few years later by Korda as *The Divorce of Lady X.*

On a far lesser level, Arthur Rosson came over in 1932 to direct two Paramount-British productions, *Ebb Tide* and *Women Who Pay*. In 1934, he directed *Forbidden Territory*, starring Russian-born actor and director Gregory Ratoff. Rather than return to Hollywood, Ratoff remained in England, appearing in two further films, released in 1935, *18 Minutes* and *Hello, Sweetheart.* Ratoff also wrote the story for *18 Minutes*, directed by Monty Banks, in which he appears as a circus lion trainer forcing into marriage a girl played by Katharine Sergava, also like Ratoff of Russian origin and also like Ratoff having a film career in Hollywood. Surprisingly, Paramount purchased the rights to *18 Minutes* for American release in 1935, changing the name to *This Woman Is Mine*. Two years later, in 1937, a play *Autumn*, translated from the Russian by Ratoff, with Margaret Kennedy, opened in London at the St. Martin's Theatre, but Ratoff is not in the cast. Ratoff was back in England in 1960, directing *Oscar Wilde*, with Robert Morley in the title role.

The reality, of course, is that the majority of American directors who came over to Britain in the 1930s were far from being in the first rank of filmmakers. Alfred Goulding directed one prominent American film, the Laurel and Hardy vehicle *A Chump at Oxford*, appropriate perhaps because of a brief British career in 1936 and 1937, but his American films were basically unimportant. While in England, Goulding concentrated on musicals or comedies with musical numbers, including a tribute to the Boy Scouts and their annual stage entertainment produced by Ralph Reader and titled, like the 1937 film, *The Gang Show.*[38] If nothing else, the film provides a glimpse of a very "camp" Reader, who seems to take perverted pleasure in dressing in female attire his Boy Scouts, some of whom are quite young. Italian-born

Anthony Varney had virtually no career as a director in the United States and basically ended it with five British films in the early 1930s: *The Road to Fortune* and *The Eternal Feminine* (1930 and 1931, respectively, which he also produced for Paramount release), *The Wrong Mr. Perkins* and *Immediate Possession* (both 1931, for Fox release), and *Almost a Divorce* (1931, for which he also provided the original story).

James A. FitzPatrick was a stocky, smiling, curly-haired Irish-American, born in Shelton, Connecticut, who has a unique place in film history thanks to the *FitzPatrick Traveltalks*, which he narrates and which successfully manage to present the world to moviegoers without hinting at any controversy, ugliness, or poverty. They provide an image of lands peopled by happy natives, and all viewed through rose-colored, or more accurately Technicolored, glasses. Certainly, FitzPatrick deserves credit for pioneering travel shorts in color, but he also was prominent in British film production in the late 1920s and 1930s. In biographical information provided by MGM in 1940, FitzPatrick is credited with "about 50 shorts on personalities" produced between 1924 and 1928 and "nearly 200 Traveltalks" produced between 1928 and 1940. He also worked in Britain, directing the 1928 feature *The Lady of the Lake*, starring Percy Marmont and Benita Hume, together with eight quota quickies produced for MGM at the Sound City Studios at Shepperton.[39] FitzPatrick had an obvious love for Britain, and his last *Traveltalks* from 1950 were *Touring Northern Ireland*, *Land of Auld Lang Syne*, and *Life on the Thames*. From 1954–64, he produced thirty-minute travelogues for television under the title of *Travelcades*, and in 1967, in London, he formed FitzPatrick Pictures, Ltd., to produce a ninety-minute feature, *The Courageous Capt. Cook*.

If there is one thread that links several of the American film directors working in British studios in the 1930s, it is their prolificacy. And there is no better example of this than William Beaudine, who began his career as an assistant director in 1910 and ended it as a television director in 1968. He was responsible for nearly 500 films and more than 300 television programs. In 1934, he directed the W. C. Fields vehicle, *The Old Fashioned Way*, for Paramount, and he should have been in heavy demand by the Hollywood studios. But he wasn't, and so he accepted an offer from Walter Mycroft, production manager at British International Pictures, to come to England and make a film titled *Dandy Dick*, part of an effort to turn music-hall comedian Will Hay into a film star. Combined as it was with Beaudine's twentieth wedding anniversary, providing a second honeymoon at British International Picture's expense, the offer was most appealing. With the four

Will Hay films that he made, it is to Beaudine that credit must ultimately go for creating the bumbling, slightly sleazy characterization that the comedian perfected on screen, particularly that of a harried schoolmaster in *Boys Will Be Boys* (1935).

Beaudine, who also collaborated on the script for *Dandy Dick*, explained,

> His timing [was] perfect. He [knew] instinctively to the split second when to say or do a thing. . . . Will is to England the type of comic that Will Rogers was to America. He can play "down to earth" characters in his own inimitable manner. It [was] my idea that he should be associated with these characters.[40]

Beaudine returned to America at the end of 1934, but when Irving Asher at Warner Bros.-British offered him a three-picture deal, the director decided to return, bringing his family with him, in January 1935. In all, Beaudine made six films for Asher, as well as a further six for other British producers,[41] and also made another crossing to New York and back again to England. It is an anomaly that here is an American director capable of shaping British comedic talent, not just Hay, but also Max Miller, billed as "The Cheeky Chappie," because of his risqué jokes, George Formby, the comedy team of Jimmy Nervo and Teddy Knox, and Hay's comedic, graceless sidekicks, Graham Moffatt and Moore Marriott.

With *Mr. Cohen Takes a Walk* (1936), Beaudine shows a sensitive style in his handling of this touching tale of a Jewish businessman (played by Paul Graetz) who grows tired of his son's handling of his department store and becomes an itinerant tinker. The conflict between youth and old age is handled in a non-aggressive, mild manner. German Paul Graetz is outstanding in this adaptation of a Mary Roberts Rinehart story, urging, "It's time for the best of all religions to get together for peace." For an American in Britain, Beaudine makes good use of English locations, including Bentalls department store in Kingston-upon-Thames and London's Berwick Street Market.

Mr. Cohen Takes a Walk did not fare well in New York, despite producer Asher's cutting more than a reel from the film, but Warner Bros. in Burbank did sign Paul Graetz to a contract at $150 a week.

Legal and tax problems forced an end to Beaudine's British stay, just as he was about to work on a production for Alexander Korda, and he returned to the United States at the end of 1937.

In the final years of his life, and after his death, Bernard Vorhaus gained "cult" status as a director of British quota quickies. The post-career fame is thanks to another and more prominent director, David Lean, who worked as an editor for Vorhaus and once casually described him as his "greatest influence." Historian Charles Drazin has written of a "symbiotic relationship between the two men,"[42] while Geoff Brown has posited that Vorhaus "stands as proof-positive than no matter how low the budget or how bad the script, a good director can make a difference."

Vorhaus began his American directorial career in 1928 with a two-reel silent short. With the coming of sound, he had difficulty finding employment and came to England, where he worked at Twickenham Studios for infamously cheap producer Julius Hagen, who somehow had a knack for spotting equally cheap talent. At Twickenham, Vorhaus directed *The Ghost Camera* (1933), which introduced Ida Lupino to the screen and featured a young John Mills. His best film is generally considered to be *The Last Journey* (1936), a melodrama involving a train driver, who foolishly believes he is about to lose his job, and his wife, and drives the packed London-to-Manchester express train with suicidal intentions.[43]

In 1937, Vorhaus was persuaded back to Hollywood with a Republic contract, but in the early 1950s, he and his wife were accused of being Communists, and therefore blacklisted; the two returned to Britain, where Vorhaus remained for the remainder of his life and never worked again in the film industry. His films were rediscovered in the 1980s, and I had the good fortune to know him at the end of his life and to edit for publication his autobiography, *Saved from Oblivion*.

Unlike Vorhaus, Tim Whelan came to Britain while at the top of his form. He had worked as a writer on a number of Harold Lloyd features, as well as the brilliant 1927 Beatrice Lillie vehicle, *Exit Smiling*. It was in England that he made his directorial debut in 1928, with *Adam's Apple*, starring comedian Monty Banks, and released in the US as *Honeymoon Abroad*. As cinematographer Ronald Neame recalled,

> Whelan and Banks were great friends and complemented each other. Tim was soft-spoken and charming while Monty was volatile and more crass. Between takes they would roll dice on the floor, money changing hands as the unit gathered around to laugh and root for one or the other. If a game became heated, we simply delayed shooting.

Production chief Walter Mycroft recalled the arrival of the Americans at Elstree:

> There were three of them to begin with—Monty Banks, his director Tim Whelan, and writer Rex Taylor, who wrote the scenario of my *Under the Greenwood Tree* [released September 1929]. They appeared startlingly one winter evening in the vestibule of our studio. Everything about them was startling: their outlandish golfing suits and shoes and gangster hats, their idiom, their scarcely veiled, but good humoured contempt for things English in general, and for an English studio in particular; above all their specific and sincere belief that the United States won the war, that other war that Hollywood had glorified in *The Big Parade*, without a British, or come to that a French soldier, in sight. . . . Setting aside their and our national prejudices, I soon found there was much to learn from our visitors and set about doing so."[44]

Adam's Apple was followed by *When Knights Were Bold*, dismissed by one critic as "when gags were old," which is important in that its leading lady, the stage actress Miriam Seegar, became Mrs. Tim Whelan. Whelan returned to England in 1932, and remained there for seven years, directing some first-rate comedies and occasional dramas, including *The Divorce of Lady X* (1938), *St. Martin's Lane/The Sidewalks of London* (1938), *Q Planes* (1939), and *The Thief of Bagdad* (1940), which he and Alexander Korda completed in Hollywood.[45] Also in England, Whelan screen-tested two Irish beauties, Geraldine Fitzgerald and Maureen O'Hara.

Whelan continued to work in the United States into the 1950s. At the time of his death, columnist Louella Parsons wrote that he was "one of [the industry's] finest men and most distinguished directors."[46]

Whelan, Vorhaus, and Beaudine are not only prolific but also have reputations. Unfortunately, there is also Frank A. Richardson, who belongs here, and he is an American who is only prolific. He worked in Hollywood as an assistant director in the late 1910s and 1920s, directed a few short subjects, and then came to Britain, where he made twelve forgettable films for UK release by Fox, Universal, Warner Bros., and others between 1931 and 1937.[47] Richardson then appears to have retired—or at least given up directing films—until 1950, when he returns with one last British film, *Bait*, starring Diana Napier and John Bentley, a crime drama concerned with a female gang leader, and based on a play that he had written.[48]

Two American "stars" of British cinema in the 1930s were neither actors nor directors, but editors. Elmo Williams became a prominent editor in the United States and later a producer, most notably of the 1970 film, *Tora! Tora! Tora!* He came to England in 1933 as an assistant to his friend, Paramount editor Merrill White. White had been sent over by Paramount to edit *The Queen's Affair*, which the studio planned to produce at Elstree, starring Jeanette MacDonald and Herbert Marshall, and with Lubitsch directing. After Lubitsch pulled out, the studio also lost its stars, and Herbert Wilcox took over the production as a vehicle for Anna Neagle. Williams learned his craft under Wilcox, and when the producer came to America, along with Anna Neagle, Williams returned to his homeland and edited the producer's first four films there, *Nurse Edith Cavell* (1939), *Irene* (1940), *No, No, Nanette* (1940), and *Sunny* (1941).[49]

William Hornbeck was rightly described by Frank Capra as "without doubt the greatest film editor in the history of motion pictures." And his formative years as a feature film editor were spent in England. Hornbeck had commenced his career in 1916 as an editor with Mack Sennett, but when the producer went bankrupt in the early 1930s, Hornbeck was out of work for the first time in his life. He took a tramp steamer to Britain and wrote ahead to friend and fellow editor, Harold Young, that he was on his way and in need of work. Alexander Korda hired him, and Hornbeck worked for the producer, often with the credit of supervising editor, on twenty-six films, beginning with *The Scarlet Pimpernel* in 1934, and ending with *The Thief of Bagdad*, which had started shooting in England, at Denham Studios, in 1939, but was completed in Hollywood. Hornbeck's involvement with Korda did not end with the return to Hollywood; he worked there with the producer on *Lady Hamilton/That Hamilton Woman* (1941) and *Jungle Book* (1942).

Korda urged his editor to become a director, but as Hornbeck recalled, "It was all very flattering, but as much as I loved film—loved physically handling and working with it—I just couldn't stand to give that up, as wonderful as directing would have been."[50]

CHAPTER SEVEN

Hollywood Producers and British Film Production in the 1930s

THE 1927 CINEMATOGRAPH FILMS ACT HERALDED THE AGE OF THE "quota quickie" with its requirement that a specific number of films distributed and screened in Britain must be produced in Britain. Seventy-five percent of the salaries had to go to British subjects, including a British writer, and 7.5 percent for distributors and 5 percent for exhibitors of all films were to be British. As cynics point out, there was no requirement as to quality. The act was a dilemma for American producers and distributors who were now forced to ensure that in order to release vast quantities of their product in Britain, a percentage had to be British. The outcome was that American distributors either produced films in Britain for British consumption but with no intention of distributing them anywhere else or purchased films from independent British producers to add to their British release schedule. Legend has it that MGM found a unique solution to the problem. It would release its quota of British films in Britain but screen them at theatres only in the mornings when the buildings were closed to the public and the audience comprised of the theatre cleaners.

In 1931, it is reported that the seven major American distributors had their forty-four quota films supplied by thirty-six different British producers.[1] Some American distributors were more heavily involved in actual British productions than others. There was small interest in quality, and the bottom line was that the films should cost the American distributors as little as possible. It was often claimed that the production cost for British quota quickies was one pound for each foot of film. Thus, a seventy-minute feature, 7,000 feet in length, would cost in its entirety 7,000 pounds.

As Peter Noble records,

> A well-known screenwriter . . . asserts that it was quite usual for a group of writers to start work on Monday morning and produce a "shooting script" on a given theme by Saturday. The film was then cast over the week-end and completed within a fortnight![2]

Paramount-British was set up in 1930, and the studio leased a sound stage at the British & Dominions Studios for quota production. Two major non-American producers, Alexander Korda and Herbert Wilcox,[3] were initially involved, and some American talent was imported. Harry Lachman, primarily an artist who had worked at Rex Ingram's Victorine Studios in Nice and who had also been associated with British International Pictures[4] and made one British film for MGM, *The Outsider* (1931), was hired and he directed three Paramount-British films in 1932: *Aren't We All?*, based on the Frederick Lonsdale play, *Down Our Street*, and *Insult* (1932). Perhaps more significant than bringing himself, Lachman brought to the British studios a British photographer who had been working for Rex Ingram in Nice, Michael Powell, who was to become the country's preeminent filmmaker. Lachman returned to England from America in early 1939 to direct Will Fyffe and Phyllis Calvert in *They Came by Night*, based on a play by the English writer Barré Lyndon, who had a brief career in Hollywood, most notably writing the screenplay for the 1944 production of *The Lodger*. Paramount-British's only really major success was its first one, *Service for Ladies/Reserved for Ladies* (1932), produced and directed by Alexander Korda, and starring Leslie Howard and Benita Hume. Reference should also be made to *Man of Mayfair*, released in November 1931, an inconsequential film except that it starred Jack Buchanan, who had enjoyed a Hollywood success the previous year in Paramount's *Monte Carlo*, directed by Ernst Lubitsch and co-starring Jeanette MacDonald, and was about to become certainly the most popular British male film star of musical comedies if not all genres.

Clive Brook, who had been a major Hollywood leading man since the mid-1920s, told Paramount, to whom he was under contract, that he was willing to appear in its British productions, but added, "When Paramount British films are being shown all over the United States I should like nothing better than to play in them."[5] The actor obviously knew there was little likelihood of that happening. As Paramount-British executive J. C. Graham commented, "These pictures have no more chance of getting into America that I have to jump across the Atlantic Ocean."[6]

The studio had high hopes for *Lily Christine*, a 1932 screen adaptation of the popular Michael Arlen novel, for which the author is also credited with the dialogue. Paul Stein directed, and the title role was played by former silent star Corinne Griffith, making an inauspicious talkie debut, opposite British actor Colin Clive, who had made a name for himself in Hollywood with *Journey's End* (1930) and *Frankenstein* (1931). Prior to its April 29, 1932, opening at London's Plaza Theatre, there was a special midnight matinee performance for the Prince of Wales. However, when the film opened as the second half of a double bill at a Mamaroneck, New York, theatre, *Variety* (September 20, 1932) was scathing:

> *Lily Christine* is a bad picture. Even British audiences have probably stamped it as a bore, and there's nothing tolerant about American patrons where their screen fare is concerned, regardless of the source. . . . The picture's screaming deficiency is a complete disregard of tempo. It drags and it drags. No effort in direction or cutting to relieve the situation.

Film Weekly reported,

> It was one of the most expensive and lavishly produced films ever turned out in a British studio.
>
> It was made with a cast that included that great favorite of the silent days and a Hollywood gilded star, Corinne Griffith.
>
> And it was . . . "just another motion picture."

After viewing the film, in the spring of 1932, the studio decided to cease direct involvement in British productions. That was now left directly to British & Dominions, which continued operation at Elstree through 1936, when a fire forced a move to Pinewood. Paramount British's last British film appears to be *Incident in Shanghai*, released in January 1938, with Anthony Havelock-Allan producing (a task he had undertaken since 1934) and John Paddy Carstairs directing.

The former production head of Paramount's Hollywood studio, Jesse L. Lasky, came to London in August 1936. "I have come to England to look around," he told *Film Weekly*. "Fortunes will be made over here during the next few years."[7] Lasky was not among those who made them, despite or perhaps because his notion of a perfect British film was to pair Nino Martini and Francis Lederer, an Italian and a Czech.

Paramount leading lady of the 1920s, Gloria Swanson, had first entered film production, not entirely with success, in the United States. In February 1932, the actress came to London on honeymoon with her fourth husband,

Michael Farmer. After the birth of their daughter there, Douglas Fairbanks, Sr., suggested Swanson form a production company and make a film in England, to a certain extent because as Farmer was British, Swanson also had British citizenship and certain tax advantages. Funding came in part from United Artists, in part from South African investors, and primarily from the sale of Swanson's stock in United Artists.

Veteran British actor and writer Miles Malleson provided the story for *Perfect Understanding*, in which a newly married couple confess their past affairs, while Michael Powell was involved in the screen adaptation. Laurence Olivier was an ideal choice to play opposite Swanson, although ten years her junior. Initially, Swanson had asked Edmund Goulding to direct, an ideal choice, but he proved unavailable, and she settled for the far less talented Cyril Gardner, whom she described as "a bit inexperienced but keenly intelligent."[8] For the second female lead, Swanson chose Hollywood leading lady Genevieve Tobin, who later pronounced the trip a waste of time as so much of her role was cut.[9]

Lily Christine (1932), with Colin Clive and Corinne Griffith.

The film was not a success, either in the UK or in America, when it opened in the spring of 1933. In her autobiography, Swanson describes the American critics as "indifferent," adding that after the national bank closure and the introduction of the New Deal, "Americans were consequently in no mood to see a group of high-born Britishers engage in well-spoken dramatic squabbles in the courts and on the French Riviera."[10] (The film was partially shot in Cannes.) At the time, the actress blamed most of the problems with the film on the British:

> Trying to turn out a picture in English is like trying to swim the Channel with your hands and feet tied—and with the current against you. . . . In Hollywood, the heads of production departments are so experienced and resourceful that you are spared all the little problems. But in England, every tiny technical detail awaits your decision. You must worry about everything.
>
> I suppose I'm too American, too used to direct methods, to adapt myself to the British tempo.[11]

Perfect Understanding (1933), with Gloria Swanson and Laurence Olivier.

The British responded that Swanson began production with no organization, constantly changed her plans, and insisted on supervising all aspects of the production herself.

Fox British Pictures, Ltd., was established at Wembley Studios in the summer of 1932, with its primary director, as well as board member, being Albert "Al" Parker. Parker had enjoyed a prominent career as a silent director in America in the 1920s; his career had started as an actor, and later director, with Douglas Fairbanks, Sr., and he was responsible for one of the actor's best known and admired films, *The Black Pirate* (1926). Why he came to Britain in the early 1930s, abandoning a Hollywood career, is uncertain, but come he did, and he made fourteen uninspired films for Fox from 1932 through 1938.[12] Ronald Neame, who photographed a number of Parker's films, recalled him as "fierce-tempered, heart-of-gold."[13] From directing, he made a career change to actors' agent, with clients including James Mason, Trevor Howard, Susannah York, Glynis Johns, and Helen Mirren. He also continued his association with Fox, serving as a talent scout for the successor company, 20th Century-Fox.

In 1929, the distinguished theatrical producer Basil Dean established Associated Talking Pictures, with studios at Elstree, and in 1931, he formed an alliance with RKO Radio Pictures, the latter providing technical expertise and distributing his films primarily for the British market. Films under this alliance would begin with the familiar RKO radio tower logo, sending out Morse code signals, followed by the British company logo with the Morse code signals continuing. Audiences were assured via a main title that the film presented "stars of the British Stage and Screen Photographed and Recorded under American Supervision and Produced by Basil Dean in England."

The arrangement was terminated a year later, but not before RKO had sent over editor Otto Ludwig to help in the production. In 1934, producer Julius Hagen was signed to make one film a month for RKO at Ealing Studios.

Later, films were acquired from minor British producers for UK release, and in the summer of 1937, the studio signed a contract with Herbert Wilcox to produce films for RKO release both in Britain and, more importantly to Wilcox, in the United States. The first was *Victoria the Great*, with Anna Neagle in the title role and a short Technicolor sequence at the film's close, released in September 1937. It was followed by yet another version of *The Rat*, released in November 1937, and with Anton Walbrook in the role made famous by Ivor Novello. A second Queen Victoria bio-production, *Sixty*

Glorious Years, released in September 1938 and shot entirely in Technicolor, led to Wilcox and Neagle's coming to the United States and embarking on a Hollywood career, beginning with *Nurse Edith Cavell*, released in October 1939.

After discovering that it could pass off Australian and Canadian productions as British, so far as the quota was concerned, Columbia made little effort to acquire independent British films for release. The studio produced only one film, over which it had complete control, in England, and that was *The Lady Is Willing*, shot in the summer of 1933 and released in January 1934. Studio head Harry Cohn came over to Elstree and the British & Dominions Studio, and he was joined by Columbia cinematographer Joe Walker, Columbia soundman Edward Bernds, Columbia's laboratory head in Hollywood, George Seid, and director Gilbert Miller, a prominent Broadway producer making his first and only film. The cast was an excellent one, led by Leslie Howard, supported by Cedric Hardwicke, Binnie Barnes, and Nigel Bruce. There were problems. Cohn was not happy with British working methods. The British Board of Film Censors objected to some aspects of the story, which involved a group of investors hiring a detective to kidnap the wife of the man who has defrauded them. According to Joe Walker, Gilbert Miller "gave the definite impression he couldn't be bothered with a mere motion picture,"[14] and was eventually replaced by Lewis Milestone.

Despite problems, *The Lady Is Willing* was relatively successful in the US, with Mordaunt Hall writing in the *New York Times* (August 11, 1934) that "it is a farce of the Parisian variety [based on a play by Louis Verneuil] which possesses something of the effervescent quality René Clair gives to his pictures. Although the action is stilted here and there, obviously occasionally because of censorial deletions, the film has the compensating virtues of excellent acting, scintillating lines and original, but decidedly mad, escapades."

At least through the mid-1930s, Universal had virtually no interest either in producing or purchasing for release British films. Indeed, prior to 1936, it appears that the only Universal film emanating in England was the serial *Lloyd of the C.I.D.*, consisting of twelve two-reel episodes released in 1932. Muriel Angelus has some name recognition as the leading lady, but the leading man, Wallace Geoffrey, has none. He appeared in only a handful of films and was probably more active on the stage, co-writing the play *The Perfect Woman*, which had a fairly successful run in 1948–49. Incredibly, to direct, Universal sent over Henry McRae, who had been working for the studio since 1912, had some connection with Universal's American serials, and whose career as a director came to an end a year later. *Lloyd of the C.I.D.* was released in the United States as *Detective Lloyd* and was also recut as a feature for British release under the title *The Green Spot*.

In 1936, Universal began its own production at Sound City Studios (Shepperton), and announced, hopefully but with little chance of reality, that its films would be "of such a box-office quality that they will be released throughout the world."[15]

The only American entity that demonstrated any concern for quality was United Artists, which, as a distribution outlet, had no studio in America and had always counted on the productions of others for its releases. In the United Kingdom, it relied heavily on the "quality" producers there, most notably Herbert Wilcox and Alexander Korda. In fact, as Rachael Low points out, "There were few United Artists imports from America, and the company was not in need of a quota."[16] Indeed, two-thirds of the films released in Britain by United Artists were British-made.

The one American company with a formidable production schedule and its own studio in Britain was Warner Bros., which operated there under the name of Warner Bros.-First National Productions, Ltd., In 1931, it took over the lease of the Teddington Studios overlooking the River Thames just outside of London. The property had been used as a film studio as early as 1912 when it was owned by Ec-Ko Films. In 1931, it was acquired by E. G. Norman and actor/director Henry Edwards, but they made only one film there, *Stranglehold*, which Edwards directed, before passing it on to Warner Bros. The first Warner Bros. production at the studio was *Murder on the Second Floor*, which included exterior scenes on Teddington High Street, based on a 1929 play by Frank Vosper, and released in January 1932. *Film Weekly* was particularly critical, writing that "the work of some of the players would scarcely pass muster in an amateur theatrical show."[17] *Murder on the Second Floor* was photographed by American Charles Van Enger and directed by American William McGann. At that time, the studio boasted of having the first camera dolly in the United Kingdom.[18]

The Teddington studios contained three stages, allowing for the production of two films simultaneously. There was also a boat moored at the studios, and which was to take part in the evacuation from Dunkirk in 1940. Key technical personnel at the studio were studio manager Harry Larraine, chief cameraman Willard Vananger, sound recording head George Groves, and publicity director George Ayre.

McGann was one of three American directors at Teddington on a long-term basis, with the other two being Ralph Ince and Roy William Neill.[19]

McGann had started his career as a cinematographer before promotion to "B" picture direction at Warner Bros. in 1930. McGann was very busy at the studio in 1932, but returned to the United States the following year. He remained at Warner Bros., becoming a special effects director in 1944 and head of the department in 1950; he retired in 1953.

Ralph Ince had worked in the American film industry as an actor before becoming a director at Vitagraph in 1912, and was incredibly busy, although he never achieved the fame or the reputation of his brother, producer Thomas H. Ince. He was an old-fashioned actor and an old-fashioned director, and, from a modern perspective, might seem an ideal contender for a later career in British films. Two years after a 1932 marriage to a third wife, Ince signed a contract to work for Warner Bros. in England, in all probability because jobs were scarce for fifty-year-old men in Hollywood. In all, he directed eighteen films for Irving Asher,[20] and was loaned out to British Lion in 1936 to direct one, *It's You I Want*, starring Sir Seymour Hicks and Marie Lohr. It was convenient having a director such as Ince under contract in that his past acting experience meant that he could always play appropriate roles in his films when necessary. Ince's career was abruptly ended in April 1937 when a car in which he and his wife were traveling was involved in an accident which proved fatal for the actor; he died a wealthy man, with an estate valued at $65,000.

Either by design or happenstance, Roy William Neill created an aura of mystery about himself, commensurate with some of the films in the mystery and horror genres which he directed. He may have been born in Ireland or on a boat off the coast of Ireland, near Dublin or near Cork. In all probability, he was born in San Francisco in 1887. He adopted an accent described by some as that of "an educated Irishman, somewhat British sounding, but with just a hint of the Irish lilt or brogue."[21] After a stage career (dating back to at least 1911) and a film career (which began in 1915), Neill signed a contract with First National Productions in 1936, and embarked on a new career as a British director, making fourteen films up until the outbreak of the war. The most prominent is *Dr. Syn*, released in August 1937, starring Margaret Lockwood and George Arliss, and the only film that Neill shot in England not made at Teddington—it was a Gaumont-British production.[22]

With America's entry into the war, Neill returned to the United States, and in 1942 directed *Sherlock Holmes and the Secret Weapon*, one in the series of Universal-produced Sherlock Holmes films starring Basil Rathbone and Nigel Bruce, with which Neill was to be closely associated for the next four years. In all, Neill directed, and later also produced, eleven Sherlock

Holmes films through 1946. With the war's end, Universal decided to send Neill back to England, where he was to make an untitled Technicolor feature; there was also talk of a Technicolor remake of *The Sign of the Four*, starring Rathbone and Bruce. However, Roy William Neill died—like his birth, with something of a mystery involved—before production began—he may have died on board the *Queen Elizabeth* or he may have died on December 14 in London.

One British director who refused to work at Warner Bros.- British was Walter Forde, because, as he told me, the studio paid so little.[23]

The American directors at Twickenham were not apparently held in high esteem by Jack L. Warner back at the Warner Bros. headquarters in Burbank. He described them as "old-fashioned has-beens who have been making . . . drek."[24]

Three men were involved in the actual running of the studio and the Warner Bros. operation in Britain: Max Milder, Ananda Max (Doc) Salomon, and Irving Asher. All three had a long association with the company.

Born in Zanesville, Ohio, and formerly US eastern division domestic manager for the studio, Max Milder was appointed managing director of Warner Bros. Pictures (London) Ltd., in 1931. He also held the title of director of First National Film Distributors, Ltd., Warner Bros.-First National Productions, Ltd., and Warner Bros.-First National Pictures, N.V. (Holland). Milder's primary function was running the company's distribution setup in Europe, as well as theatres in which it had a proprietary interest. Most notably, this was the theatre chain of Associated British Pictures Corporation, Ltd., in which Warner Bros. had a 37 1/2 percent interest by 1946, effectively controlling the company.[25] In 1938, Milder on behalf of Warner Bros. acquired Daly's Theatre in London's Leicester Square, demolished the property, and built the Warner Theatre as a "shop window" for its non-British productions. It joined the Empire Leicester Square, owned by MGM, as one of two American theatres in the heart of London's entertainment district. Also in 1946, Milder took over Henderson Film Laboratories, Ltd., to handle the printing of Warner Bros. releases in Britain.[26]

Doc Salomon's association with the Warner brothers was a long one, and they were obviously very fond of him. Jack L. Warner wrote,

> Doc Salomon was and always will be a part of the history of Warner Bros. He was with us when we first operated a film exchange in San Francisco. He was with us when we built the old Sunset [Boulevard] studios. He was

> with us when we acquired the First National lot here at Burbank. He was with us when we made *The Jazz Singer* and introduced sound.
>
> In his early days, Doc was a stunt man and doubled for many stars. At the Sunset studios he was our chief property man and when we moved to Burbank he became chief of our plant police and protection force. . . .
>
> When we decided to produce in England, we sent Doc to Teddington as plant superintendent. That was in 1930. In 1938 he became studio manager at Teddington.[27]

The best known of the three Warner Bros. executives in England as head of production and the one most associated with the studio—he held the title of managing director—is Irving Asher, whose involvement with Warner Bros. dates back to 1919. At Teddington, he was paid 300 pounds a week, rising to 350 pounds (or $1,750) in January 1938. One of the first stars he had hoped to welcome to Teddington was George Arliss, who was under contract to Warner Bros., but despite *Film Weekly*'s (March 25, 1932) claim that he would "definitely make a picture in England this summer," the actor did not. Also announced at that time as transferring from Burbank to Teddington were two of the studio's prominent directors, John G. Adolfi and Alfred Green (who had worked with Arliss), but they never made the journey.

Asher did make use of some American talent at Teddington. A lesser Warner Bros. player, Sally Blane, came over to star in two films at the studio, *Mayfair Girl* and *Crime on the Hill*, both released in 1933. Character comedian Roscoe Ates, famous for his stutter, was starred in *Fair Exchange*, released in July 1936. Warner Bros. contract player Glenda Farrell was brought over to play opposite Claude Hulbert in *You Live and Learn*, released in August 1937, but it is unclear why either she or the studio bothered. Betty Compton was a British-born Broadway star of the 1920s, whose primary claim to fame is her 1933 marriage to New York Mayor Jimmy Walker. A year later, she was at Teddington, making her only feature film appearance, in *Too Many Millions*. Screenwriter Paul Gangelin was also busy at Teddington between 1934 and 1939, with his most prominent credit, as co-writer, being *They Drive by Night* (1939).

In 1937, the *New York Times* reported that "Mr. Asher has a plan for making British stars, his idea being to team his British contract players with stars brought over from Hollywood, so that American cinema audiences will get to know them."[28] The newspaper went on to announce the possibility of Kay Francis and Paul Muni coming to Teddington. It didn't happen.

Irving Asher and Laura La Plante in the summer of 1936.

There was an idea also that Asher would seek out British talent for recommendation to Burbank. Generally, this also did not happen, and when a British actor or actress is mentioned as having been of interest to Asher, it is obvious to a casual observer that the suggestion of American interest is ludicrous. He did apparently recommend to Burbank Ian Hunter, who played opposite Laura La Plante in *The Church Mouse*, and the actor was signed by Warner Bros. in June 1934 at $500 per week per picture, most notably for *The Adventures of Robin Hood* (1938), returning to Britain during the war. At Jack L. Warner's insistence, Robert Donat was signed to a contract in December 1934, but successfully managed to renege on the deal. The only

The similarity in appearance between Clara Bow and British silent and early sound star Chili/ Dorothy Bouchier (seen here) is quite remarkable.

important discovery of Asher's is Errol Flynn, who was starred in *Murder at Monte Carlo*. By the film's release, in January 1935, the actor was already en route to Burbank. As Asher presciently noted, "we have a big piece of property on our hands in Errol Flynn."[29]

Among the actors tested by Asher and whose tests were sent to Burbank were Oscar Homolka (date unknown), Patric Knowles (date unknown), Werner Krauss (date unknown), Fritz Kortner (November 7, 1936), Isabel Jeans (July 17, 1937), and Byron Owen (July 17, 1937). Jeans was signed to a contract. Kortner was dismissed by Warner as "too Teutonic and too heavy."[30] Asher warned Warner that Krauss had a reputation as a Nazi sympathizer, and when he appeared on the London stage in *Before Sunset* (September-October 1933), he was hissed by the audience. Krauss was not signed.

British leading lady Chili/Dorothy Bouchier, who was sometimes referred to as the British Clara Bow, was signed to a contract with Teddington on October 18, 1935. The contract was suspended on November 17, 1937, in order to permit her to come to Burbank for screen tests, etc., but nothing came of the visit.

Interest from America in the running of the studio was not substantial, although there were complaints that Teddington was not turning out films suitable for American consumption.[31] It does seem surprising that Asher signed and nurtured two comedic talents who were very English and would have stood no chance in America, either on stage or screen. Max Miller, "the cheeky chappie," was noted for his vulgarity and suggestive jokes. Claude Hulbert, the brother of the better-known Jack, was a typical silly-ass Englishman, of which there were already quite a few in Hollywood. Asher tried long and hard to promote Claude Hulbert to Jack L. Warner.

In 1935, Burbank studio production chief Hal Wallis had suggested to Jack L. Warner that the studio's adaptation of the Ian Hay and A. E. W. Mason play, *A Present from Margate*, should be filmed at Teddington, with location scenes at the south of England seaside resort of Margate. Ultimately, it was easier to change the locale and the title to *The Widow from Monte Carlo*. In May of that year, Warner was in London, staying at the Dorchester Hotel, and checking out operations at Teddington, which were presumably satisfactory. Two years later, in January 1937, Warner Bros. sent over former actor William "Buster" Collier, Jr., to see what was going on at Teddington, and it was reported that Collier complained that the films being shot there were being padded when they should have been cut.[32] For his advice, Collier was paid $625 a week.

On June 19, 1934, Asher married Laura La Plante in Paris. La Plante had been a leading female star at Universal in the 1920s and at the coming of sound, but her fame had declined in the early 1930s, as had her marriage to the much older director William Seiter. She came to England simply because she had always wanted to visit, and there she renewed her friendship with Asher, whom she had dated prior to her marriage. After three trips back and forth between England and America, she decided to stay in England for a while. La Plante's first film at Teddington, prior to her marriage, was *Her Imaginary Lover*, with Percy Marmont as her leading man, released in

October 1933. The actress made four other films at Teddington, all selected by Asher: *The Girl in Possesion* (1934), *The Church Mouse* (1934), *Widow's Might* (1935), and *Man of the Moment* (1935). "He chose what he thought was suitable for me," La Plante recalled.[33]

Both La Plante and Asher left England in October 1939. "We had two children and I had a baby who was about three months old," said the actress, "and we had planned a trip back to the States to show off the new baby. We simply moved the sailing up because of the possibility of war. The American Embassy had already suggested that any American residents who intended returning to the States should do so now."[34]

The previous year, on March 1, 1938, Asher had resigned from Warner Bros. Since 1935, he had chaffed at Jack L. Warner's appointing New York-based Sam E. Morris, vice president in charge of foreign sales, as his immediate supervisor. The final insult, as far as Asher was concerned, came when Morris forbade him to spend more than $1,000 on any original source material, novel, story, or play. "You would not want me to continue to operate in this studio as an office boy at my salary, and I am afraid I couldn't do it if you would," fumed Asher to Warner.[35] Warner had no hesitation in accepting Asher's resignation, telling Morris, "He is too big a man to make pictures at Teddington of the type we need and which we can stay in business with."[36] Warner Bros. had been paying Asher's parents $150 a week and employing his brother on the Burbank lot at $100 a week. The brother was fired and payments to the parents were ordered to cease immediately. Asher filed suit in New York against Warner Bros., and the matter was settled out of court in August 1939. In the meantime, Jerome Jackson replaced Asher as supervising producer.

After leaving Warner Bros., Asher became an associate producer with London Films and later an executive producer with Columbia's British arm. For Columbia, he produced *The Spy in Black* and *Q Planes/Clouds over Europe* (1939), both of which were also an Alexander Korda presentation, as well as *Ten Days in Paris* (1939). In Hollywood, Asher worked as a producer at MGM, but by 1944, as Major Asher, he was serving on Admiral Mountbatten's staff in Asia. There is no accurate record of the number of films that Asher produced at Teddington, but by my count they are in excess of ninety.

With Asher's departure, Doc Salomon took over as head of production at the studio. He was keen to cut costs wherever possible, following Warner's dictate that "we can only take so much in on the pictures being made at Teddington, and we should not spend any more than necessary."[37]

On *Murder Will Out*, released in July 1939, the director Roy William Neill was paid 1,000 pounds in total to both produce and direct the film, with leading man John Loder receiving 1,200 pounds.

Salomon tried hard to promote a young Scottish-born director, David MacDonald, to Warner as having Hollywood potential. In 1939, a print of MacDonald's latest film, *This Man Is News*, was shipped to Burbank, with Salomon noting that MacDonald is "the fastest director I have seen yet,"[38] with the film costing a mere 16,600 pounds to produce. Ultimately, MacDonald stayed in Britain.

With the outbreak of war, Teddington closed briefly, but was reopened with Warner Bros. trying to continue British production despite problems with limited personnel because of military service. "Even unknown names are difficult to obtain," wrote Max Milder to Warner, complaining that actress Renee Houston was demanding 10,000 pounds per picture.[39] For his part, Warner decreed there should be no more costume pictures made at Teddington. He urged Milder to persuade Noel Coward, without success, to sign over the rights to *Blithe Spirit*. He advised against suggesting that Laurence Olivier and Vivien Leigh should be signed for a Hollywood production: "They are good British citizens and are exactly where they belong—helping to save their country."[40]

Warner had far from kinds words about Anton Walbrook, whom Teddington had been trying to sign for an unidentified film with the working title of *Jewel Robbery*, and who was demanding 1,000 pounds a week together with various perks:

> I am happy that you did not sign Anton Walbrook . . . because anyone as temperamental as this guy is, especially at a time when millions of people are giving their children and their own lives and being forced to give up their countries and homes, should be ashamed of himself, demanding the things he is. I don't know if Walbrook is an English citizen or not. If he isn't he should be more ashamed than ever and should be the last one to take advantage of people in whose country he has taken refuge.[41]

Doc Salomon at the studio and Max Milder at Warner House on Wardour Street in London's Soho district continued to handle Warner Bros. interests in Britain. They did not allow the war to prevent them from signing up in April 1942 at least one actress under contract, Anne Crawford. As part of the war effort, directors at Teddington were now receiving between 3,500 and 5,000 pounds per film. Crawford was starred opposite Ben Lyon

in *The Dark Tower*, shooting at Teddington in October 1942 for 1943 release, and based on a play by Alexander Woolcott and George S. Kaufman. In November 1942, Milder was able to report to Warner that the company's James Cagney/George M. Cohan musical *Yankee Doodle Dandy* had grossed 14,429 pounds in its first four weeks at the Warner Theatre, "the biggest revenue we ever had on any picture."[42] On a more personal level, Milder was also able to deliver fifty Havana cigars as a gift from his boss to Lord Louis Mountbatten.

As the war progressed, Warner Bros. tried with difficulty to produce three films a year at Teddington. There was discussion as to whether to cut down production to only one feature film and to rent out the studio to others. As it happened, within two years, the discussion was irrelevant. Warner asked Salomon to record the sound of V1 flying rockets, or "robot bombs" as they were called by the Americans, on Wednesday, July 5, 1944. Salomon already had made recordings of many sounds from the London Blitz for use by Warner Bros. as background to its films.

At 8:40 P.M. that evening, a V1 flying bomb hit the power house at the studios, causing a fire that basically destroyed the entire facility and also killed Salomon and two other workers.[43] Milder heard the news while having dinner in central London and rushed to the scene. Because highly flammable nitrate films were not permitted to be kept in central London, all the Warner Bros. prints were stored at Teddington, but, incredibly, they survived. The negative of the last film to be shot at the studio, *Flight From Folly*,

Teddington Studios, photographed with snow on the ground in December 1937.

Teddington Studio the day after being hit by a V1 rocket.

a musical starring Pat Kirkwood and Hugh Sinclair, was at a film laboratory, and also survived. Because of wartime censorship, it was difficult for Milder to get word to Burbank about what had happened, but with the help of the head censor he was able to advise Warner of the tragedy without actually mentioning the location of the studio, the time, or the cause of the fire.

Ironically, it was at Teddington that a major film dealing with a bombing raid on Berlin had been made late in 1941. *Flying Fortress*, directed by Walter Forde, concerns itself with an American pilot, played by Richard Greene, who joins the RAF.

Jack L. Warner was devastated at Doc Salomon's death, which he described as in the line of duty. He ordered the suspension of all work at the Burbank studios on July 7 for a two-minute silence, arranged a memorial service that same day for close friends and colleagues, and announced that all studio flags would be flown at half-mast for thirty days.

Reconstruction at Teddington began in 1946, and the studio was officially opened two years later by Danny Kaye. It became a television studio in 1959, when it was acquired by ABC Television (no relation to the American entity) and used for filming the popular series, *The Avengers*. In 1968, ABC became Thames Television and the studio continued to prosper.

Warner Bros. returned to studio ownership in Britain in 2010, when it purchased the Leavesden Studios, twenty miles northwest of London, near Watford, a former aerodrome first used as a studio facility in 1995 for the making of the James Bond feature, *GoldenEye*. The new Warner Bros. studio was officially opened by Prince William and Prince Harry on April 26, 2013, and the first Warner Bros. film to be shot there after the opening was the Tom Cruise science fiction vehicle, *Edge of Tomorrow* (2014). All the Harry Potter films were shot at Leavesden, and in 2012, it became the site of the Warner Bros. Studio Tour—London, devoted entirely to "The Making of Harry Potter."

Fox British Pictures was formed in July 1932, and later that same year, it began production at the Wembley Studios in North London. Fox, now 20th Century-Fox purchased the studios outright in 1936, but ceased filming there two years later. Earlier and during the same period, producer George King was also making films for Fox and later 20th Century-Fox elsewhere. In 1936, Robert T. Kane, who, with the exception of *George White's Scandals* (1934), had been involved in the production of "B" pictures for the studio in Hollywood, announced that he was to make British films for 20th Century-Fox at the Denham Studios, beginning with *Wings of the Morning*.

One of the lesser-known but important American producers at work in England in the 1930s was Richard Wainwright, whose films, Rachael Low writes, "were distinguished by good casts and greater sophistication than usual and, although not widely known, were greatly admired by a select few."[44] Born in Chicago in 1895, Wainwright had been trained as a chartered accountant before joining the pioneering Selig Polyscope Company during World War I. He worked as a distributor and producer in Hollywood before forming Hagenbeck Films in Berlin, followed by Cherry Kearton Films. The latter specialized in animal subjects, and its 1929 production of *Tembi*, set in Africa, had the distinction of being viewed by Queen Mary in February

1930. It was reported that she was so absorbed that she stayed for the next picture, a Douglas Fairbanks, Jr., vehicle, but walked out halfway through. "It is a pity I cannot come more often," she told the theatre manager.[45] It was in 1930 that Cherry Kearton announced the crowning achievement of his life to be the making of a filmed record of the life of the penguin.[46]

Wainwright began producing fictional features in England with *Forbidden Territory* in 1935, directed by American Phil Rosen. It was followed by an English-language version of *Emil and the Detectives* and *Sleeping Car*, directed by Anatole Litvak and starring Ivor Novello. In 1936, Wainwright announced the formation of Universal-Wainwright Studios, producing films for British release by Universal, including *The Crimson Circle* and *Wolf's Clothing*, both released in March of that year.

Wolf's Clothing was directed by Andrew Marton—his first British film, which he described as "a better grade slapstick spy story."[47] Marton, who is generally known as a second-unit director—most notably on *Ben-Hur* (1959)—was born in Hungary and had come to Hollywood in 1923, working as an assistant director and editor. He left for Germany, but then came to Britain to escape the Nazis, and began a career with Wainwright, following *Wolf's Clothing* with *The Secret of Stamboul* (1936). The latter was based on Dennis Wheatley's novel, *The Eunoch of Stamboul*, with the title change demanded by the censor, shot on location in Turkey, and starring James Mason. Marton's last British film of the 1930s, *I Met a Murderer*, released in February 1939, was an independent production starring Mason and his wife, Pamela Kellino, photographed by Kellino's father, Roy, and written by the three of them. Marton claimed to have had "an indefinite contract"[48] with Wainwright, but with the outbreak of the war he decided to move on to Hollywood.

Marton's best film for Wainwright was undoubtedly *School for Husbands*, released in August 1937, and starring Rex Harrison and Diana Churchill. A farce, it was released in the US by a very minor distributor, J. H. Hoffberg Company, and opened at New York's Little Carnegie Playhouse on February 6, 1939. According to Frank S. Nugent in the *New York Times* (February 7, 1939), it "has a shin-bruised look, a slightly downtrodden look, the look, in fact, of a well-worn Yorkshire pudding, which, in lightness, it rather resembles."

The director was involved in one other film with British connections, and that is the 1950 release, *King Solomon's Mines*, on which he replaced Compton Bennett, and which marked the Hollywood screen debut of Stewart Granger (although the film was actually shot in Africa). Wainwright

Joe Rock.

continued on in Britain, serving as managing director of London & District Cinemas, Ltd., which operated eight theatres. He was still active in the 1960s, heading Tele-Ventures London, Ltd.

Another forgotten American producer who was exceedingly active in Britain in the 1930s is Joe Rock (1891–1984), whose career in the American film industry dates back to 1916, making two-reel comedies at Vitagraph. Rock's British films of the 1930s are generally mediocre, often featuring actor-comedian Leslie Fuller. But Rock was responsible for the financing of one major production of the period, and that is Michael Powell's *The Edge of the World*, the story of a group of islanders off the far North coast of

Scotland. The film was released in the summer of 1937, around the same time that Rock's studio went bankrupt.

Rock had come to Britain in 1933 from Java, after producing the short subject, *Krakatoa*, which won the Academy Award for Best Short Subject—Novelty.[49] He remained in Britain during the war, returning to the United States as an executive at Universal in February 1946. At that time, it was announced that he owned the rights to ten BBC *Scrapbook* programs, dealing with British history.

In June 1935, Douglas Fairbanks, Jr., set up Criterion Film Productions, which made three films the following year, for release by United Artists. Fairbanks, Jr., starred in all the productions, the first of which was a costume picture, *The Amateur Gentleman*, co-starring Elissa Landi, an Italian-born actress who had made her stage and screen debut in England in the mid-1920s, and had gained considerable fame in the United States with her starring role in Cecil B. DeMille's *The Sign of the Cross* (1932). Directing was Thornton Freeland, an American who had made *Whoopee!* in 1930, starring Eddie Cantor, and who was responsible for another eight British films between 1934 and 1939, as well as a handful in the 1940s. Freeland's only complaint was that he found "British humor slower and heavier than ours."[50]

Dolores Del Rio came over to co-star with Fairbanks, Jr., in his second production, *Accused*, with a story and script by Zoe Akins, who probably did not travel to England for her contribution. The production was again directed by Thornton Freeland, who had earlier directed Del Rio in Hollywood in *Flying Down to Rio* (which the actress regarded as the first film in the revival of her career). The final Fairbanks, Jr., production, *Jump for Glory*, began production in November 1936, with American character actor Alan Hale in the cast and Valerie Hobson, who had made a handful of Hollywood films between 1934 and 1936, as the leading lady. It was, according to Frank Nugent in the *New York Times* (June 15, 1937), "a glib little crime-without-punishment film." Directing was the gruff and reliable Raoul Walsh, a major Hollywood talent and quite a boost for British cinema. According to actor/producer Brian Forbes, Walsh was a passionate Anglophile.[51] If he was, the director was not a great admirer of British speech, and in 1930, it was reported that Walsh could not understand much of the English he heard in London theatres and that in his considered opinion, the screen adaptation of *Journey's End* would be incomprehensible to American ears.[52] Walsh also directed a second British film in 1936, *O.H.M.S.*, released in the US as *You're in the Army Now*, and starring American Wallace Ford. *O.H.M.S.* was promoted as the first British film made with the cooperation of the army, and the *Los Angeles Times* noted the presence of "the Argyle and Sutherland Highlanders, whose kilted uniforms all cause a sigh in many a feminine breast."[53] The critic in the *New York Times* was disinterested in the military presence and complained only of the use of antiquated US slang.

Walsh had planned to make a third British film, based on Rudyard Kipling's "Soldiers Three," and starring Victor McLaglen, but nothing came of the idea. Walsh brought with him from Hollwood, as his assistant director, David MacDonald, who was Scottish-born but who had been working in America with Cecil B. DeMille and others after giving up life on a Malaysian rubber plantation.

Despite the ultimate failure of Criterion, Fairbanks, Jr., spoke of its efforts fondly at a 1936 National Board of Review luncheon:

> It was like Hollywood fifteen years ago, that pioneer spirit. It was interesting and very exciting. They didn't have any nationalistic feeling about it—saying "British pictures! Hooray!" Their main consideration was English-speaking pictures. It was an international feeling. Here we are, more or less related, the only countries in the world that can call each other cousins literally.[54]

Aside from his own productions, Fairbanks, Jr., starred in Alexander Korda's production of *Catherine the Great* (1934) and *Mimi* (1937), opposite Gertrude Lawrence. Irving Asher had helped Fairbanks finance Criterion, and, in return, the actor agreed to star opposite Laura La Plante in Asher's production of *Man of the Moment*, shot on location in Monte Carlo, which would, in all probability, have been considered too minor a film to attract the attention of Fairbanks, Jr.

As he recalled, "Professionally, *Man of the Moment* was not at all what I should have done at that period. But Irving hoped that with my name and Laura's, a good supporting cast and direction by an ex-Hollywood comedian whimsically named Monty Banks, Warners would overlook the picture's quota category and release it in the States and Canada. Although they never did, I had the best time imaginable making the movie."[55]

There was always something very English about the American Douglas Fairbanks, Jr. He himself has noted that he could speak good "English-English" and that he was frequently cast by Hollywood producers in British roles.[56] He is always vaguely and disturbingly "snobbish," with his fondness for the British aristocracy and his wartime service under Lord Louis Mountbatten, all of which led to a honorary knighthood in 1949. When

he embarked on a television career in the 1950s, it was not surprisingly at Elstree Studios with *Douglas Fairbanks Jr. Presents* (1952–55), a syndicated anthology series which was quite popular in the United States. Fairbanks hired many American actors in England, hiding out from the blacklist, in part, it was claimed, because American television viewers could not understand British accents. Fairbanks also starred in a number of British feature films of the 1950s, beginning with *State Secret* and *Mr. Drake's Duck* (both released in 1950).

The one British actor who reminds one most of Fairbanks, Jr., is Barry K. Barnes, who has much the same suave and debonair manner. Barnes is the perfect passive leading man—as in *The Ware Case* (1938), as the half-hearted, frustrated lover—and he is good in costume drama, as witness *The Return of the Scarlet Pimpernel* (1937), in which he stars opposite Merle Oberon as Sir Percy Blakeney.[57] What a pity that he never had the opportunity of a Hollywood career.

Dolores Del Rio and husband, MGM art director Cedric Gibbons, arrive at London's Waterloo Station on March 4, 1936.

Douglas Fairbanks, Sr., and his third wife, Lady Sylvia Ashley, in London in the 1930s.

Douglas Fairbanks, Sr., made his farewell to the screen in Alexander Korda's London Films production of *The Private Life of Don Juan*, released in the summer of 1934. Fairbanks was separated from Mary Pickford, and he welcomed the opportunity to be in London and to be close to Lady Sylvia Ashley, who was to become the second Mrs. Douglas Fairbanks, Sr., following the 1935 divorce from Pickford. The film provides its star with the opportunity to leave the screen gracefully, although there is perhaps a little too much of a similarity between the aging lover who is the legendary Don Juan and the aging screen legend who is Douglas Fairbanks, Sr. It also gives Korda's wife-to-be, Merle Oberon, the opportunity to sparkle as dancer Antonita.

While arguments might appropriately be put forward in the names of Alexander Korda or Herbert Wilcox, there is one producer who really, decade after decade, represents British cinema at its best, and that man is Michael Balcon. As head of production at Gaumont-British from 1932–36,

Michael Balcon (left) meets with Louis B. Mayer (center) and MGM executive William Goetz, as he arrives at the Santa Fe Station, Los Angeles, on April 12, 1935.

he was consistently making quality "A" pictures for both the British and American markets. He had under contract some of the brightest stars of British cinema—George Arliss, Madeleine Carroll, Jessie Matthews, and Conrad Veidt—and some of its best directors, including three who made names for themselves in Hollywood—Alfred Hitchcock, Robert Stevenson, and Victor Saville. Balcon understood the need in British cinema for major Hollywood stars, and he tried, unsuccessfully as it happens, to persuade, among others, James Cagney, Grace Moore, Spencer Tracy, and Robert Young to work for him.

In December 1936, Balcon left Gaumont-British to become director of production for the British branch of Metro-Goldwyn-Mayer. MGM, which had previously acquired films from various British distributors to meet its quota requirements under the supervision of its managing director, Sam Eckman,[58] had decided to drastically change its image in Britain. It would make films there comparable in quality, star power, and commercial potential to its Hollywood productions, and such films were intended as much for the American market as the British. The company rented space at Denham Studio and Balcon spent the first half of 1937 at the MGM studios in Culver City, California, planning a production schedule. There were various potential ideas, including the "aerial adventure" *Shadow of the Wing*, to star Clark Gable, along with an adaptation of James Hilton's *Rage in Heaven* and an adaptation of *Silas Marner*, to star Lionel Barrymore.

Unfortunately, Balcon and MGM's studio head, Louis B. Mayer, were not compatible. It became clear that supervision of the British films would come from Hollywood rather than Balcon in England. The autonomy that Balcon had been promised was not forthcoming, and he resigned after completion of the first film, *A Yank at Oxford*, to be replaced by British director Victor Saville, working under the supervision of American executive producer William Goetz. No scenes were permitted to be filmed at Oxford, and some scenes were later reshot in Culver City.

A Yank at Oxford provided a perfect vehicle for MGM contract star Robert Taylor in the title role, and, thanks to Balcon, the love interest was provided by Vivien Leigh, who had yet to star in *Gone with the Wind*. The director, Jack Conway, the cinematographer, Harold Rosson, and the editor, Margaret Booth, all came over from Culver City. The film offers a whimsical, if athletic, concept of student life at Oxford, with Leigh playing a married woman who is available to offer solace to the students. Despite her future fame, Leigh does not receive top female billing, with that going to Maureen O'Sullivan.[59] Leigh and Taylor were co-starred by MGM in *Waterloo Bridge*, and in 1942, the studio produced a film with the same basic idea, *A Yank at Eton*, with Mickey Rooney in the title role, supported by a group of Britishers, headed by Edmund Gwenn as the headmaster (continuing on in an academic role he had played in *A Yank at Oxford*), and including Freddie Bartholomew, Peter Lawford, Alan Mowbray, Alan Napier, and others.

The second MGM film, *The Citadel*, an adaptation of the A. J. Cronin novel, went into production in June 1938. The director, King Vidor, was again American, working under MGM contract producer Sidney Franklin, as was cinematographer Harry Stradling, with a British leading man, Robert Donat,

A Yank at Oxford (1938), with Griffith Jones, Maureen O'Sullivan, and Robert Taylor.

and an American leading lady, Rosalind Russell. Russell replaced the original choice of Elizabeth Allan (a British actress under contract to MGM). The film cost a reported \$1 million and grossed \$2.5 million. It was far more successful than *A Yank at Oxford*, receiving three Academy Award nominations and being named Best Picture by the National Board of Review.

The third production was a sentimental tale of an aging schoolmaster, whose career is basically a failure, and whose only comfort is a wife, who dies, and the boys whom he teaches. Robert Donat stars in this adaptation of a James Hilton novella, with Greer Garson making her screen debut as the wife. From Culver City, Sidney Franklin supervised the production and the editing, with the direction handled by Sam Wood. The film was primarily shot at Denham but some location scenes were filmed at Repton College. As H. Mark Glancy has commented, "When it was released in the summer of 1939, *Goodbye, Mr. Chips* seemed to be a sad farewell to all things English, and it became the most popular of the three MGM-British films."[60]

Elizabeth Allan (right) and Diana Wynyard, two British stars of the 1930s under contract to Metro-Goldwyn-Mayer.

Donat received the Academy Award for Best Actor for his work in *Goodbye, Mr. Chips* and was scheduled to star in a fourth MGM film, *Busman's Honeymoon*, based on a Dorothy L. Sayers mystery novel, but he was far from happy with the studio and, indeed, refused to journey to Culver City for two further films, *Standby for Action* and *Beau Brummell*. (Reportedly, MGM had offered Donat a seven-year contract at 60,000 pounds a year. The actor rejected the offer because it would have limited his ability to appear on stage, and a compromise four-year contract had been suggested by the studio.)[61] *Busman's Honeymoon* began filming in August

1939, only weeks prior to Britain's declaration of war with Germany. Its new leading man, Robert Montgomery, playing Lord Peter Wimsey, happened to be in England. The leading lady, Constance Cummings, as Harriet Vane, was already a resident. Richard Thorpe directed, and the film was completed in April 1940, by which time Montgomery had left England for America.

In the *New York Times* (November 3, 1940), Bosley Crowther described the film, released in the US as *Haunted Honeymoon*, as "a bit of amiable sleuthing." The critic in the *Los Angeles Times* (August 21, 1940) commented that "the picture was produced amidst the turmoil of war, which is probably one of the reasons it doesn't come off."

With the advent of World War II, both director Victor Saville and actress Greer Garson fled Britain for California, ostensibly and conveniently to fulfill their contracts. As noted, Robert Donat remained in Britain, and made two further films for MGM during the war: *Sabotage Agent/The Adventures of Tartu*, produced by Irving Asher and directed by American Harold S. Bucquet (1943), and *Perfect Strangers/Vacation from Marriage* (1945).

Robert Morley, having returned from playing in Hollywood in *Marie Antoinette*, visits Robert Donat and Rosalind Russell on the set of *The Citadel* (1938).

CHAPTER EIGHT

Diversity—Female Filmmakers, African American Performers, and Others

AT THE BEGINNING OF THE BRITISH CINEMA, AN OCCASIONAL PERSON of color might be seen on screen, more often as an entertainer rather than an actor. Such an individual cannot be defined as "African American" in that he or she was from the British West Indies, as, for example, in the case of Bermuda-born Ernest Trimmingham, who appears in a supporting role in the 1912 release of *Dick Turpin—The King of Highwaymen*, and is, in all probability, the first British film actor of color.

The most prominent of African Americans to appear in British films on a regular basis is Paul Robeson, who appeared as Othello at London's Savoy Theatre from May through July 1930, with a supporting cast that included Maurice Brown as Iago, Ralph Richardson as Roderigo, Peggy Ashcroft as Desdemona, and Sybil Thorndike as Emilia. When the play closed, Robeson continued at the theatre for a further week in a concert engagement, which also included his performance in the first scene from Eugene O'Neill's *Emperor Jones*. The following year he appeared at the Ambassadors Theatre in O'Neill's *The Hairy Ape*, and in 1933, he played the Piccadilly Theatre in O'Neill's *All God's Chillun Got Wings*.

There was little racial prejudice in Britain at this time, in large part, perhaps, because the non-white population was small. When Robeson and his wife were denied entry into the Savoy Grill in London, for example, mass outrage was expressed in both the press and in Parliament, and the suggestion was made that such discrimination was the result of American influence rather than a British trait. As early as August 23, 1939, Robeson appeared on British television in a short musical recital broadcast live by the BBC.

As a frequent visitor to Britain in the 1930s (and later), not surprisingly, Robeson was approached with film offers, the first from Alexander Korda, then preparing a screen adaptation of the 1930 Edgar Wallace novel, *Sanders of the River*. Some second-unit footage was shot in Africa, but the film was primarily made on the backlot at Shepperton Studios and at the Worton Hall Studios. It is surprising that the actor failed to realize how patronizing and racist his part would be, but he claimed enthusiasm for the role of Bosambo, the petty criminal who is appointed N'Gombi tribal chief by the British District Commissioner in Nigeria. "For the first time since I began acting, I feel that I've found my place in the world, that there's something out of my own culture which I can express and perhaps help to preserve," Robeson told the British Sunday newspaper, the *Observer* (July 29, 1934).

In reality, *Sanders of the River* provides nothing more than a positive view of British colonial rule in Africa, with all the characters, be they natives or British, nothing more than imperial stereotypes. As biographer Karol Kulik notes, producer Alexander Korda was "a confirmed Anglophile who saw the Empire builders as the embodiment of all the most noble traits in the

Sanders of the River (1935), with Paul Robeson and Nina Mae McKinney.

English character and spirit."[1] Released in July of 1935, *Sanders of the River*, directed by Zoltan Korda, co-stars Leslie Banks as Commissioner Sanders, a role that had been turned down by both Ralph Richardson and Raymond Massey, who were perhaps a little more savvy than Robeson in understanding the reality of the characterizations.

Robeson claimed to have been tricked into playing the role, which he later condemned as a "slanderous attack on African natives."[2] Such is obviously not the case, although it may well be that in the editing stage, and after Robeson had completed his role, changes and additions were made to the film. At worst, Robeson is a tool of British imperialism. His son, Paul Robeson, Jr., credits *Sanders of the River* with helping his father discover his African roots and also claims that he was radicalized after a meeting with one of the extras, Jomo Kenyatta, who was later to become the first president of Kenya. Less supportive was Marcus Garvey, who wrote in *Black Man* (June 7, 1935) that "the Producers have been using Paul Robeson, from *Emperor Jones* to *Stevedore*, to put over a vile and vicious propaganda against the Negro. . . . Anyone who has seen *Sanders of the River* can readily grasp the significance of the surrender of the Negro to all that is cultural, civilized, lofty and high, which mark him as being unworthy for a competent place at the present time in the civilization of the world . . . he has been made to look like a savage alongside of the white man. A picture like this, shown to the majority of people of ordinary intelligence, can only tend to inflame them against the black man. . . . The wonder is that Paul Robeson cannot see that he is being used to the dishonour and discredit of his race."

Sanders of the River was rife for parody, and in 1938, Will Hay played a bumbling Commissioner Tibbetts in *Old Bones of the River*. The role of Bosambo was taken by British Guiana-born Robert Adams, who appears in later Robeson British films and is his stunt double in *The Proud Valley*.

Despite Garvey's criticism and the negative comments of others, Robeson continued to work in British films. In *Song of Freedom* (1936), he plays a London-born dockworker, John Zinga, who becomes an opera star and travels to Africa to find his roots. The reality of the Africa that he finds is that its natives are poor, ignorant savages. Robeson spoke highly of the film in *Film Weekly* (May 23, 1936): "I believe *Song of Freedom* is the first picture to give a true picture of many aspects on the life of the coloured man in the west. Hitherto on the screen, he has been caricatured or presented only as a comedy character. This film shows him as a real man with problems to be solved, difficulties to be overcome." The critic of the *Times* (London) wrote, in the issue of September 21, 1936, that

> the whole story may be melodramatic and not well constructed but Mr. Robeson has an astonishing power of giving dignity and emotional significance to every event in which he appears, and that even when he only uses his voice in speech. When he sings, as he often does in the course of the film, he at once raises the whole level of the production above that of popular entertainment or that of a simplified message and moral.

Graham Greene was of the opinion that Robeson overcame the limits of the film, its story, and its inexpensive look: "A sense stays in the memory of an unsophisticated mind fumbling on the edge of simple and popular poetry."[3]

Robeson's love interest here and in his next film, *Big Fella* (1937), is provided by Elisabeth Welch, whose work, along with that of Adelaide Hall, is discussed in Chapter Eleven. *Big Fella*, with its unappealing title, and equally unappealing child actor in the shape of Eldon Grant, is set on the docks of Marseilles, with Robeson finding a lost English boy.

Robeson led an all-star cast in Gaumont-British's 1937 adaptation of H. Rider Haggard's *King Solomon's Mines*. Here, he is an African leader, Umbopa, "not just . . . a splendid savage but a man of real thoughts and ambitions,"[4] facing off to a group of white adventurers, Cedric Hardwicke, Roland Young, Anna Lee, and John Loder. In *Jericho/Dark Sands* (1937), Robeson plays an American soldier, Jericho Jackson, who is serving with his regiment in Europe during World War I, but flees to Africa after killing a bullying sergeant. The director was the American Thornton Freeland, and comedy is provided by white American actor Wallace Ford. North African location shooting in Egypt added to the film's appeal, as did British actor Henry Wilcoxon, who returned to Europe to make *Jericho*, after success as Cecil B. DeMille's leading man in *Cleopatra* and *The Crusades*.

It was Robeson's last British film, *The Proud Valley*, which he acknowledged in later years as the only one for which he retained respect. Released in January 1940, Robeson plays a Negro stoker who helps unemployed Welsh miners reopen a mine and is killed in the process. As Jeffrey Richards has commented, "*The Proud Valley* sought to do justice both to the aspirations of the working class and of the black man in Britain. . . . It is imbued with a respect for its subjects that is as moving as it was rare in British cinema of the 1930s." In many respects, *The Proud Valley* is socialistic in approach to its subject and very much politically correct in its view of white and black races working equally together, as one man with no racial divide. Indeed, at one point the Welsh choirmaster, played by Edward

Chapman, comments, "Damn and blast it, man, aren't we all black down that pit?"

The film owes much to left-wing stage producer Herbert Marshall, who wrote the story for Robeson, novelist Louis Golding, who worked on the script, and, above all, the young director Pen Tennyson, an Oxford-educated filmmaker with a strong working--class understanding, and who was killed in a plane crash early in World War II. The film suffered in part because a more popular and more entertainment-oriented mining story had just been released, *The Stars Look Down*, and perhaps because it was viewed as overly simplistic and somewhat clumsy in construction. Graham Greene was not particularly enthusiastic, writing in the *Spectator* (March 15, 1940) that

> colour prejudice is dragged in for the sake of Mr. Paul Robeson who plays the part of a big black Pollyana, keeping everybody cheerful and dying nobly at the end (Mr. Robeson's fat sentimental optimism seemed to me a little revolting) . . . The direction of the quiet documentary scenes is good, but Mr. Pen Tennyson, who may have been handicapped by an undistinguished cast and a wobbly script, seems ill at ease with drama.

In the film, Robeson, sings two songs, both accompanied by a Welsh choir: "Lord God of Abraham," from Mendelssohn's *Elijah*, and the Negro spiritual "Deep River." He is also heard over the final scene, singing what is considered the Welsh national anthem, "Land of My Fathers." Robeson retained his affinity for the Welsh people, and in October 1957, while he was still prevented from traveling by the US government, some 5,000 gathered in South Wales to hear him sing and talk with them over the transatlantic telephone cable. The following year, Robeson was able to travel in person to Wales and visit those whom he might well have considered as his people. With every Robeson film, the appeal is as much with the songs—usually two per production—as with his performance. The songs are generally inferior, as Graham Greene noted at the time, and un-African, despite the background. But they are generally charming—particularly when Robeson is coupled with Elisabeth Welch.

Playing opposite Robeson in *Song of Freedom* is South Carolina-born Nina Mae McKinney, who came to fame in 1929 as the female lead in King Vidor's all-black production of *Hallelujah*. In the 1930s and after World War II, McKinney toured Europe, appearing in nightclubs billed as "The Black Garbo." It was claimed by *Film Weekly* that she left Hollywood in the spring of 1933 because she was refused "a permit" to make a "mixed color" story,

Paul Robeson visits London's Trafalgar Square in July 1958.

although the language used in the news report is confusing.[5] McKinney's first appearance in a British film is in the musical *Kentucky Minstrels*, released in November 1934, the sentimental story of an old-time blackface minstrel facing hard times. *Film Weekly* (May 24, 1935) described the film as "nigger minstrel entertainment," but noted, "Nina Mae McKinney, as the star of the final spectacular revue, is the best thing in the picture—and she, of course, has nothing to do with the plot." After *Song of Freedom*, McKinney made two further British films, both concerned with broadcasting. In the first, a 1935 short subject titled *B.B.C. the Voice of Britain*, she sang "Dinah," and in the second, *On Velvet* (1938), in which a Cockney bookie and a Jewish punter set up their own television station, she sang "Swanee River." According to her successor as Robeson's leading lady, Elisabeth Welch:

> She turned out to be a swine. As a lot of people do, she thought that being a star, you must be temperamental, your must be nasty. She used to tear off her costume, shouting that it didn't suit her, it wasn't fitted right.

> [Impressario C. B.] Cochran said he gave her money to bury her father at least four times and her mother twice.[6]

Actors of color were to be found later in British films and on British television, but they came not from the United States but from what had been the British West Indies, and, more and more, they were native-born Britishers.

If Paul Robeson dominates among African American entertainers in Britain, then there is one Chinese American performer with similar appeal, and with a British film career basically equal to that of Robeson, and she is Anna May Wong. In all, the actress appeared in five British films of the late 1920s and 1930s, and also made her legitimate stage debut there.

Los Angeles-born Anna May Wong or Wong Liu Tsong (meaning Yellow Frosted Willow) had made her screen debut, as an extra, in 1919, and came to fame in 1922 playing the leading role of Lotus Flower in the first Technicolor two-color production, *The Toll of the Sea*. Despite the importance of the production in screen history and its being a starring role, Wong's career in America during the remainder of the decade was far from prestigious, with many of her subsequent parts being small—influenced, of course, by her ethnicity. As an Asian woman, she could not be cast in a romantic role opposite a Caucasian leading man. Thus, she was both happy and eager to accept a contract to appear on screen in Germany, under the direction of Richard Eichberg. Something of Wong's prominence upon arrival in Germany in 1928 is evidenced by a well-known photograph of her by Alfred Eisenstaedt in Berlin, showing her in the company of Marlene Dietrich and Leni Riefenstahl. The actress had a contract for five films, but made only two before leaving for London.

Here, she made her legitimate stage debut, opposite Laurence Olivier, in *The Circle of Chalk*, a historical Chinese drama, which opened at the New Theatre on March 14, 1929, and ran for five weeks. There were complaints that Wong's accent was difficult for audiences to comprehend; it was not the Chinese accent to which there were objections but rather her American accent. Producer Basil Dean pronounced it "as thick as the smog that now smothers their cities."[7]

Shortly prior to her stage debut, Wong had made her British film debut, playing the leading role in German director E. A. Dupont's production of *Piccadilly*, which also starred British actor Jameson Thomas and American performer Gilda Gray, famous for her "shimmy" dance. The film positively sparkles with life, energy, and vitality. Dupont is a director for whom silent

film is the perfect medium; here, there is none of the plodding dullness and lack of life so evident in his 1929 British talkie, *Atlantic.*

As Shosho, Wong makes her first appearance in a restaurant kitchen, dancing seductively on a table, her nipples quite clearly visible through her sweater, with the sense of eroticism profound. It is almost as if Gilda Gray symbolizes what was erotic a few years earlier, while Anna May Wong is the new sensuality, about to herald a new decade in this, her last silent film. In the British fan magazine, the *Picturegoer*, Marjory Collier wrote,

> In *Piccadilly*, she played the vamp—very successfully. A. E. Dupont's production, if it sometimes repels, is always arresting.
>
> He allows no milk and water effects. Whether as a slattern of the scullery, or with ivory skin showing through transparencies and black lace sleeves or engirdled by her dancing apparel, Anna, under his direction, dominates the singularly drab and uninspiring plot.
>
> By her immobility, her reposeful body movements that are certainly her Oriental heritage, she gave a touch of dignity to the siren she portrayed. Nevertheless she remained a siren—nothing more.[8]

Anna May Wong is introduced dancing on the table in the restaurant kitchen in *Piccadilly* (1929).

Piccadilly (1929), with Jameson Thomas and Anna May Wong.

Piccadilly opened in New York as an "art house" presentation at the Little Carnegie Playhouse on July 13, 1929, with a brief, final scene in sound. Sime Silverman in *Variety* (July 24, 1929) agreed with his fellow critics that Anna May Wong "outshines the star" (Gilda Gray), while describing her character as that of "a chink dancer." However, he was far from enthusiastic about either the story, an original by famed novelist Arnold Bennett, or Dupont's direction.

The New York newspaper critics were most enthusiastic. In the *World*, Quinn Martin wrote that "the Dupont settings, the atmosphere of Piccadilly and of Limehouse and of Soho, are very well managed, and the acting of the leading man, Jameson Thomas is extremely effective. Mr. Thomas is not unlike Ronald Colman either in appearance or in method." The *New York Times* critic wrote, "Mr. Dupont is noted for his unusual touches, and he has not spared them in this production. Even the opening, which ordinarily is but a staid prosaic list of characters, has become almost part of the picture. The director has managed to get the most from his situations without overdoing them." The *Evening Post* critic urged, "Anyone seeking a good silent picture, intelligently handled from start to finish would do well to visit the Little Carnegie Playhouse in Fifty-seventh Street, this week."

After appearing as herself in a satire on *The Taming of the Shrew* in the primitive, but still entertaining, revue film, *Elstree Calling* (1930), Wong returned to Berlin to make one further film for Richard Eichberg, *The Flame of Love*, released in German, French, and English versions. It was then back to Hollywood, where she had a couple of good parts, Princess Ling Moy in *Daughter of the Dragon* (1931) and Hui Fei in Josef von Sternberg's *Shanghai Express* (1932). In the former, she plays the daughter of villainous Fu Manchu and the woman with whom Sessue Hayakawa, playing a Chinese rather than Japanese part, and not doing it very well, falls in love.

Wong was back in Britain in 1933 and 1934. Not even the editing of David Lean can salvage the poor direction and pacing by J. Elder Wills in her first film on this visit, *Tiger Bay*, released in September 1933. The location of the story is somewhat confusing in that Tiger Bay is an area of the Welsh capital, Cardiff, known for its large Jamaican population. The setting of the film appears to be London's Limehouse district, but, in reality, the film takes place in an unidentified South American port. Here, Wong is running a Chinese nightclub which is little more than a café, and caring for her British "ward," played by Rene Ray. There is more than a hint of a lesbian relationship between the two women, perhaps more so on the part of Wong's character, Lui Chang.

Anna May Wong is the star here, and she is also the arbitrary star of her next British film, *Chu Chin Chow*, released in May 1934. Based on the popular 1916 musical by Oscar Asche, the film is well directed by always-reliable Walter Forde, who had tried without success to persuade producer Michael Balcon to allow him to shoot in color, which would certainly have added much to the film's entertainment value. The production features a polyglot cast, with British George Robey and German Fritz Kortner playing the male leads.

Based on the story of Ali Baba and the Forty Thieves, *Chu Chin Chow* features Wong as slave girl Zahrat, who saves Ali Baba and his family, but, unlike the original source, is not permitted to fall in love with Ali Baba's son. While arguably somewhat slow and old-fashioned for American audiences of the 1930s, *Chu Chin Chow* was released in the United States and opened at New York's Roxy Theatre on September 21, 1934.

Wong's last British film, *Java Head*, released in July 1934, and with impressive technical credits, including assistant director Carol Reed, art director Edward Carrick, and film editors Thorold Dickinson and David Lean, is the most important of her films for one reason. At a time when it was unthinkable to show a Chinese and a Caucasian kissing, *Java Head* features not one but two kisses between its leading players, Anna May Wong and the British John Loder, playing her husband. Obviously, the latter enjoyed the experience, as, according to producer Basil Dean, he and Ralph Richardson, playing Loder's brother in the film, "spent most of their time standing on the sidelines, drooling at the celestial beauty of Anna May."[9] *Java Head*'s director was J. (Jacob) Walter Ruben, an American screenwriter, director, and producer who made only this one British film.

Java Head eventually made it to America a year after its British release, opening at New York's Cameo Theatre in July 1935. It was not well received, with *Variety* (August 14, 1935) complaining of the lack of warmth to Wong's performance. It found similar fault with second female lead, Elizabeth Allan, and was not particularly impressed with Edmund Gwenn's performance as the father, despite his being already signed to a contract with MGM.

The Wong character takes opium to end her life in *Java Head*, thus freeing her husband to marry a nice English girl. Similarly, in *Tiger Bay*, she kills herself at the film's close, while in *Piccadilly* she is killed by her jealous lover. It is generally the lot of Anna May Wong that she must die at a film's conclusion. Perhaps if she had stayed longer in Britain, she might have found a role that allowed her to live a good, long life after the end credits and even perhaps to indulge in more interracial kissing, but there were no further British films on offer.

It is not known how the Chinese community in Britain regarded Anna May Wong or her screen characterizations. In May 1931, Dr. C. Kuangson Young, the Chinese Consul General in London, did contact *Film Weekly* to express the distress of the Chinese colony in London at the manner in which the Chinese had been presented on screen in offensive characterizations:

> The feeling of my countrymen is that the continual representation of Chinese in the characters of villains and criminals, in such films as *Dr. Fu Manchu* and *The Yellow Mask* [a 1930 British adaptation of an Edgar

> Wallace novel] tends to give a false impression of China to British filmgoers.
>
> We have crooks in China just as there are crooks in Great Britain and America; but we also have many splendid characters of historic interest and many treasures of natural and artistic beauty. I wish film producers would turn their attention to these aspects of Chinese life instead of concentrating on the traditional "Chinese villain." Truthful representation on the screen of Oriental subjects would lead to better understanding between the people of Great Britain and China.[10]

British women did hold creative roles behind the camera during the silent era, with some even working as directors. Ethyle Batley and Jakidawra Melford were the first, active as early as 1912, and there was also Dinah Shurey in the late 1920s. A number of British actresses, like their American counterparts, had their own production companies, and women were also to be found among the ranks of screenwriters, but nowhere as many as there were in the American film industry of the silent era.[11]

Jacqueline Logan had appeared in the Ziegfeld *Follies* prior to beginning a film career in Hollywood in 1921. She was by all accounts well educated and had worked as a newspaperwoman prior to entering the entertainment world. The most famous of Logan's silent screen roles is as Mary Magdalene in Cecil B. DeMille's production of *The King of Kings* (1927). Like DeMille, she was a conservative, and at his death, she sent a telegram to *Variety*, noting that "he spent the last of his energy trying to perpetuate his high ideals."[12] With the coming of sound, Logan came to London in January 1930, supposedly to appear on the stage although there is no record of her involvement with the theatre there. In 1930, she did co-star, playing the second female lead, in *The Middle Watch*, a silly comedy involving two female passengers on a naval vessel. The film opened in New York at the Roxy Theatre on December 19, 1930, cut by twenty minutes from its original British release length. *Variety* (December 24, 1930) was quite positive in its comments on Logan, noting,

> She radiates crispness until it seems to reduce to an appreciable extent the slowness of her fellow performers in this film. The dialog writer has used excellent judgment in working in a deal of American slang for Miss Logan. Another reason for the feature having a good chance over here is that Miss Logan does a [Clara] Bow with the British navy, outwitting all of the officers and the admiral himself.

Jacqueline Logan at her grand piano, at which publicity has it she spends many moments.

The Middle Watch was followed by *Shadows*, also from British International Pictures and released in March 1931. It was an exceedingly minor production with an obscure director, Hungarian-born Alexander Esway, and a cast of minor players. Logan is an American kidnap victim, saved by the son of a newspaper proprietor.

As early as 1921, Logan had written on her biographical sheet for Samuel Goldwyn Productions that she had the "ambition to be a director."[13] That ambition became reality in Britain a decade later. On August 25, 1931, *Variety* reported that British International Pictures was to allow her to produce and direct a film, based on her own, unpublished magazine story. That film was *Strictly Business*, released in January 1932, and co-directed with Mary Field. The latter had been active as a documentary and educational filmmaker since 1927 and she was later to head the Children's Film Foundation, making appropriate (and vastly unpopular with their intended audience) feature films for young audiences.[14] Described by journalist Nerina Shute as

"Downright Practical," she was "just the right person to collaborate with Jacqueline Logan." Logan, whom it was explained knows about lighting, camerawork, and cutting, presumably thanks to her work as an actress in Hollywood, would "lend the more delicate touches."[15]

A comedy involving an heiress and a blackmailer, *Strictly Business* was, as *Variety* (January 19, 1932) pointed out,

> essentially a small picture. Mainly interesting on account of the fact it was made by two women, one well known over here [Britain] for her documentary film work, and the other known both here and in American for her acting. . . . Just a small comedy for the small halls; it would have been better if they had spent twice as much money on it. It would equally have been worse had they spent less.

The Middle Watch (1930), with Jacqueline Logan and Owen Nares.

Variety did praise obscure leading lady Molly Lamont:

> Perhaps the best thing in its favor is the work of Molly Lamont as the juvenile lead. This girl has been nursed by B.I. for about 15 months, and now emerges as the best thing to look at on the English screen. She'd make good in Hollywood with a quarter of a chance. Looks fairly camera-proof, too.

South African-born Molly Lamont did make it to Hollywood in the mid-1930s, taking small roles in films such as *Mary of Scotland* (1935) and *The Awful Truth* (1937). She retired in 1951 and died in Los Angeles fifty years later. Jacqueline Logan returned to the United States and retired from films in 1934. In later years, she was involved in right-wing political activities, working out of her home in Florida, where she died in 1983.

The most interesting of creative women to come to Britain from Hollywood, and, at least in my opinion, the most important was Dorothy Farnum. Born in New York in 1897, she had been writing screenplays from 1919 onwards, initially for independent producers and then for Warner Bros. (including the 1924 production of *Beau Brummel*, starring John Barrymore). From 1924 until 1931, Farnum was under contract to Metro-Goldwyn-Mayer, for whom she wrote a considerable number of major films for the company's major contract stars. For Garbo, she wrote *The Torrent* (1926), *The Temptress* (1926), and *The Divine Woman* (1928). For Blanche Sweet, she adapted *Tess of the d'Urbevilles* (1924). For Joan Crawford, she wrote *Dream of Love* (1928). For Ramon Novarro, she wrote *The Pagan* (1929) and *Call of the Flesh* (1930). For John Gilbert, she wrote *Bardeleys the Magnificent* (1926) and *Redemption* (1930). And for Grace Moore, she wrote *A Lady's Morals* (1930) and *Jenny Lind* (1931).

In 1923, Farnum married Toledo, Ohio, financier Maurice Compton Barber, and the two traveled frequently to Europe from 1925 onwards, coming first to London in November 1927. In the early 1930s, the couple would appear to have decided to make their home in England. Farnum entered the British film industry, concentrating on scripts for romantic dramas, again starring major names: Victoria Hopper in *The Constant Nymph* (1933) and *Lorna Doone* (1934), Ivor Novello in *Autumn Crocus* (1934), and Evelyn Laye in *Evensong* (1934). She also worked on three films for Paramount in Paris in 1930–32, and in 1936, she was reportedly working on a film version of the life of Pavlova.

The most interesting and important of the films Dorothy Farnum wrote in England is the 1933 screen adaptation of the Lion Feuchtwanger novel *Jew Suss* for Gaumont-British. The story is set in eighteenth-century Wurttemberg, with anti-Semitic laws but tolerance of Jews because of their

Dorothy Farnum.

wealth. The wealthiest is Joseph Suss Oppenheimer, who is appointed tax collector for Count Weissensee, with whose daughter Oppenheimer has fallen in love. Eventually, Oppenheimer is put on trial for the crime of having a sexual relationship with a Gentile and is hanged in rather spectacular fashion. A subplot involves Prince Karl Alexander's attempt at seducing Oppenheimer's daughter, Naemi,[16] and her jumping from a window to her death rather than give in to him.

The film was written and produced concurrent with the introduction of new anti-Semitic laws in Nazi Germany, and it is obviously conversant with what is happening in Germany based on the use of the line, "They will

Conrad Veidt in the title role of *Jew Suss* (1934).

always persecute us." The production stars Conrad Veidt in the title role and is directed by the American-Jewish Lothar Mendes, who also directed *The Man Who Could Work Miracles* (1936) and *Moonlight Sonata* (1937), starring Jan Paderewski, in Britain. Making her screen debut as Naemi is Pamela Ostrer, the daughter of Isidore Ostrer, who, with his brother, Maurice, owned Gaumont-British. The Ostrers ownership of Gaumont-British led to its being labeled "Gaumont-Yiddish" by those in the industry and even, apparently, the British government.[17]

Jew Suss boasts sumptuous sets and a star-studded cast that also includes Cedric Hardwicke as Rabbi Gabriel, Benita Hume as Marie Auguse, and Gerald du Maurier as Count Weissensee, in his last screen role, dying prior to the film's release. Publicity reports indicate it was nine months in production and it was claimed to be the most expensive British film up to that date, costing 125,000 pounds to make. (In 1935, Alfred Hitchcock's *The 39 Steps* was produced for a mere 58,000 pounds.) The world premiere took place simultaneously on October 4, 1934, in London, New York, and Toronto. The British premiere was attended by the Duke of Kent. Unfortunately, the film is all scenery and costumes, and devoid of life. *Film Weekly* (January 4, 1935) dismissed it as "too slow and ponderous to be very entertaining," continuing, "In spite of its pageantry and its profusion of scenes and characters, the film's ultimate fate may very well rest upon the personal popularity of Conrad Veidt."

Variety (October 9, 1934) reviewed the film under its American Fox release title of *Power*, cut by some fifteen minutes because of sequences which could not be approved by the Production Code Administration. The trade paper was highly impressed by the film but questioned its box-office appeal, commenting,

> In transmuting Feuchtwanger's weighty exposition to the screen, Director Lothar Mendes and his collaborative scriptists manifested much ingenuity and skill in edition, elision and selection, to paint in celluloid what the new expatriated German author did in his powerful novel, *Jew Suss*. But, despite the Hollywood background of Mendes and adaptor Dorothy Farnum, they didn't quite choose hard and close enough.

In 1940, the same novel was adapted for the German screen under the title of *Jud Suss*, and it became what is generally identified as the most anti-Semitic film of all time. In view of the easy manner in which the plot could be manipulated, it is perhaps not surprising that there were objections to the British film from Jewish groups.

Dorothy Farnum ceased working in the film industry after *Jew Suss*, but she and her husband remained in Europe until after the outbreak of World War II. On November 23, 1940, they left Lisbon for New York, arriving on December 4. The couple did not return to Europe again, and nothing is known of their later life. Farnum's husband is believed to have died in 1950. Farnum's date of death is unknown.[18]

Wings of the Morning (1936), with director Harold Schuster and star Annabella.

CHAPTER NINE

Technicolor Comes to Britain

TECHNICOLOR IS (OR RATHER WAS) A COLOR PROCESS MOST CLOSELY associated with American film production. It was invented in the United States, and the most famous of all Technicolor films—*Gone with the Wind*—is a classic of American cinema. Dr. Herbert T. Kalmus introduced the process, which was initially a two-color one, in the late 1910s. Full-color or three-color Technicolor was introduced in 1932 with the Disney animated film, *Flowers and* Trees, followed by the first three-color Technicolor feature, *Becky Sharp*, in 1935.

Technicolor was the industry standard for color film through into the 1950s, when basically it was replaced by Eastman Color. Certainly, Technicolor played a part in British film history—it was more important in British film production than any American-based producer—and nothing is more demonstrative of that claim than the publication of an entire book on the subject of *British Technicolor Films* by John Huntley in 1950. There is a famous quote, falsely attributed to George Bernard Shaw, that England and America are two countries divided by a common language. Nothing more exemplifies this perhaps better than the color system and corporate name of Technicolor, which is known in the United Kingdom as Technicolour. All British films are shot in Technicolour, while all American films are shot in Technicolor. A compromise was necessary, and British films shot in Technicolor would bear the credit, "Colour by Technicolor."

Wings of the Morning has obvious historical importance as the first Technicolor feature film to be shot in Europe. Aside from that distinction, the film has considerable charm and appeal. It is the first film to illustrate what most cinematographers were later to realize: that the light in England

and Ireland is much softer than in California—or for that matter, in the rest of Europe—and it provides for a more subdued pastel effect than in most color films shot in the United States. Further, *Wings of the Morning* helped begin Harold Schuster's directorial career, and laid the groundwork for Technicolor's expansion into the British market, including the opening of a London plant within months of the film's completion.

In April 1935, producer Michael Balcon had commented that "England is interested in color but is doing nothing about it because the American process is not available here."[1] As if in answer to Balcon, a month later Dr. Herbert T. Kalmus of Technicolor announced that his company planned to establish plants in both London and Paris. Technicolor acquired an eleven-acre site on London's Great West Road and built a $1.5 million laboratory. By April 1936, the trade press was announcing that every major British studio would have at least one color feature in its 1936–37 schedule—something of an exaggeration—and Kay Harrison, Technicolor's new British managing director, told reporters that six British companies had signed with her company to produce twenty-four features and numerous short subjects. The first feature was to be *The Sport of Kings*, which became *Wings of the Morning*, followed by *Lawrence of Arabia* (which was to remain only a project until 1962). At the same time, other non-American color systems were being promoted; Associated Talking Pictures at Ealing announced that it would film *Hassan* in British Raycol, but the production was canceled, Dufaycolor was in general use, and Harmonicolor was announcing ambitious plans.

The man behind *Wings of the Morning* was American producer Robert T. Kane, who had been involved in European production for both Paramount, heading the Joinville Studios in Paris, and Fox, prior to returning to the United States in 1933. Kane returned to Europe in 1936 to produce four films for his British-based New World Pictures, subsidized by 20th Century-Fox, with the first production being *Wings of the Morning*, budgeted at $500,000.

In the late spring of 1936, a contingent of Americans came over from Hollywood to commence work on the production at the newly opened Denham Studios, the home of Alexander Korda's London Productions. *Wings of the Morning* was announced as the first film to be made at Denham, although other features were in simultaneous production there. Leading man Henry Fonda, on loanout from Walter Wanger Productions, made his first visit to England, and while filming *Wings of the Morning* met his future wife, Frances Seymour Brokaw. (Brokaw was a wealthy Canadian-born socialite who committed suicide on her forty-second birthday.) René Hubert was costume designer. From the Technicolor Company, both Dr.

Kalmus and his ex-wife, Natalie, made the trip, along with cinematographer Ray Rennahan. Dr. and Mrs. Natalie Kalmus (1882–1965) were married from 1902–21, re-married in 1923 and continued to live together until 1948, when they were divorced yet again. Under the terms of the divorce settlement, Natalie Kalmus was to receive credit as color supervisor on all of the Technicolor productions and was a formidable force in regards to color control on sets and costumes. Some more prominent directors fought her participation, but generally she was heavily involved in the production of Technicolor films until 1948. In more recent years, it has been fashionable to denigrate her work and suggest that she contributed little to the "look" of the Technicolor films, but this is obviously not true and she had a thorough understanding of the medium of color, what colors worked together and which did not.

What is so impressive about Technicolor feature films of the 1930s and 1940s, be they American or British, is not the storylines, the direction or the acting, but Natalie Kalmus's color coordination. The immediate reaction of the viewer upon seeing the films is how well those gloves match that dress or how well the trousers set off the color of the shirt. If Technicolor films can be said to have an auteur, then that auteur is Natalie Kalmus.

Glenn Tryon, a former light comedian, was the assigned director. Indeed, the only major technical credit that did not go to an American was that of art director, handled by former British architect Ralph Brinton. Tryon oversaw some of the location shooting in Ireland as well as the filming of the Derby, the famous race for three-year-old colts and fillies which has been held annually since 1870 on Epson Downs. However, following a disagreement with Kane, Tryon was taken off the film, and by July 1936, he was back in Hollywood. To replace Tryon, Kane selected Harold Schuster, a thirty-four-year-old editor who was already in London, hired to work on the film in that capacity. Schuster had been active in films since the making of *The Birth of a Nation*, in which he appears as a child, and his finest achievement as an editor is his work on F. W. Murnau's *Sunrise* (1927). He recalled,

> I had never been to Europe before. It all happened so fast. Bob Kane was a friend—I had worked with him in the early days. It was a very happy relationship. I don't know why he selected me, to tell you the truth, although I was pretty well versed in film.[2]

The choice of Schuster may well have been made in part by 20th Century-Fox production chief Winfield Sheehan, who had written of the editor, "He has the experience, character and mentality for a good director." Sheehan was later to write directly to Schuster:

> I am sure you will give a good account of yourself in your first job of direction, although the additional burden of color is on your shoulders. The worst you can get out of it is a lot of hard experience which will stand you in good stead in the future. I think that a couple of years in London directing pictures will do a world of good, and give you a broader and more international slant on life and people. I am sure that one day you will be a successful director, because I believe you have vision, initiative and imagination, in addition to technical knowledge and experience.

In the *International Photographer* (December 1936), Ray Rennahan reported,

> The Denham plant is equipped with the very latest types of Mole-Richardson lamps. . . . As we were shooting Technicolor, our set was naturally rigged with Mole-Richardson "H.1. Arcs," side arcs and scoops, exactly as though we were in Hollywood. Denham has enough modern Mole-Richardson equipment to take care of all the companies their six stores accommodate at once, and arcs enough to meet any demand a Technicolor unit might make.

On the negative side, Rennahan found the fog very troublesome—it even got on the sound stages—and noted that the weather could destroy a standing set in less than a year. On a personal level, he was disappointed that "grips" were virtually unknown, that property men were not reliable, and, above all, that the electrical crew did not understand lighting and were of little help to the cameraman in preparing a set for his style of lighting.

If Rennahan was not too happy with some of his British co-workers, many of them were far from enthusiastic about Robert Kane's working methods. There were complaints that the unit displayed a total disregard for the health and welfare of its crew, who were expected to work sixteen hour days, beginning at 7:30 in the morning, seven days a week. On more than one occasion, technicians complained they worked over 100 hours, straight time a week. The British technicians also protested the non-payment of overtime, suggesting that if the British producer paid his British employees on an American basis, they could almost pay off Britain's war debt to the United States.

The operating cameraman on the film was Englishman Jack Cardiff, who had been chosen from half-a-dozen assistant cameramen at a late-night secret meeting at Denham some months prior to when production began. Unable to answer the technical questions posed by Technicolor's representatives, Cardiff discussed the lighting used by the great masters in their paintings. The next morning he was informed that he was the company's choice. Some years later, he wrote,

> I shall always remember the first sight of the Technicolor camera emerging, like Botticelli's painting of Venus rising from the sea. As the unpacking continued, it became apparent that Technicolor's camera equipment and efficient methods of working were greatly ahead of our own. Everything connected with the camera was first-class—like a Rolls Royce.

Stage Two of the Denham Studios was utilized for the film, with the first interior in Technicolor to be shot on British soil—in June 1936—being that of French actress Annabella in the prologue, which involves the marriage of the Irish Lord, played by Leslie Banks, to a gypsy girl. This was Annabella's first English-language film, and the assistant to the producer, William Burnside, had to teach her English. The gypsy encampment, featuring prominently in *Wings of the Morning*, was built on the banks of the River Colne, which flows through the Denham grounds.

John McCormack, the great Irish tenor, was not signed until well after the film was underway, in July 1936, and his casting was obviously an afterthought by Robert Kane. It is an unfortunate afterthought, for although McCormack's voice is as gorgeously mesmerizing as always, the three songs he sings slow the film down badly. However, it must be admitted that without one of them, "Killarney," it would not have been possible to introduce some beautiful shots of the Irish countryside, photographed by the second unit over a two-week period.

Shooting was completed by September 1936, and Schuster returned to Hollywood to edit the production. Because there was not an operating Technicolor laboratory in England during the production, Schuster could only view the rushes in black-and-white.

The film tells the story of Marie, Queen of the Gypsies, who returns to Ireland, where she had married some forty-seven years earlier the Earl of Clontarf, and, following his death, been cursed for the next three generations of her family. In Ireland, she is joined by her daughter Maria (also played by Annabella), who has escaped from a revolution in Spain. Maria falls in love with a Canadian horse trainer, Kerry (Henry Fonda). Following various misunderstandings, the chief of which is Kerry's thinking that Maria is a boy, Kerry trains Maria's horse, "Wings of the Morning," to win the Derby. The curse is lifted, and Kerry and Maria are married.

Despite its melodramatic and rather cumbersome plotline, which is adapted from a short story by Irish-American writer Donn Byrne, *Wings of the Morning* has a winsome charm. It is colorful in every sense of the word. The shot of a red London double-decker bus takes on a rare beauty. A yellow signpost for the Automobile Association seems almost lyrical. At times, the colors are positively ravishing, and at other moments, particularly the scenes of the Irish countryside, the color is subtle; the sky is grey and the "green" hills and vales of Ireland appear mystically subdued. As British critic and documentary filmmaker Basil Wright rhapsodized in the British periodical, the *Spectator*, "There is a bloom which the black and white film can never achieve." Further, *Wings of the Morning* vividly illustrates a comparison made a little earlier by Pioneer Pictures publicist Paul Snell, who likened black-and-white films to Harlem in a snowstorm, and Technicolor pictures to a field of spring flowers.

Mrs. Natalie Kalmus explained the coordination of the colors in *Wings of the Morning*:

> In this picture we have tried to preserve one level of color throughout. Over half the picture was filmed out-of-doors, so that in these scenes the predominant color is the soft and restful green of the English countryside [she meant Irish countryside]. Even in the gypsy prologue to the picture, where some of the costumes are very vivid, they are offset by the masses of green. When we cut from these exteriors scenes to interiors we try to preserve the same "high level." Our sets are brown, grey and green—warm, rich shades of color for walls, furniture, tapestries and curtains, but all soft and tending to absorb light rather than reflect it. In this way the colors of the interiors and exteriors are kept at the same level.
>
> In the preparation of a color picture such as *Wings of the Morning* we read the script and prepare a color chart for the entire production; each scene, sequence, set and character being considered. This chart may be compared to a musical score and amplifies the picture in a similar manner.
>
> If colors are properly handled it is possible to make it appear as though the actors were standing there in person, thus creating the illusion of the third dimension.

> There was one slogan too, which everyone applied: "Color is not the star of the pictures—it is an additional factor. Don't use color for color's sake."

If the color is above criticism in *Wings of the Morning* (and it is), the pacing is not. At best, it is leisurely, and at worst, slow. It moves along at its own speed, at times seeming to hesitate as to which plot route to take, at other times throwing in incidents which have no relevance to the story. If the direction seems a little haphazard, it is also genuinely sincere and sensitive to its subject matter. Perhaps, as one critic wrote at the time, *Wings of the Morning* breaks every canon of decent filmmaking. Yet surely, *Wings of the Morning* is a revolutionary film in its way, and should look, in every sense of the word, different from other films of the period.

Certainly, although the critics were dubious as to the film's importance as a motion picture in and of itself, they were wildly enthusiastic about the color cinematography. "The film justifies the whole business of colored films more than it is possible for me here to convey," wrote the often feisty critic James Agate in the British *Sunday Times*. *Time* magazine wrote of its "impudent, abstracted charm." *Variety* considered *Wings of the Morning* to be "one of the few features in color which is not merely a demonstration of color."

Harold Schuster, Robert T. Kane, René Hubert, and Annabella were reunited for *Dinner at the Ritz*, also shot at Denham for an October 1937 release, with Phil Tannura as the black-and-white cinematographer. Schuster directed one final British film in the spring of 1938, *Queer Cargo*, a modern drama of piracy off the coast of China, released in the United States as *Pirates of the Seven Seas*. His later career in the United States was not particularly distinguished, although he was a busy director, responsible for such popular titles as *My Friend Flicka* (1943) and *So Dear to My Heart* (1948).

In July 1937, Dr. Kalmus announced that Alexander Korda had signed a contract with Technicolor to produce six films (of which five were made) in the process at Denham, beginning with *The Divorce of Lady X*, starring Merle Oberon, Laurence Olivier, and Ralph Richardson. Unlike previous productions, as John Huntley has pointed out, this comedy of marital problems was relatively small scale, but *Film Weekly* declared that "its Technicolor is said to be among the best yet."[3] American Tim Whelan handled the directorial chores, unlike the later Korda productions, which took advantage of stories and scenery—*The Drum* (1938) and *The Four Feathers* (1939), directed by brother Zoltan, and *The Thief of Bagdad* (1940), directed, in part in Hollywood, by Ludwig Berger and Michael Powell. Immediately

Dinner at the Ritz (1937), with Annabella and David Niven.

prior to the last production, Korda made, at Denham, *Over the Moon*, a relatively unimportant and forgotten Merle Oberon vehicle, with Thornton Freeland handling the direction.

Veteran American composer and director Victor Schertzinger, whose career dated back to the 1910s, with an emphasis on musicals in the 1930s, was hired in the summer of 1938 to direct a Technicolor screen adaptation of Gilbert and Sullivan's *The Mikado*, utilizing members of the D'Oyly Carte Opera Company, as well as American radio singer Kenny Baker and British stage star Jean Colin. The film was not entirely faithful to the original in that a number of lines, scenes, and songs were cut and a prologue added. Most happily, it does preserve a record of the work of Martyn Green, who had appeared with the D'Oyly Carte Opera Company from 1923 through 1951. *The*

Mikado was released in the United States in the summer of 1939 and was well received, with the *Los Angeles Times* (June 9, 1939) praising the "radiant color, enchanting melody, superior performances and the charm of great novelty." It was sufficiently popular in America that it was reissued in 1948.

The makeup and wigs for the actors in *The Mikado* were handled by Ern Westmore, one of Hollywood's famed Westmore brothers. It was reported that he received 150 pounds a week for his work, and the makeup budget was 4,000 pounds. "Never before has so much money been spent on this department in a British film," reported the fan magazine *Picturegoer*.[4] Wax models of the actors in makep and costume were created by Westmore for diplay at the "Woman's Fair" at London's Olympia facility.

The Mikado was photographed by American William V. Skall, who was just beginning a very distinguished career as a cinematographer with a specialty in color. Immediately prior to its production, he was responsible for the cinematography on Herbert Wilcox's *Sixty Glorious Years* (1938), with Anna Neagle as Queen Victoria and Anton Walbrook as Prince Albert. C.

The Mikado (1938), with Kenny Baker and Jean Colin.

Aubrey Smith returned from Hollywood to take on the role of the Duke of Wellington.

Mrs. Kalmus was to remain in London, supervising the productions. Also at Denham, Lawrence Butler, director of special processes for London Films, became the first man to achieve optical double-printing in the Technicolor process, superimposing a shot of the Denham Laboratories upon another shot of the River Colne. By the end of 1937, Technicolor was able to report that its London plant was working at full capacity, processing two million feet of film a month.

Replacing Mrs. Kalmus in Technicolor's British operation was Joan Bridge (1912–2010), who had studied art at Britain's Birmingham University and written her dissertation on color. In 1937, she was hired as color director by Duyfacolor, and five years later, she was appointed Technicolor's color consultant. In all, Bridge worked on some seventy-six Technicolor films, with *Caeser and Cleopatra* (1945) being the first upon which she received credit. In later years, she changed careers and became a prominent British costume designer, receiving an Academy Award, with Elizabeth Haffenden, for her work on *A Man for All Seasons* (1966).

The 1940s was a "golden age" for British Technicolor films. Certainly, there were a few lesser features: *The Great Mr. Handel* (1942), documenting the composer's time in England; *Western Approaches* (1944), a tribute to the British Merchant Navy, which must have been difficult to shoot in view of its documentary approach to the subject; the African-based *Men of Two Worlds* (1946); the Anne Ziegler and Webster Booth musical, *Laughing Lady* (1946); *The Man Within* (1947); the period melodrama *Jassy* (1947); and *Blanche Fury* (1947). Michael Balcon produced *Saraband for Dead Lovers* (1948) and *Scott of the Antarctic* (1948), and David Niven excelled in the title role of *Bonnie Prince Charlie* (1948).[5] Most importantly, the decade saw the release of Michael Powell and Emerich Pressburger's *The Life and Death of Colonel Blimp* (1943), *A Matter of Life and Death/Stairway to Heaven* (1946), *Black Narcissus* (1947), and *The Red Shoes* (1948); Noel Coward's *This Happy Breed* (1944) and *Blithe Spirit* (1945); Laurence Olivier's *Henry V* (1944); Gabriel Pascal's *Caesar and Cleopatra* (1945); and Alexander Korda's *An Ideal Husband* (1947).

Caesar and Cleopatra was received with superlatives by British critic Peter Noble, who wrote that "the use of Technicolour [*sic*] here is perhaps the most advanced of any other film, British or American, while the settings designed by John Bryan and fashioned by Harold Batchelor are, to quote

Wesley Ruggles, in England to direct *London Town*, meets with one of the city's Pearly Queens.

Peter Burnup, English editor of *Motion Picture Herald*, ‘of immensity and beauty unsurpassed hitherto on this side of the Atlantic.’”[6]

Constance Cummings co-starred in *Blithe Spirit*, as did Kim Hunter in *A Matter of Life and Death/Stairway to Heaven* (and also briefly in the US release version of *A Canterbury Tale*) and Paulette Goddard in *An Ideal Husband*. Fredric March and his wife, Florence Eldridge, had the leading roles in *Christopher Columbus*. But otherwise, there was no American presence here outside of the Technicolor brand, except for *London Town*, with its American director, Wesley Ruggles.

J. Arthur Rank obviously craved a reputation outside of his native country. He wanted Americans to recognize him as *the* preeminent British producer and showman, and to that end he determined to make a musical that would be on a par with the best America had to offer. The first step was to hire an American director, albeit one who had never made a musical and whose most important film, *Cimarron*, winner of the 1931 Academy Award

Kay Kendall in *London Town* (1946).

for Best Picture, is generally considered to be the worst film ever so honored. Rather than rely on British technical talent, Rank hired a German-American cinematographer, Erwin Hillier, who had never previously made a color film, and German-American art director Ernst Fegte. For the costumes, he hired one of Hollywood's top designers, Australian-born Orry-Kelly. For the choreography, he turned to Agnes de Mille. To ensure an authentic "British" script, two Americans, Sig Herzig and Elliot Paul, were brought over, aided by at least one competent British writer (and later director) Val Guest. The songs were not assigned to a reliable British composer, such as Noel Gay, but to Americans Jimmy Van Heusen and Johnny Burke. At least the composers had the common sense to base the main song, "The 'Ampstead Way," on Gay's "The Lambeth Walk."

The somewhat slight story involves a youngish comedian, played by Sid Field, who comes to London, with daughter Petula Clark, with the promise of a position as chief comedian at the New Hippodrome, run by Greta Gynt. The reality is that Field is to be understudy to comedian Sonny Hale. Clark, with the aid of Hale's dresser, Claude Hulbert, keeps him offstage by providing him with soap that colors his face green; Field goes on in his place and is a huge success. A distraught Clark reveals the truth to her father, but all is OK after Gynt offers Hale a new, more serious acting position.

London Town began production in September 1945 at Sound City Studios, Shepperton, which had for the previous six years been utilized for aircraft production. The film allows Sid Field, a popular music-hall and revue star, to preserve on celluloid two of his best-known sketches, "The Golf Lesson" and "The Photographer."[7] It also introduces Kay Kendall, as Field's love interest, to moviegoers, and gives music-hall singer/comedienne Tessie O'Shea an opportunity to perform a couple of songs. Those were the good things to come out of the film. The bad things all boiled down to one: the Americanization of a British musical, filled with everything that Americans expect of London life, including pearly kings and queens, jovial cockneys, an entertainer with incredibly bad teeth, boating on the river at Windsor, and boys from Eton College in formal school attire.

For glamour, the film features the "Dozen-and-One Lovelies," who might have looked refreshingly pleasing and English had they not been so heavily made up. The final production number, "The 'Ampstead Way," which is interminable, features a massive thirty feet long and thirty feet wide grand piano, with eight keyboards and sixteen pianists. The whole enterprise cost a reported $2,600,000, was one year in production, and was described by *Variety* (September 4, 1946) as "a misfire" and "thoroughly American." The thoroughly American director returned to Los Angeles in the same month as *Variety*'s review, announcing, "The British film industry is progressing amazingly fast, and their standards are high." They might have been higher without the presence of Wesley Ruggles.

While agreeing that the customers got "value for their money," *Motion Picture Herald* (September 21, 1946) complained of "technical faults . . . galore" and "a maze of Technicolored ballet and splendor piled on splendor." In the British *News Chronicle* (August 31, 1946), Richard Winnington wrote,

> The finished work *London Town* is a flaccid, ugly, ill-assembled film running for two hours and yielding a total thirty minutes of fun (for which you have to wait an hour) and a couple of numbers that will be whistled,

played and hummed around. The fun consists of Sid Field being his inimitable and brilliant self in his established stage turns. Elsewhere he is lost, with Sonnie Hale and Claude Hulbert, in a film that distresses by its poor continuity, shoddy dialogue and general ineptitude. . . .

Mr. Ruggles' London is evoked by a few shots on the Thames, Cockney landladies, pearly kings and queens and the inescapable Dozen and One. In that respect the film is the purest Hollywood, which is, I take it, what Mr. Rank wanted. . . .

But I still can't see the point of importing an American director and giving him all the time and money in the world to play with when we can make bad musicals on our own, and quicker.

Despite the American presence and the money poured into production, *London Town* was not released in the United States until July 1953, when United Artists distributed it in truncated form under the title of *My Heart Goes Crazy* (the title of the first, very long production number).

So is *London Town* as bad as suggested? No. To a large extent, it is no worse than many a Hollywood Technicolor musical. It is too Americanized, and certainly it wastes the talent of a young Petula Clark, who doesn't get to sing. The first Sid Field song, "You Can't Keep a Dreamer Down," is quite pleasant. It is slightly off-putting to have Kay Kendall appear at its conclusion and announce to the audience that Field does not wish to be mistaken for the effeminate, gay character he plays in "The Photographer" sketch. At least the comment is somewhat diminished in its offensiveness to a gay audience in having Field then come on and speak to the audience in the same "camp" fashion as he had adopted for the sketch. The film closes with a title announcing the characters are all fictitious. One sincerely hopes so.

With the 1950s, Technicolor's reign came to a close, as it was replaced by Eastman Color. The last British films actually shot in Technicolor are *The Lady Killers* and *The Feminine Touch*, both in 1955. The British Technicolor plant continued in operation through 1978, making UK release prints of *Star Wars* and other major films using the dye-transfer process. Ironically, it was only the British who go to see these films in superior quality prints. Jack Cardiff recalled,

In fact Technicolor in England had gained a rather enviable reputation, where the Americans thought the colour was so good it must be down to the quality of English water used in the processing. Absolute nonsense, of course.[8]

CHAPTER TEN

A Golden Age for the British in Hollywood

IN 1933, GOSSIP COLUMNIST JIMMY FIDLER POINTED OUT THAT IT WOULD be a catastrophe if British stars in Hollywood were to return to Elstree. "The British haven't 'gone Hollywood,'" he claimed, "but Hollywood has gone British." As proof, he mentioned not merely all the British players currently active and generally starring in Hollywood, but also British films such as *Rome Express*, *Be Mine Tonight*, and *After the Ball*, which "rank with Hollywood's best efforts."[1]

The first four British films to open at New York's Radio City Music Hall were *The Private Life of Henry VII* on April 12, 1933, *Fire over England* on March 4, 1937, *Wings of the Morning* a week later, on March 11, 1937, and, almost a year later, *The Divorce of Lady X* on March 31, 1938. For the first time, British films were screened at America's most prominent showcase. *The Divorce of Lady X* also generated a major rave review from Frank S. Nugent in the *New York Times* (April 1, 1938), who announced, "The British are coming again!" Nugent went on to praise producer Alexander Korda, writers Lajos Biro and Robert Sherwood, and stars Merle Oberon, Laurence Olivier, and Ralph Richardson. Korda and Olivier were, of course, associated with both *Fire over England* and *The Divorce of Lady X*, and both, ironically, were directed and photographed by Americans. Nevertheless, the films paved the way for Hollywood careers for the producer and his stars, and, possibly, Vivien Leigh's performance in *Fire over England* may well have influenced David O. Selznick to cast her as Scarlett O'Hara in *Gone with the Wind*.

From October 1934, films produced by Gaumont-British were screened on a regular basis at New York's Roxy Theatre. *Chu Chin Chow* had a two-week run there, resulting in a telegram from William Randolph Hearst and Marion Davies, congratulating Michael Balcon on its quality.[2]

The Radio City Music Hall and Roxy screenings were not in any way the initial presentation of British films in the United States. They had been seen on American screens in New York and elsewhere since the beginning of the twentieth century, when films from a variety of pioneering British companies were released over here.[3] In the April 4, 1908, issue of the American trade paper *Views and Film Index*, George Kleine, a US distributor of foreign films, wrote of the success of English Gaumont and Urban productions. By 1907, the films of Cecil Hepworth and Robert W. Paul were distributed in the United States by Philadelphia-based Williams, Brown & Earle, and in his autobiography, Hepworth boasted that he could rely on "a standing order from America of either thirty or forty copies—at our discretion—of every subject that we have produced."[4]

In 1912, Hepworth created the Hepworth American Film Company, with Albert "Blinkie" Blinkhorn as president. Blinkhorn resigned from the Hepworth Company at the outbreak of World War I, and began distributing British films, including those of Florence Turner, independently. Aside from Blinkhorn, other American distributors would pick up the occasional British film. Arguably, the first major British film to receive a major US release was George Pearson's *The Better 'Ole*, based on the cartoon character created by Bruce Bairnsfather, distributed by the World Film Corporation, and hailed by Julian Johnson in *Photoplay* (May 1919) as "novel and different." The film opened at New York's Strand Theatre on February 23, 1919, and was only the fourth British film to be reviewed by the *New York Times* (February 24, 1919), which found it "weaker in characterizations and atmosphere than the stage production." *The Better 'Ole* was remade in the United States in 1926 by Warner Bros., with British-born Syd Chaplin giving a memorable performance.

British films continued to be released in the United States through the 1920s, with more than thirty receiving reviews in the *New York Times*. Such reviews, unfortunately, were generally negative if not downright embarrassing: *The Bohemian Girl* was "lifeless" (February 5, 1923). *Woman to Woman* contained "too much agony and too little real action" (April 1, 1924). *The Vortex* "can hardly be called a pleasant or a stirring study" (August 27, 1928). *Kitty* was "weak on drama but strong on scenery" (June 11, 1929).

The occasional British film did garner a major US distributor. United Artists released *Carnival*, starring Matheson Lang and Ivor Novello, in May 1921. Metro-Goldwyn-Mayer released *Chu Chin Chow* (1923), thanks, of course, to its American star, Betty Blythe, and *A Little Bit of Fluff* (1928), under a more understandable US title of *Skirts*, thanks not so much to its leading lady, Betty Balfour, but her leading man, Syd Chaplin, who dominates the production.[5] Despite Betty Balfour's being identified as "the British Mary Pickford," and her obvious talent and personality, the actress's films appear to have done poorly in the United States; some were released on a limited basis but there was no firm offer of a deserved Hollywood contract.

Poor Cecil Hepworth never achieved any later success in the United States. His films were available over here, but reviews were dismissive. Of what is generally considered to be his classic, *Comin' thro' the Rye*, released in November 1923, *Photoplay* (March 1925) commented,

> You'll enjoy this picture better if you stay at home. One dislikes to say unpleasant things about a visitor but we wish they had kept this picture in England. If there is one redeeming feature in the whole thing it is the lesson which it furnishes—how not to make a picture. . . . In picture production it is about thirty years behind American films. The story is poor, the settings are poor, the costumes are poor, the acting is worse and the whole thing just gives one a desire to shoot everybody that had a hand in its making.

The individual most prominently associated with the distribution of British films in the United States was New York-born Arthur A. Lee, who began releasing them on a states-rights basis through the Lee-Bradford Corporation and later Artlee Pictures in the mid-1920s. In 1925, he established AmerAnglo Corporation, and by the end of the decade had become the exclusive US distributor for British Instructional Films, Ltd., Gainsborough Pictures, Ltd., Gaumont Co., Ltd., Piccadilly Pictures, Ltd., and Welsh, Pearson, Elder Films, Ltd. With the coming of sound, AmerAnglo Corporation ceased business, and Lee became head of Gaumont-British's American division. He resigned in April 1940, and died on February 22, 1943, when the Yankee Clipper on which he was flying crashed in the Tagus River, near Lisbon, Portugal; injured in the same crash was singer Jane Froman.

The only other major US distributor of British films in the late 1920s was World-Wide Films, Ltd., based in New York and founded by American J. D. Williams and British studio executive John Maxwell. World-Wide planned to distribute more than fifty European films a year, including the entire output from British International Pictures, with its first releases in 1928 being *Moulin Rouge* and *Tommy Atkins*.

Also in the 1920s, two British showmen tried to break into the American market. G. B. Samuelson was an enthusiastic, if not exactly visionary, businessman, who had been operating a British film studio since 1912 and was later to operate a fleet of mobile fish and chip shops. Disappointed at the lack of interest in distribution of his films in the United States, Samuelson decided to embark on production here, renting space at Universal Studios in December 1919. He brought over American-born director Alexander Butler, along with contract players Madge Titherage, C. M. Hallard, and Campbell Gullan. British actress Peggy Hyland had made her debut in England in 1914 and was put under contract to Fox in Hollywood in 1918. She was loaned out to Samuelson, who also hired Universal cameraman Fred Leroy Granville and promoted him to the ranks of director. Granville and Peggy Hyland were married in 1923.

Prior to returning to Britain in April 1920, Samuelson produced seven feature films at Universal: *David and Jonathan*, *Her Story*, *The Night Riders*, *At the Mercy of Tiberius* (released in the US as *The Price of Silence*), *Shifting Sands*, *Love in the Wilderness*, and *The Ugly Duckling*. The last, starring Florence Turner, never did get released in the US, while the other titles eventually found American distributors after a couple of years.

Sir Oswald Stoll was a formidable figure in British theatre, operating a large chain of legitimate theatres and music halls. He entered film production at London's Cricklewood Studios, and while he was not interested in American production, he was keen to control the release of his films here. To that end, he sent up the Stoll Film Corporation of America, with offices in New York, presided over by George King, and with former *Moving Picture World* editor George Blaisdell as director of advertising. Less than a dozen Stoll films were actually released in the United States, beginning with *Squandered Lives*, starring Guy Newall and Ivy Duke, and *Mr. Wu*, with Matheson Lang in the title role. Surprisingly, Stoll was able to promote a feature article on Newall and Duke in the April 9, 1921, issue of *Movie Weekly*, in which they were described as "the 'Mary and Doug' of English Films." An imminent visit to America was announced, as well as the couple's availability for American film work. There was no interest. Stoll ended his US operation at the start of 1922, and became highly critical of America's failure to recognize British films.

The British film industry seemed unprepared for the coming of sound, and, as a result, at least three British productions were produced in whole or part at a Hollywood studio. Herbert Wilcox understood the importance of sound. He arranged that the first "talkie" from his British & Dominions

Film Corporation, *Black Waters*, should be shot entirely at the Sono Art World Wide Studios in Hollywood; there was actually nothing about the production, released in May 1929, to suggest it was British, with American director Marshall Neilan at the helm and American stars, Mary Brian and James Kirkwood, although the third lead was British actor John Loder. Coincidentally, this story of a mad sea captain murdering the passengers on a fogbound ship was reviewed in *Variety* the same day—July 10, 1929—that Hitchcock's first talkie, *Blackmail* was also reviewed. While *Black Waters* was described as "too much talk with mellerish action," *Blackmail* was hailed as "not just a talker, but a motion picture that talks."

Variety (June 12, 1929) was as negative towards Victor Saville's *Kitty* as it was in regard to *Black Waters*. "*Kitty*, with or without its dialog, is useless," it opined. Based on a popular novel by Warwick Deeping, *Kitty* began as a silent film at Elstree, and sound sequences were added at the Paramount-Astoria Studios in New York. As leading man John Stuart recalled, he opened a door at Elstree and came out the other side in Astoria, New York.

Finally, of these hybrid so-called British talkies, there is *Journey's End*, a co-production between British Gainsborough Pictures and Welsh-Pearson Elder and the American Tiffany-Stahl. The much underrated and unfairly forgotten silent director George Pearson served as supervising producer of the screen adaptation of R. C. Sheriff's antiwar play which remains overwhelming some seventy-five years since its original production, despite what often amounts to stilted and dated dialogue.

At the directorial helm of *Journey's End* was James Whale, making his screen debut. Born in the depressingly industrial city of Dudley, in the center of what is called the Black Country (and it is black and gloomy with Birmingham at its heart), Whale did not have the background to suggest a sophisticated manner and stylish approach to films. But he did, and he made some of Hollywood's finest horror productions of the 1930s, including *Frankenstein* (1931), *The Old Dark House* (1932), *The Invisible Man* (1933), and *The Bride of Frankenstein* (1935), as well as one of the greatest musicals of all time, *Show Boat* (1936).

Whale was a gay man, and he was not the only British director so defined. There was also Edmund Goulding, who at times appears to have had a healthy sexual interest in both men and women. He was at his best directing female stars, including Greta Garbo (*Love* and *Grand Hotel*), Bette Davis (*The Certain Woman* and *Dark Victory*), and Gene Tierney (*The Razor's Edge*). Ivor Novello—"Dear Ivor" as his fans called him—was determinedly gay, and he enjoyed an on-and-off relationship with Hollywood. The

Alexander Korda and his new bride, Merle Oberon, in June 1939.

Welsh-born actor and composer enjoyed some success in America with his British films. In 1923, D. W. Griffith starred him in *The White Rose*, onc of the director's less-successful efforts. Novello starred opposite Ruth Chatterton in *Once a Lady* (1931) and provided the dialogue for MGM's 1932 release of *Tarzan, the Ape Man*. Another member of the British-gay fraternity in Hollywood, although there is no evidence they ever socialized, was novelist-screenwriter Hugh Walpole, actually born in New Zealand but generally identified as English.

The link between the first three British films at Radio City Music Hall is producer Alexander Korda. It is Hungarian-born Korda who produced some of the greatest British international successes of the 1930s, including *Catherine the Great* (1934), *The Ghost Goes West* (1935), *Rembrandt* (1936), *The Four Feathers* (1939), and *The Thief of Bagdad* (1940, begun in England in 1939 and completed in Hollywood). And it is Korda who helped find

Ruggles of Red Gap (1935), with Charles Laughton in the title role.

international fame for British stars of the period, including Robert Donat, Rex Harrison, Charles Laughton, Gertrude Lawrence, Sabu, Conrad Veidt, and, of course, Merle Oberon (whom he married in 1939 and divorced in 1945).

If *The Private Life of Henry VIII* made Charles Laughton an international star, it is *Ruggles of Red Gap*, produced two years later by Paramount, that truly endeared him to Americn audiences. In this adaptation of a 1915 novel by Harry Leon Wilson, Laughton plays a stereotypical British butler who is won in a poker game by a self-made American millionaire. It is not a relationship that the butler appreciates. At the film's climax, butler Ruggles enters the Silver Dollar Saloon and to the astonishment of its rough, ill-educated patrons, he recites the Gettysburg Address. It is a memorable and

Frank Lawton on the set of *David Copperfield* (1935).

moving performance by Laughton, who later told the *Saturday Evening Post* (May 28, 1949) that it was "one of the most moving things that ever happened to me."

The other "Lawton," Frank, was one of a group of actors brought over to Hollywood by Fox to appear in its 1932 production of Noel Coward's *Cavalcade*. This distinguished, impressive, deeply patriotic, and profoundly moving production was made in Los Angeles by the Fox Film Corporation in the summer of 1932 and hailed by many British critics as the best British film ever produced.[6] To a large extent, with its depiction of life above and below stairs at the home of a wealthy London family, it is the forerunner of television series such as *Upstairs, Downstairs* and *Downton Abbey*. *Cavalcade* is the story of Lady Jane and Sir Robert Marryot from the Boer War and the siege of Mafeking through into the Jazz Age. It begins on New Year's Eve 1899 and ends on New Year's Eve 1932. It is a tale of tragedy and also hope for a better world, although it is perhaps difficult not to be cynical towards the film's hopes and aspirations for the future, in view of all that has passed since its release.

Fox made a perfect choice for director in Frank Lloyd, a Britisher born in Glasgow in 1886, who had been active in films since the early 1910s, and was the only British-born director to be nominated for an Academy Award in the 1920s and who had shown a natural affinity for British-related films, such as *A Tale of Two Cities* (1917), *Oliver Twist* (1922), *The Sea Hawk* (1924), *The Divine Lady* (1929), *East Lynne* (1931), and *Berkeley Square* (1932).

Cavalcade had opened at London's Drury Lane Theatre on October 13, 1931, and ran for 405 performances. Fox paid Noel Coward $100,000 for the screen rights, including the use of his music. From the original production, the studio brought over Una O'Connor (Ellen Bridges), Merle Tottenham (Annie), and Irene Browne (Margaret Harris). It ignored star-to-be John Mills, who was in the cast, while Binnie Barnes turned down the studio, disliking the adaptation. Clive Brook and Diana Wynyard replaced the original stage performers, Edward Sinclair and Mary Clare, in the leading roles. The film is very much an all-British production in front of the camera, with other Britishers in the cast including Ursula Jeans, Herbert Mundin, Beryl Mercer, John Warburton, Tempe Piggot, Desmond Roberts, Lionel Belmore, and Dick Henderson, Jr. From the Empire, represented by Australia, came Billy Bevan and Montague Shaw. Many became popular character players in Hollywood, such as short, cheeky, and cheerful Herbert Mundin, perfect in working-class roles, whom David Niven described as "a great entertainer of legendary conviviality."[7]

The film received its world premiere at Grauman's Chinese Theatre in Hollywood on January 12, 1933. It played a three-week run at London's Tivoli Theatre, and in the words of the *New York Times* (April 9, 1933), it gave "the British nation the finest 'boost' it has ever had on screen." Of course, there were detractors, who found the theme of Empire offensive. The critic in the *New York Herald Tribune* (January 29, 1933) wrote, "Mr. Coward has turned into a sort of moral Fascist.... Like all other Fascists, political, religious or intellectual, he couches his new beliefs in terms far too simple to ... carry even a modest burden of truth." But it mattered little what the naysayers thought, in large parts thanks to Diana Wynyard's performance and her manner in

On the set of *Cavalcade* (1933), from left to right, Bonita Granville, Ursula Jeans, director Frank Lloyd, and Una Merkel.

delivery of the speeches (particularly the closing toast). The *New York Journal* (January 6, 1933) described her as "a gracious lady, a gentlewoman of charm, of dignity, of patrician breeding. . . . The pride that is England is evinced in her every word and gesture. Her characterization is flawless and her acting completely overshadows that of everyone else in the cast."

As early as August 9, 1926, the London *Evening News* claimed to have counted "25 women and 89 men from Britain working in important roles in Hollywood." The number seems somewhat high and impossible to verify.

British actors and actresses active in Hollywood during the silent era include James Aubrey (born in Liverpool), Eric Campbell (born in Dunoon,

Scotland), Wilfred Noy (born in London, and also active as a director), House Peters (born in Bristol), and David Powell (born in Glasgow). Leicester-born Walter Butler had been successful as an actor in England, but in America, his name was the same as that of the British commander responsible for the Cherry Valley Massacre during the Revolutionary War,[8] and he had to change it to Walter Byron. Ivy Close, the mother of cinematographer-director Ronald Neame, and a noted British beauty and film star, came over to America in 1916 to work for the Kalem Company. Directors at the height of their success during the silent era who were born in Britain include Reginald Barker (born in Bothwell, Scotland), Charles Brabin (born in Liverpool, and the husband of Theda Bara), Colin Campbell (born in Scotland), Arthur Maude (born in Pontefract, and also an actor), Arthur Rosson (born in London), and Edward Sloman (born in London).

Jameson Thomas had been a prominent British leading man of the 1920s, who made an easy transition to sound films. Sadly, his wife contacted tuberculosis, and after completion of the Anglo-German production, *Night Birds*, released in October 1930, Thomas decided to move himself and his wife to the beneficial, warmer climate of Los Angeles. His first role in Hollywood was an uncredited one in *Body and Soul* (1931), and that was an unfortunate sign of what lay ahead—not necessarily uncredited roles but certainly small parts. Tragically, not only did Thomas's wife die, but he also contacted tuberculosis, and in his later years his income was supplemented with a small payment from the Motion Picture Relief Fund. He died at a tubercular rest home in Sierra Madre, just outside of Los Angeles, in January 1939 at the age of forty-five, after a last uncredited role in *Marie Antoinette* at MGM. His Hollywood career ended as it had begun.

Gibson Gowland is best known for his performance as McTeague in Erich von Stroheim's *Greed* (1925), and it is perhaps difficult to believe he is an Englishman. But Gowland was born in County Durham in the north of England, and had come to the United States in 1913. Prior to *Greed*, Gowland had appeared in a couple of British feature films and made a handful of British films in the 1930s. The most memorable of his British work is as Angus in the unintentionally hilarious *The Secret of the Loch*, released June 1934, and starring a demented Sir Seymour Hicks in search of the Loch Ness monster. Gowland is an appropriately menacing presence, with a respectable Scottish accent and with a far better understanding of how to wear a kilt than Mel Gibson ever had in *Braveheart*.

Active first as a screen comedian and then a director from the 1920s through into the 1940s, Walter Forde was one of the most talent and vastly underappreciated of British directors, particularly in the 1930s. He could handle any genre—comedy, drama, musical—with consummate skill and ease. He retired to Los Angeles, where his parents had been living for a number of years, in 1954, but he had made an earlier visit there in 1922 and 1923. After appearing in a series of two-reel British comedies, Forde was approached by Harry Spoor, the British manager of the Essanay Company, who suggested that the comedian try his luck in America. Forde was given an introduction to Essanay's co-founder George K. Spoor in Chicago, but when he got there, after knocking on Spoor's door and trying to explain who he was, Forde found the door slammed in his face. Undaunted, Forde made his way to Hollywood. He recalled finding a five dollar bill on the sidewalk and spending the next thirty minutes touring the neighborhood in the hope of finding another.[9] Eventually, he did make two films at Universal, *Good Deeds*, directed by William Watson and released July 23, 1922, and *Radio Romeo*, directed by Lloyd Bacon, and released June 25, 1923, but was then let go. Unwanted by the film industry, he became a house painter. "There are still one or two houses which I see, to which I gave three coats out, three coats in," he told me.[10] His wife, Culley, did not get along well with Americans, and after nine or ten months, Forde returned to England and to what was probably a more illustrious career than he would have enjoyed in Hollywood.

In the 1930s, Percy Marmont was the personification of an English gentleman, notably as the chief constable father of Nova Pilbeam in Hitchcock's *Young and Innocent/The Girl Was Young* (1937). London-born Marmont had earlier enjoyed a prominent Hollywood career as a silent leading man, always somewhat anguished-looking, opposite such stars as Leatrice Joy in *The Marriage Clause* (1922), ZaSu Pitts in *The Legend of Hollywood* (1924), and Clara Bow in *Mantrap* (1926). He became a star in 1923 in the adaptation of A. S. M. Hutchinson's *If Winter Comes*, for which he returned to England for location scenes in London, Canterbury, Brighton, and at Leeds Castle. Marmont returned permanently to Britain in 1928.

On the distaff side, enthusiasm for British stars was almost nonexistent. The major British female stars of the day, Betty Balfour and Mabel Poulton, did not even consider an American film career, and certainly Poulton's harsh cockney accent would have prevented her having any appeal in American talkies. In its October 24, 1925, issue, *Picture* Show commented that "it is common gossip that America has made very definite attempts to woo her [Betty Balfour], but she has remained loyal to England."[11] There were, however, two British leading ladies who tried their luck in America, neither with any great success.

Pretty, dark-haired ingénue Flora Le Breton had been seen in British films from 1920 and made something of an impact in J. Stuart Blackton's *The Glorious Adventure*. In 1924, she and her mother made the journey to America with very limited success. The actress played second lead in four poverty-row productions, made between 1924 and 1925, and also appeared in a lesser role in one major studio production, First National's *The White Monkey* (1925), based on one of John Galsworthy's Forsyte Saga novels. She was back on screen in 1930, playing with Charles Ruggles in the first sound version of *Charley's Aunt*, but again not in the leading female role. On stage, initially, Flora Le Breton did somewhat better. She had studied at the Royal Academy of Dramatic Art, and that certainly must have helped in her being hired for the title role in the comedy *Lass o' Laughter*, which opened on Broadway on January 8, 1925. The passing years were not kind to the actress, and in her last Broadway appearance, in *The Chinese Nightingale* (1934), she was cast as a kitchen maid. The production ran a mere eight performances. Le Breton died in Brooklyn, at the age of fifty-three, in 1951.

Arguably, Estelle Brody is out of place in this chapter in that she was actually born in New York—in 1900—and had appeared on the American stage as a dancer prior to coming to Britain in the early 1920s. Her first starring role on screen was as *Mademoiselle from Armentieres*, released in September 1926. The film was widely popular in Britain and well received by the critics, but when it opened in New York at Loew's Lincoln Square Theatre on June 30, 1928, released by MGM, recut, and with comic titles by Ralph Spence, it was not too enthusiastically reviewed by *Variety* (July 18, 1929), which commented, "This may be *The Big Parade* for England but it will never get beyond some of the poorer second runs in America, unless deliberate advantage is taken of its excellent title."

In that the film was considered a British response to *The Big Parade*, Estelle Brody's American birth was regarded as inappropriate. She was, therefore, "reborn" as a Canadian, and remained such for the rest of her career. Nobody could question her credentials as an English actress with her performance in *Hindle Wakes*, released in February 1927, in which Brody plays to perfection a working-class Lancashire girl. In the last two films, Brody had John Stuart as her leading man, and he again played opposite her in *Kitty*, her first part-talkie, for which she returned to New York for the sound sequences.

In 1929, Brody returned to America and made a number of unidentified short subjects in both Hollywood and New York. Back in England, she explained to *Film Weekly* (August 15, 1931) that had she had been studying the sound film in the country of its birth, adding,

> As regards British pictures in America, it is nonsense to say, as several prominent people have done, that the American public do not want films made in Great Britain. But they will not tolerate some of the second-rate pictures which have been exhibited in the U.S.A. as typical British productions. Who can blame them? If we want to capture some of the American market we must send them really first-class pictures.

To all extents and purposes, Estelle Brody's career was over; she married a London agent and appeared occasionally, often uncredited, in later films and on television. I met her in 1969, just as she was preparing to move with her husband to Malta. She was very elegant, very well-spoken, with no hint of an American accent. Her somewhat extreme right-wing politics made Malta, with its Communist government, a strange choice as a future domicile. However, she remained and died there in 1995, at the age of ninety-four.

Charles D. Hall's credits as an art director include some of the most famous Universal productions of the 1920s and 1930s—*The Phantom of the Opera* (1925), *All Quiet on the Western Front* (1930), *Dracula* (1931), *Frankenstein* (1931), and *Show Boat* (1936)—and he was born in Norwich.

Empire-born, in India, Roy Pomeroy was the "technical wizard" who parted the Red Sea in Cecil B. DeMille's *The Ten Commandments* in 1922 and created the flying sequences for the original screen version of *Peter Pan* in 1924. He remained with the same studio, Paramount, as head of the special effects department, helped in the making of *Wings* (1927) and, as a result, became the first Englishman to win an Academy Award—for "Engineering Effects." It was Pomeroy who tested all the Paramount contract players as to their worthiness to work in talkies and directed its first all-talkie production, *Interference*, in 1928. At that time, the British fan magazine *Film Weekly* headlined "World's Greatest 'Sound' Expert an Englishman."[12] He disappeared from public view in the mid-1930s and died a decade later.

The list of Britishers in Hollywood in the 1920s and 1930s is a long and distinguished one, including Brian Aherne, George K. Arthur, Leslie Banks, Freddie Bartholomew, Eric Blore, Clive Brook, Nigel Bruce, Constance Collier, Ronald Colman, Donald Crisp, Reginald Denny, Ralph Forbes, Alec B. Francis, Reginald Gardiner, Cary Grant, Sydney Greenstreet, Edmund

Clive Brook, the very personification of an Englishman at rest in Hollywood.

Gwenn, Cedric Hardwicke, Bob Hope, Leslie Howard, Vivien Leigh, Doris Lloyd (born in Liverpool), Dorothy Mackaill (born in Hull), Herbert Marshall, Ray Milland, Alan Mowbray, Reginald Owen, Claude Rains, Basil Rathbone, Henry Travers, Henry Wilcoxon, and Roland Young. Some—notably Charlie and Syd Chaplin—never became American citizens. Most did not become Americanized but rather became more stereotypically English both on and off screen, although it must be acknowledged that Ronald Colman enjoyed the distinctly un-British hobby of square dancing in his spare time.

Most Englishmen and women would agree that God is quite definitely an Englishman, and so, appropriately, his son was portrayed on screen in his first two major appearances by Englishmen: Howard Gaye in *Intolerance* (1916) and H. B. Warner in *The King of Kings* (1927).

It is not just God who is an Englishman, but apparently all major figures in history, as depicted by Hollywood and impersonated by George Arliss. As *Newsweek* (February 18, 1946) wrote at the time of his death,

> Because of him, millions of movie-taught Americans visualize the dominant characters of the eighteenth and nineteenth centuries as strangely alike: sad-eyed men with long faces, long noses, and long upper lips.

The British presence in Hollywood was not limited to leading players. In 1935, Central Casting reported that 2,500 English men and women were registered for extra work.[13]

Curiously, Hollywood did not sign up the most effervescent singing and dancing personality of British cinema in the 1930s, Jessie Matthews. Her American fame was such that in August 1936, celebrated artist James Montgomery Flagg traveled to London to sketch her. Fred Astaire had suggested she come to Hollywood and become his dancing partner but Matthews's British studio commitments would not allow it. Unquestionably, the films of Matthews were some of the most popular British films to play the United States. One journalist declared that she had assumed a prestige unrivaled by the most famous of Hollywood stars. "She was accepted by Americans as a symbol of care-free gaiety; a creature with a dash of the right kind of sex appeal; something which in America completely knocked on the head the ugly impression created by a woeful line of British films."[14]

The American critic Don Herold described her as "the best woman dancer on the screen, one of the best song putter-overs, one of the most delightful persons, and the possessor of two of the loveliest legs in two hemispheres."[15]

Jack L. Warner tried without success in February 1936 to persuade the star to sign a contract with Warner Bros. He had plans to star her in remakes of two earlier studio musical adaptations, *Sally* and *The Desert Song*, and seemed surprised that any actress would reject the offer to star in a new version of *Sally*, associated previously with Marilyn Miller.

In October 1937, Matthews announced that she was to sign a three-year contract with MGM, followed by an arrangement with 20th Century-Fox, whereby she and husband Sonnie Hale would have their own producing unit, but nothing materialized. She did come to America in 1941 to star on Broadway in *The Lady Comes Across*, but the show closed almost immediately after its opening. The New York trip did lead to a brief visit to Los Angeles and work on the patriotic, historical drama *Forever and a Day*.[16] According to Matthews, she spent three days working on the film, which constitutes her only American screen appearance.

"I believe in buying British and selling British," said Gracie Fields to a British fan magazine, "I can make more money in English studios than I can possibly do on the other side of the Atlantic. In other words—Hollywood can't pay me enough."[17]

Forever and a Day (1943), with Jessie Matthews and Ian Hunter.

Gracie Fields was Britain's biggest star of the 1930s—on screen and on the variety stage—whose rapport with her audience was unprecedented. She was working class, from Lancashire, but her appeal was to all strata of society and she also enjoyed limited success in the 1930s in the United States. It was producer Basil Dean who crafted her film success, beginning with her second production, *Looking on the Bright Side*, in 1932. As Jeffrey Richards has pointed out, Gracie provided an anthem for the Depression, "Sing as We Go," and another for the first days of World War II, "Wish Me Luck as You Wave Me Goodbye."[18] She might have continued in Britain and gained even greater popularity during World War II, except that her second husband, director/comedian Monty Banks, was an Italian citizen who would have been

Gracie Fields with her second husband, comedian/director Monty Banks.

interned when Italy entered the war against Britain in 1940. The couple first came to Canada and then moved on to the United States, where Banks was able to assume US citizenship, having been brought up there. The move to America was regarded as nothing less than an act of treason by the British press. She had betrayed her country when it needed her most, despite her working strenuously on behalf of British War Relief in the United States. In all, Gracie made five films in America, *Holy Matrimony* (1943), *Molly and Me* (1945) and *Paris Underground* (1945, released in the UK as *Madame Pimpernel*), as well as the Technicolor short, *Young and Beautiful* (shot in 1941 and released in 1942), and *Stage Door Canteen* (1944), in both of which she appears as herself, singing in the last "The Lord's Prayer," which seems both inappropriate for her and for the soldiers gathered around her, who might have appreciated something a little more entertaining.

Fields was eventually rehabilitated in her homeland in the late 1940s, and the 1950 death of Monty Banks probably helped. She remains one of the few British music-hall stars to have lasting popularity and fame in America.

Charlotte Greenwood, who was obviously influenced by a similar performance style, proclaimed of Cicely Courtneidge that "her humour is broad enough to please everyone, yet she has a subtlety underlying it which pleases intellectually."[19] One intellectual who did not agree with Greenwood's assessment was Graham Greene. Reviewing Courtneidge's performance in *Me and Marlborough* in the *Spectator* (September 6, 1935), he wrote, "She is not an actress who can suggest pathos or romantic love. . . . I found myself too embarrassed by Miss Courtneidge's facial contortions to appreciate their share. Miss Courtneidge is used to throwing her effects to the back row of a theatre gallery, and the camera is not kind to her exaggerations."

Film historian Rachael Low is kinder, describing her as

> a warm personality, eager but coy, formal and polite and just a little arch, she accentuated her size and ungainliness and guyed herself, but retained her natural charm. She was a gifted comedienne and with sympathetic material could be extremely funny, and became a much-loved aunty figure to British audiences.

Metro-Goldwyn-Mayer determined to co-star Courtneidge in its 1935 production of *The Perfect Gentleman*, released in Britain as *The Imperfect Lady*, which had been conceived initially as a vehicle for Frank Morgan, who receives top billing. The studio borrowed the actress from Gaumont-British, to which she was under contract, and in return loaned out Madge Evans and Jean Parker to the British company. The comedy concerning an aging English aristocrat who teams up with a music-hall performer might have been adequate, and was certainly helped by director Tim Whelan, familiar with his star in England. Unfortunately, according to Courtneidge, "I arrived at the M.G.M. Studios in great excitement and anticipation of success. . . . It was a bad film and the part was quite wrong for me." Her producer was not the most understanding of men, asking her, "Now, Miss Courtneidge . . . tell me what do you do in England? What kind of part do you play?"[20]

A new producer was found and, according to Courtneidge, the story was rewritten to revolve around her and not Frank Morgan. She spent three months in Los Angeles, and at one point she was joined by husband Jack Hulbert, who tried to help with the storyline. A preview did not go over well, and the studio decided to rewrite the ending. To no avail. "I thought it was rubbish," declared the star. "We remade the rubbish twice with different directors."[21] There is no way to verify the actress's comment.

It must be admitted that, unlike so many British films of the 1930s, the Cicely Courtneidge vehicles are not pedantic. Whatever else they are or are

The Perfect Gentleman (1935), with Frank Morgan, Herbert Mundin, and Cicely Courtneidge.

not, they are seldom dull. Unfortunately, the same could not be said of Anna Neagle's films, produced and directed by husband Herbert Wilcox. They were little more than history lessons. They might prove, as was suggested at the time, that Neagle's acting was comparable to that of Helen Hayes on the stage, a highly debatable claim, but they also seemed to suggest a limited personality. Watching Neagle's films one is always aware that she has a lover-husband-director who truly adores her, idolizes her, and can see nothing wrong in anything she does. The scripts have not been viewed with a critical eye, and neither have the performances. Neagle spent time, she claims, on research, discussing her role as Queen Victoria in *Sixty Glorious Years* (1938) with the last surviving lady-in-waiting to the monarch. Both *Sixty Glorious Years* and its predecessor *Victoria the Great* (1937) played Radio City Music Hall, and, as a result, Neagle and Wilcox were offered contracts by RKO. There were wonderful notices for the films, but as Neagle told me, "Once we got into the country, it didn't mean a thing. Anton Walbrook [as Prince Albert] wasn't known. I wasn't known. Herbert said they didn't know about Queen Victoria, they didn't even know where England is."[22]

As a British fan-magazine writer of the time explained it,

> I don't think the Americans want mighty two-hour costumed double-portioned slices of our imperial history; what they want and will fall for in a big way are good comedies, carefully written and intelligently cast, solid earthy stories of English life with a semi-documentary interest and, perhaps, a sidelong glimpse of history in a minor key, like *Tudor Rose*, very different from the "glorious" full-blast march-pasts we have been surfeited with.[23]

The 1936 film *Tudor Rose* starred child actress Nova Pilbeam, and she had made quite an impact in America with her few screen appearances. Had she signed a contract, she might well have developed into a major international star. She certainly had the talent.

Anna Neagle and Herbert Wilcox seemed willfully ignorant of what Americans wanted, and their first RKO film was *Nurse Edith Cavell*, released in October 1939, and based on the life of the World War I nurse executed in Belgium by the Germans. Again, it was a serious subject. Lighter subjects were put into production—*Irene* (1940), *No, No Nanette* (1940), and *Sunny* (1941). Again, the choice was misplaced. Old stage musicals do not make good modern films, even if there had been screen adaptations a decade earlier. Neagle is a good, competent dancer, but she is not a singer—she has a slight voice—and starring her in musicals was always a mistake by an overindulgent lover, who was to become her husband in 1943. The couple returned to England, believing sincerely that they should contribute to the war effort in their own country, and the actress returned to playing British heroines, from pioneering aviatrix Amy Johnson in *They Flew Alone* (1942) to Florence Nightingale in *The Lady with the Lamp* (1951).

If Anna Neagle was too serious for American audiences, then Laurence Olivier displayed too much of his feminine side. In *Fire over England* (1937), he is shown crying at the sight of his father's ashes at the foot of the stake. American audiences tittered nervously and then laughed out loud at the sight of an English actor crying on screen. Americans expect their heroes to be strong; they cannot "blubber." And so the scene was cut. Olivier was to prove sufficiently brooding as Heathcliff in *Wuthering Heights* (1939) and sufficiently stoic as a hero, playing Lord Nelson in *Lady Hamilton/That Hamilton Woman* (1941), but, basically there was no real American film career on offer. And, arguably, Britain had far more to offer him in the way of prestigious projects, on screen and stage, and honors, including a life peerage in 1970.

Anna Neagle as Nurse Edith Cavell (1939).

Olivier notwithstanding, at one point it had seemed that the British would actually triumph over Americans in Hollywood. "Will you make room over there for any American studio executives? Will there be a place in England for Hollywood producers if local businesses fail?" one British actor was asked. "Certainly," he replied, "After all, we must have someone to empty the waste baskets."[24]

CHAPTER ELEVEN

British Cinema at War

BRITAIN'S DECLARATION OF WAR WITH GERMANY IN SEPTEMBER 1939 failed to bring an immediate halt to American production there, in part because an embargo on the export of box-office profits meant that American studios could not enjoy the financial success that their films generated. The *New York Times* reported that MGM had derived an annual revenue of $15 million from Britain prior to the war; that sum was now cut in half and the studio "will be compelled to spend the money in England if that market is to contribute any profit."[1] With funds frozen in the United Kingdom, at least one American studio decided to continue not only with production of an individual film but with a series, which just happened to be based on a British character. That character was Simon Templar or "The Saint," created in 1928 by Leslie Charteris, who was actually born in Singapore but had British citizenship thanks to its being a colony. The first of The Saint films to be shot by RKO in England, prior to the war, was *The Saint in London*, starring George Sanders in the title role, with Sally Gray as his leading lady and John Paddy Carstairs as the director.[2] Sanders was already a Hollywood star when he was sent back to England, where he had been brought up by British parents who happened to be in Russia when he was born.

The outbreak of World War II did not permit Sanders's return for a second film, but the American studio formed a new company, RKO Radio British Productions, with producer William Sistrom in charge, and selected a new leading man, Hugh Sinclair, to play The Saint. Sally Gray was again the leading lady, and RKO was so impressed with her performance that it offered the actress a Hollywood contract, which she rejected. Leslie Fenton directed *The Saint's Vacation*, which was well received at its New York opening at the Rialto Theatre. The critic in the *New York Times* (June 13, 1941) noted that "although Hugh Sinclair . . . lacks a bit of George Sanders' sardonic suavity, he's a capital fellow nonetheless."

The *New York Times* ignored the third and final British production in the series, *The Saint Meets the Tiger*, which Paul Stein directed and in which Hugh Sinclair's leading lady was Jean Gillie. Indeed, the film was considered unreleasable by RKO, which sold it to Republic which in turn waited until 1943, two years after shooting had been completed, before adding it to its schedule.[3]

Given similar treatment by RKO was its 1941 British production of *Dangerous Moonlight*, starring Anton Walbrook, again with Sally Gray as the leading lady, and directed by Brian Desmond Hurst. Despite its being a superior effort, the story of a Polish pianist who flies in the Battle of Britain, thanks obviously to producer William Sistrom, and its introducing the popular "Warsaw Concerto," written by Richard Addinsell, the film was again rejected by RKO and passed on to Republic, which released it in the United States as *Suicide Squadron* in April 1942.

William Sistrom (1884–1972) was British-born, and early in his career, in the 1910s, had worked as a studio manager at Universal. In 1935, he joined RKO, where his producer credits are many but unimpressive. Sistrom did not end his British career with *Dangerous Moonlight*. In 1943, he produced a pair of Two Cities films, both released the following year—*Tawny Pipit*, written by, directed by, and starring Bernard Miles, and *Mr. Emmanuel*, directed by Harold French, and starring Felix Aylmer and Greta Gynt. After the war, Sistrom produced *Hungry Hill* (1947), directed by Brian Desmond Hurst, and starring Margaret Lockwood and Dennis Price, and *Woman Hater* (1948), directed by Terence Young, and starring Stewart Granger and Edwige Feuillere.

Republic did produce at least one wartime film which was shot in part on location in London, and that is *Thumbs Up*, released in the summer of 1943. The story of an American entertainer, played by Brenda Joyce, working in a Piccadilly nightclub was to have featured a number of Britishers, including comedian Vic Oliver, Jack Hylton and His Orchestra, and singer Ray Noble, but none were in the film as released. *Thumbs Up* did provide employment for a handful of Britishers in Hollywood, notably Elsa Lanchester, Queenie Leonard, Molly Lamont (born in South Africa), and André Charlot as a theatrical entrepreneur. The latter casting is an example of art imitating life in that Charlot had been responsible for various theatrical revues first in Paris and later in London. He came to America in 1937 and his career took a rapid decline, with a couple of stage productions in Hollywood, *The Charlot Revue of 1940* and *Charlot's Revuette* in 1941 before a career on screen from 1942 through 1956, which consisted of little more than "bit" parts and extra work.[4]

Herbert Wilcox and Anna Neagle were both under contract to RKO when war broke out, and they asked to be released from that contract and returned to Britain, where Wilcox directed his wife in two films for RKO. In *They Flew Alone/Wings and the Woman*, shot in the fall of 1942, Neagle plays pioneering British aviatrix Amy Johnson. *Yellow Canary*, filmed in the spring of 1944 from a script by American DeWitt Bodeen, is a contemporary wartime drama.

There were two further RKO British productions released in 1945 at war's end. Based on a novel by Eric Ambler, *Hotel Reserve* is set in France in 1938, stars James Mason and Lucie Mannheim, and has a trio of directors: Victor Hanbury, Lance Comfort, and Max Greene. *Great Day* is a tribute to the British women's institutes, stars Flora Robson, and is directed by Lance Comfort.

The quota restriction was revised in 1938 and suspended in October 1942, although it had little relevance in terms of US involvement in British films at that time. As discussed in Chapter Seven, the Cinematograph Films Act of 1938 had lead to a number of first-class American-financed films being produced in Britain. However, in 1942, the war was more of a deterrent to American-sponsored film production than any suspension of any government restriction could counter.

The one major exception is *Way to the Stars*, a Two Cities Films production shot early in 1945 that might be defined as a British film but was made with the cooperation of both the British and American air forces. Anthony Asquith directs, with a screenplay by Terence Rattigan, based on an original story by Rattigan and American Richard Sherman. The cast includes Michael Redgrave, John Mills, Trevor Howard, and, as the American airman, Douglass Montgomery, who was at that time serving with the Canadian Air Force, his father being Canadian. As Jeffrey Richards has perceptively commented, the film's aim is to demonstrate that "what links Britain and America in the end is shared sacrifice."[5]

Way to the Stars was voted the most popular film of World War II by readers of the British right-wing newspaper the *Daily Mail*. It was released in the United States under the title of *Johnny in the Clouds*, the title of the poem that serves as a moving epilogue to the film, read by Michael Redgrave. The US release by United Artists was not particularly successful. It opened at New York's Winter Garden Theatre, replacing another British

New York-born Bonar Colleano specialized in playing GIs in British films of the 1940s, with his first success being in *Way to the Stars* (1945).

film, *Blithe Spirit*, on November 15, 1948. Bosley Crowther commented in the *New York Times* (November 18, 1945), "Douglass Montgomery jumps around a bit too coyly as the American pilot who moves in and other American parts are played too fliply, but we'll overlook them."

On a much more formal level, the British and US governments combined to support production of *The True Glory*, a compilation of newsreel footage assembled by the British Carol Reed and the American Garson Kanin, showing the invasion of the European mainland from D-Day to V-E Day. Described as "conceived by Gen. Dwight D. Eisenhower as the full film record of the European war," *The True Glory* opened in New York on September 7, 1945, as a Columbia release, and went on to win the Academy Award for Best Documentary Feature.

The anti-Nazi feature, *Freedom Radio*, starring Diana Wynyard and Clive Brook, was produced by Columbia Pictures in England in 1940 (released in 1941). Its young ingénue, Joyce Howard, was offered a seven-year Hollywood contract by the studio, but her response was, "No, no, no . . . the war had just started and I wasn't going to go to Hollywood. . . . Leave all my chums, so many of them off to the front, no way."[6]

Columbia Pictures was more aware it seems than British studios in recognizing the potential that some British talent had in wartime. It signed Vera Lynn, the most popular of all entertainers during World War II, known as "The Forces Sweetheart," and she appeared in three Columbia productions, shot at the Riverside Studios at Hammersmith in North London: *We'll Meet Again* (1942), *Rhythm Serenade* (1943), and *One Exciting Night* (1944, and released in the US as *You Can't Do Without Love*). *We'll Meet Again* takes its title from the 1939 song, made famous by Lynn, and one of the great songs of World War II. Lynn's recording is also used over the final scene of Stanley Kubrick's British-produced 1964 film, *Dr. Strangelove or: How I Learned to Stop Worrying and Love the Bomb*.

Columbia also signed the best known British screen comedian of the period, George Formby[7] (who also co-produced the first two of the Vera Lynn films), and it is something of a culture shock to watch one of Formby's Columbia films with its glossy Hollywood logo rather than a drab British opening credit card. Either Columbia did not understand that Formby was basically a comedian and ukulele-playing singer and not a typical leading man or Formby had pretentions that he was a sex symbol. In *I Didn't Do It*, released June 1945, for the most contrived reason, he removes his shirt and keeps it off for much too long, revealing a very white and very flabby chest that cannot have been appealing to any female member of the audience. The film involves a murder mystery and lacks sufficient musical numbers, although it does provide Ian Fleming (no relation to the author) with the opportunity to demonstrate his talent as a police inspector of gravitas despite the comic mayhem surrounding him.

Suprisingly perhaps, George Formby did have some reputation in the United States. He was the subject of a feature article in the *New York Times* in 1940, in which it was noted that

> although he has headed the poll as the best British star for the past two years, Formby is no Gable or Boyer. His is a face which combines the less attractive features of a discouraged horse and a friendly cow, and whose outstanding characteristics are a merry eye, a rumpled head of hair and prominent teeth.[8]

The piece coincided with the American premiere, on December 9, 1940, of his latest film, *It's in the Air*, at New York's Little Carnegie Playhouse. It was the second Formby film to be released (by B.S.B. Corp.) in the United States, preceded by *Let George Do It* (released in 1940 by Film Alliance of the US, and reissued in 1942 under the title of *To Hell with Hitler*). In his review in the *New York Times* (December 10, 1940), Bosley Crowther wrote, "Americans . . . who delight in the antics of, say, Joe E. Brown or possibly Laurel and Hardy, will undoubtedly find it enjoyable." The comparison is more than a little odd in that the cited comedians do not sing or play the ukulele and might well be considered positively sophisticated in comparison to Formby.

It is ironic that because of America's neutral stance in World War II prior to December 1941, and Pearl Harbor, there was no reason why American-produced British films might not be shown in Nazi-occupied Europe. It is certainly true that one Warner Bros.-British production, *They Drive by Night*, shot at Teddington (which the Nazis were later to destroy) was released both in the Netherlands and Norway in August 1941, despite the Nazi takeover of the former in May 1940 and the latter in April of the same year.[9]

During World War II, the British did relatively well in the Academy Award stakes. In 1941, there were special awards to the National Film Board of Canada for its documentary *Churchill's Island* and to the British Ministry of Information "for its vivid and dramatic presentation of the heroism of the R.A.F. in the documentary film, *Target for Tonight*." In 1942, MGM's sentimental, patriotic but generally patronizing effort, *Mrs. Miniver*, was named Best Picture, William Wyler won for Best Director, Arthur Wimperis, George Froeschel, James Hilton, and Claudine West won for Best Written Screenplay, and its star Greer Garson was named Best Actress. In addition, Noel Coward received a special Academy Award "for his outstanding production achievement, *In Which We Serve*." The following year, the British Ministry of Information production, *Desert Victory*, was named Best Documentary Feature.

Despite bombing raids, despite shortages in various areas, and even despite a considerable number of actors and technicians being unavailable because of active military service, the British film industry had a good war. The government took over a considerable number of studios—Amalgamated, Imperial, and Associated British—and others were unavailable. The number of films actually produced decreased, from 103 in 1939 to as few as forty-six in 1942. But there were no more quota quickies, and, as Peter Noble commented, "conversely with the decrease in the number of films there has been a notable and inspiring increase in the general caliber and standard of the home 'product' during the war years. The British film has achieved a stature as never before and it is safe to submit that the wartime years witnessed a reorientation in our film industry, leading to a situation where British films are now rapidly taking their place alongside the finest of the world's movies."[10]

Among the British films that were well received in the United States were the Boulting brothers' *Pastor Hall* (to which Eleanor Roosevelt provided a foreword for the American release), Alexander Korda's *The Thief of Bagdad*, Laurence Olivier's *Henry V*, and Michael Powell and Emeric Pressburger's *One of Our Aircraft Is Missing*, *The Life and Death of Colonel Blimp*, and *A Canterbury Tale*. One of the three modern pilgrims, if they may be so described, in the last film is an American sergeant, John Sweet, playing the role of the fictional US sergeant Bob Johnson. Burgess Meredith had originally been considered for the part, but Michael Powell saw Sweet acting in an amateur production and selected him to play the sergeant who must deal with various Anglo-American differences, as well as give veracity to what is, in all truth, a rather silly plot. Sweet made no other film appearances and returned to America and life as a teacher, dying in North Carolina in 2011 at the age of ninety-five. Remarkably for the time, he donated his salary for the film to the NAACP.

Variety (May 31, 1944) was heavy in its praise of Sweet, noting,

> By far the best role in a well-nigh perfect cast is filled by Sgt. John Sweet, borrowed from US Army. Facing the camera for the first time, he frankly does nothing more than play himself. His reactions to English customs are guaranteed to give British audiences a real bang, just as there are millions of laughs for the GI's who have been up against all the things experienced by the Yank on the screen. In civil life, Sweet is an Ohio school teacher. He has all the earmarks of a find, reminding one of the late Will Rogers.

For the US release of *A Canterbury Tale*, additional footage was shot of Kim Hunter, playing Johnson's girlfriend. She was already in England, about to appear in *A Matter of Life and Death/Stairway to Heaven*, also for Powell and Pressburger.

One British film that was too good for American consumption, or at least whose storyline was too good for a British film that was to be released in the United States, is *Gaslight*, which Thorold Dickinson directed for British National Films in 1940. The film is based on the Victorian thriller by Patrick

Ann Dvorak and Leslie Fenton return to Hollywood after their March 1932 wedding in Yuma, Arizona.

Hamilton, whose correct title is *Gas Light*, which had a successful season on the London stage in 1939. Columbia Pictures bought the film for American release in 1942 under a new title, *A Strange Case of Murder*. In the meantime, the play had opened on Broadway in December 1941 (and was to run through December 1944) under the title of *Angel Street*, with Vincent Price as the villainous husband. MGM acquired the film rights and produced its own version in 1944, with George Cukor directing and Ingrid Bergman and Charles Boyer replacing the original stars of the British version, Diana Wynyard and Anton Walbrook. The film is important as the first featuring

British actress Angela Lansbury at the start of a seven-year contract with MGM. The British version was eventually released in the United States by Commercial Pictures, Inc., in 1953 under the title of *Angel Street.*

MGM had decreed that the negative and all existing prints of the British version be destroyed, but before this happened Dickinson and editor Sidney Cole made a 35mm print which was deposited at the British Film Institute. At the time, critic C. A. Lejeune fumed in *Cine-Technician* (January-April 1940),

> We know that if we make bad pictures in this country the Americans don't want them—even our own countrymen are not very keen on bad English pictures. Perhaps even less do the Americans want *good* British pictures. Since when has a powerful industry encouraged foreign competition.

Luckily, the British version has survived and been restored, and very obviously it is superior to the American version, with a slightly variant storyline. Diana Wynyard's performance is beyond reproach and there is something delightfully evil in the manner in which Anton Walbrook pronounces her character's name, "Bella."

A small and noble group of Americans experienced the war on a personal level, staying in Britain throughout the blitz. A couple are very well-known for their participation in the war effort, while others have received little praise or thanks. Ironically, one British screen star who might have enhanced her somewhat soiled reputation by returning to Britain at the outbreak of World War II is Lilian Harvey, London-born and one of Nazi Germany's top stars (and a very pleasing one) throughout the 1930s. Instead, she moved in 1939 to the south of France and then immigrated for the remainder of the war to the United States (where she had made four films released between 1933 and 1935).

New York-born actress Ann Dvorak (pronounced "Vorzhahk") first came to Britain in August 1932 in the midst of a contract dispute with Warner Bros. She had gone on strike demanding higher wages. Dvorak made known that she wished to appear in British films, but Warner Bros. was successful in preventing her so doing, and in October 1932, the actress returned to America with the promise of a pay raise and elevation to stardom. With her innocent brown eyes, hinting of a temper, Dvorak had specialized in playing suffering, hard-luck women, and was a well-liked actress at the studio. On March 17, 1932, she married British actor Leslie Fenton, who was also working at Warner Bros. and was anxious to become a director. The couple enjoyed a life at sea, and, when Britain declared war on Germany, it was natural for Fenton to apply for a commission with the Royal Navy.

On December 14, 1940, Dvorak followed him to England, sailing on the American Export liner *Exeter*. She threw herself into war work, initially enlisting in the MTC (the Mechanized Transport Corps) and driving an ambulance. Later, she helped put on Red Cross and USO shows (after America had entered the war). She also starred in three feature films and one short subject in Britain. Two, released in 1943, were directed by Lance Comfort and produced by William Sistrom for RKO, *Squadron Leader X* and *Escape to Danger*. While she was working on the latter, Dvorak's London apartment was bombed. In the thirty-minute short subject, *There's a Future in It*, the actress was directed by her husband, playing a woman in love with a bomber pilot. The first of the feature films, *This Was Paris*, was released in January 1942, and co-starred Ben Lyon. Utilizing footage of the German invasion of France and the seizure of Paris, the film's female lead is certainly Dvorak, but Lyon does little as an American newspaperman and the real male star is Griffith Jones, as a British Intelligence officer. *This Was Paris* was not well received, with *The Hollywood Reporter* (March 4, 1942) describing it as "confused" and *Daily Variety* (March 4, 1932) calling it "uninspiring."

Leslie Fenton was injured in the March 1942 commando raid on the Nazi submarine base at St. Nazaire and eventually invalided out of the service. The couple returned to America in 1944, and that same year they were divorced. "Put it down to a war casualty," the actress told Louella Parsons. "We just couldn't get along and our unhappiness started in England while we were working on the war effort there."[11]

Bessie Love, whose career embraced starring roles in both American silent and sound films (including *The Broadway Melody)*, had first come to England in 1934 with her husband, William Hawks, a theatrical agent and brother of director Howard, whom she had married in 1929. When it came time to divorce him, she returned to England a few months later, along with her mother and her daughter, Patricia. When the war broke out, she was determined to help, but finding little interest in her as an actress (or, for that matter, an ambulance driver), she appeared in only a couple of films, *Atlantic Ferry/Sons of the Sea* (1941) and the short subject *London Scrapbook* (1942). She next contacted Michael Balcon asking for work, and he hired her as a continuity girl (or script girl) on *San Demetrio, London* (1943), a true drama of the Merchant Navy. Love subsequently returned to acting, both on stage and screen, but never on a level of fame she had known in Hollywood and on a very spasmodic basis.

Constance Cummings and husband Benn Levy return to America from England on board the *Queen Mary*, March 22, 1937.

It was not divorce that drove (though she came willingly) Constance Cummings to Britain, but marriage. A contract star at Columbia in the early 1930s and Harold Lloyd's leading lady in *Movie Crazy* (1932), one of the comedian's best sound films, Cummings first came to England in 1933 after Columbia had failed legally to prove she was still under contract. Accompanying her was British playwright Benn Levy, whom Cummings married on June 27 of that year. On that visit, aside from the marriage,

Bessie Love and her husband William Hawks return from Europe to New York on the *Berengaria* in November 1934.

Cummings starred in two films, *Heads We Go*, released in July 1933, and *Channel Crossing*, released in October of that year.

Cummings was well-liked by both her colleagues and the British public, and she was obviously most amenable as far as promotional efforts were concerned. From March 3, 1933, through April 7, 1933, the actress wrote in *Film Weekly* of her work on *Heads We Go*, comparing its director Monty Banks to Warner Bros. contract director Archie Mayo. It is not surprising that in 1937, Robert Donat described Cummings as "an American guest—of whom we should be so proud that nothing should ever be permitted to tempt her out of England."[12]

She was back in Britain in 1936, starring in *Seven Sinners* and *Strangers on a Honeymoon*, both directed by Albert de Courville. In *Seven Sinners*, her leading man is Edmund Lowe, and the sparking, witty dialogue between the two, written by Sidney Gilliat and Frank Launder, makes them a perfect pair. The comparison between *Seven Sinners* and Hitchcock's *The Lady Vanishes* two years later, and also written by Gilliat and Launder, is startling. Hitchcock seems to try to build upon what the previous film has accomplished and does not particularly succeed. Further, the special effects, while antiquated by today's standards, are equally impressive—there is even an actual shot of a train crashing into a lorry.

Both *Seven Sinners* and *Strangers on a Honeymoon* were filmed at the Shepherd's Bush studios in a working-class area of West London. As Cummings recalled, "I remember how surprised I was when I went to Shepherd's Bush. I thought this was going to be a lovely place out in the country."[13]

Constance Cummings appeared as Mrs. Chips on stage in London, opposite Leslie Banks, in October 1938.

In March 1938, Cummings and Benn Levy returned to London, which was now their permanent home. When war was declared, there was no consideration that the actress might leave her husband in England and return to the safety of the United States. She was in Britain to stay. "It wasn't intentional," she asserted.

There were plays galore and a handful of films. "If I was doing a play with an English cast," remembered Cummings, "then I found I must get rid of my American accent to a certain extent. I never got completely rid of it. For the films, it never mattered so much. I don't know if I had some lessons or help, but I did soften it a bit. Early on I went to the Old Vic [1939]. And I did *Saint Joan*. Her accent would have been Hertfordshire or something like that. My American accent didn't matter so much."

During the war, the actress starred in three British films, *This England* (1940), *The Foreman Went to France/Somewhere in France* (1941), and *Blithe Spirit* (1944). An episodic, patriotic film, *This England* features Cummings in each episode of the story from 1086 through 1940. *The Foreman Went to France* has Cummings playing opposite British music-hall comedian Tommy Trinder, with Cornwall standing in for France. Despite its somewhat mundane title, the film, released in America by United Artists, boasts a score by William Walton and superior direction by Alberto Cavalcanti. Cummings had great admiration for her leading man and she and Benn Levy were big fans of the British music hall:

> We used to go and see Music Hall comics. I have great admiration for somebody who can stand up for twenty minutes all by himself or herself and keep the audience in fits of laughter. That's more difficult to do than do any part in a play.

Noel Coward's *Blithe Spirit* may have a cast including Rex Harrison, Kay Hammond, and Constance Cummings, but it is dominated by Margaret Rutherford as Madame Arcati, the spiritualist medium:

> She really was a character. She really was Madame Arcati. Everything would be set up and you'd be ready to take a shot and you'd say, "Where's Margaret?" And you'd find Margaret in her little dressing room on the set eating some sandwiches. She was a genuine eccentric and, of course, a very talented actress. I think she didn't know how eccentric she was. She played it straight. She was married to Stringer Davis, and he was very sweet to her. He treated her rather like a lovely Dresden thing. He looked out for

> her. I remember once, we were out shooting, and he said, "This is Queen's weather. Margaret very often has Queen's weather." I think she might have wandered off at a tangent if left to herself. He was very much like a gallant, like a nanny. She liked him there.

There were nine films after the war, the best of which is *The Battle of the Sexes* (1959), in which Cummings demonstrates her sense of comedy opposite Peter Sellers. She is the formidable American executive practicing time and motion study on an Edinburgh-based company of kilt makers, with Sellers as the chief accountant, very much set in his ways. The couple is so good together that they even eclipse the impressive Edinburgh scenery.

The films pale somewhat in comparison to Constance Cummings's later stage career, with the highlights in that medium being *Long Day's Journey into Night*, opposite Laurence Olivier, on the London stage in 1972, and Arthur Kopit's *Wings*, in New York and London in 1978, 1979, and 1983.

To her husband, she was always "Cummings," but to her friends, she was "Connie," and what a delightful, unassuming actress she was. When one arrived at the Old Church Street home in Chelsea, designed in 1936 for her and Benn Levy by Walter Gropius, and at the time the height of modernity, Connie would often fling open the window on the third level, where the living room and dining area were, shout a hello, and throw down the key. I have even known her to be standing at the ironing board, working away, when one arrived, oblivious to her attire or fame as both a Hollywood and a major British theatrical star. "From the moment I arrived here, I felt at home," she once said, and that is exactly how she made visitors feel.

The most famous American entertainers in Britain during World War II are Bebe Daniels and Ben Lyon, both of whom had been major Hollywood stars in both the silent and sound eras and had married in 1930. Bebe and Ben first came to England in 1933, with Bebe starring in the sophisticated musical comedy, *The Song You Gave Me*, for British International Pictures. Paul Stein directed, and Bebe's leading man was Hungarian-born Victor Varconi. She also starred in the far less sophisticated and more modest, *A Southern Maid*, co-starring British musical comedy star Harry Welchman. At this time, Ben appeared in *I Spy*, with American leading lady Sally Eilers. In 1936, both Bebe and Ben came to Britain, as a result of a kidnapping threat against their daughter, Barbara, and starred at the London Palladium. They stayed on and toured British music halls, and appeared together on screen in *Not Wanted on Voyage*, released in February 1938. Bebe also starred in *The Return of Carol Deane* (1938), and Ben appeared in *Mad about*

Money/He Loved an Actress (1938)—a piece of incredible mediocrity despite the presence also of Harry Langdon and Lupe Velez—*I Killed the Count* (1939), and *Confidential Lady* (1939).

In the summer of 1939, the couple returned briefly to America to find a safe haven for daughter Barbara and adopted son Richard, and then came back to Britain. "We accepted what England had to offer us in good times," they explained to me, "and so we think we should not run out when there is trouble."[14] Bebe and Ben were appearing live on stage in Blackpool on September 1, 1939, when war was declared. In response, Ben had a special visiting card printed, reading, "Mr. Ben Lyon Friendly Alien," and the two set about creating a radio variety show for the BBC. *Hi Gang!*, first broadcast on Sunday, May 26, 1940, ran for fifty-two weeks; a second series began on November 9, 1941, and ran for twenty-six weeks, and, postwar, there was an attempt at a third series, titled *Hi Gang 1949*, which ran from February through August of that year.

Hi Gang! was one of the most popular radio programs of the war, with Bebe and Ben joined by comic Vic Oliver,[15] as well as occasional visiting Hollywood stars. A film version was released in December 1941.

For Bebe and Ben, war in Britain was not without its personal trauma. The couple built an air-raid shelter in the basement of their longtime home at 18 Southwick Street, near Marble Arch. When they tried to visit America to see their children, there were problems in that they were told their passports would be seized by the American authorities and they would not be allowed to return. Bombing raids would disrupt the broadcast, and the couple might have to sleep at the studio. Their friend Arthur Woods, who had directed Bebe in *The Return of Carol Deane* and Ben in *Confidential Lady*, had joined the RAF and he was killed in action.

After America's entry into the war, Ben Lyon was appointed a lieutenant colonel in the army air force, and he and Bebe created American Overseas Artists to entertain the troops and broadcast the radio program, *The Stars and Stripes*. Bebe was the first female civilian to land in Normandy after D-Day and was awarded the Medal of Freedom for service under fire. As Ben recalled,

> She went over and recorded the American wounded, showing the speed and efficiency of the chain of evacuation. How a man could be wounded in Normandy in the morning, and be in hospital in England in the afternoon. It gave great comfort to mothers and fathers and sweethearts back in America. Later in Italy, she recorded the British wounded as well as Americans down there.[16]

Bebe Daniels and Ben Lyon.

The couple still found time to entertain, with both starring in *Gangway* at the London Palladium, which ran from December 1941 through December 1942, and Bebe starring in *Panama Hattie* from June 1943 through June 1944 (the show was revived from January through April 1945).

Their war service to Britain is incredible. And it is small wonder that even today, long after their deaths, they are held in high esteem. They did return to American in the 1940s, but were never completely happy there and returned to London in 1949. With their children, they created the radio series, *Life with the Lyons*, which ran from 1950–61, followed by a television series in 1957 and 1961. It spawned two feature films, *Life with the Lyons* and *The Lyons in Paris*, both released in 1954. Bebe Daniels died in London in March 1971. Ben Lyon returned to the United States, where he married former silent leading lady Marion Nixon. He returned to Britain for a visit in December 1975 and told me how saddened he was at what was happening to the country, how offensive was the racism he found against Asian immigrants, and how dirty everyone looked. The English, he told me, needed "a kick in the ass." Ben died almost exactly eight years after Bebe, in March 1979.

Adelaide Hall.

The other American couple in Britain throughout the war, Adelaide Hall and Elisabeth Welch, were not related, except by the color of their skin—both were African Americans—and both worked with Bebe Daniels and Ben Lyon on American Overseas Artists entertaining African American troops, with a reported 3,000 at some concerts. In addition, they were members of the British organization, ENSA (Entertainments National Service Association) and appeared throughout Europe, unlike with the American organization, in non-segregated shows. Had they been captured by the Germans or if the Nazis had invaded Britain, the two women would have been as much in danger as any Jewish-born individual.

Born in Brooklyn, Adelaide Hall made her professional debut in 1921 in *Shuffle Along* and also embarked on a career as a nightclub entertainer. The songs most associated with her are "Creole Love Call," which she introduced with Duke Ellington and His Orchestra in 1927, and "I Can't Give You Anything But Love" from *Blackbirds of 1928*. With her husband, Bert

Elisabeth Welch.

Hicks, Hall came to London, via Paris, in 1938, and consolidated her career as a leading African American entertainer. In September 1940, she was appearing at the Lewisham Hippodrome in South London when an air raid started. Rather than have the audience leave the theatre and possibly endanger themselves, Hall kept on singing, ending when the "all clear" sounded at 3:45 a.m., after performing fifty-four songs.

Hall's film career is practically nonexistent. She has one song, "Be Still, My Heart," in *The Thief of Bagdad* (1940) and sang "Shame, What a Shame" in *Night and the City* (1950), but the number was cut from the production. In 1989, a record of her in concert was filmed under the title of *Sophisticated Lady*. Hall died in London in November 1993 at the age of ninety-two.

Elisabeth Welch's film career is more substantial and more important. She was born in Manhattan and made her stage debut in 1922. Along with Adelaide Hall, she appeared in *Runnin' Wild* (1922) and was also in *Blackbirds of 1928*. In *Runnin' Wild*, Welch introduced, singing but not dancing, the "Charleston." In January 1931, Welch was selected by Cole Porter to sing "Love for Sale" in the revue *The New Yorkers*. Porter wrote a second song for her, "Solomon," introduced in London at the start of Welch's British career in 1933. Welch had great admiration and affection for Porter and for Britain's Ivor Novello, who featured her in *Glamorous Night* (1935) and *Arc de Triomphe* (1943).

In 1934, Welch made her screen debut in *Death at Broadcasting House*, appearing as herself and singing "Lazy Lady." "I always say they should have left all the other words out and just called it *Death*," she remarked.[17] In all, Welch appeared in nineteen British films, often as herself or as a nightclub singer, and was also the subject of a 1987 documentary, *Keeping Love Alive*. Derek Jarman featured her singing "Stormy Weather," which she had introduced to Britain in 1933, in his 1979 version of *The Tempest*. Her most important films are the two, *Song of Freedom* (1936) and *Big Fella* (1937), in which she is Paul Robeson's leading lady.

"A lovely man," she recalled. "We discussed politics naturally. But I'm not politically minded, although I follow. And I have my own theories. He said, you've got to be a citizen of the world because of this [pointing at the color of her skin]. I said, 'I've got so many bloods in me, I'm part of the world. I don't stand up for one or the other. Only for what's right. For decency.' He wanted to convert me [to Communism] but he was very gentle about it. I'll take anybody's arguments if they have a sense of humor with it. Paul didn't have a reputation for being difficult. It was later on. There were no lines he objected to in *Song of Freedom*."

Claiming to be half-Scottish, Welch saw no reason to take out British citizenship. "Once I'd made England my home, I'm not a mover. I didn't intend to stay there." She pointed out that there was less inclination in England to note the color of one's skin. "I was brought up in a mixed neighborhood, Sixty-third Street and Amsterdam Avenue. That was primarily Irish, secondly Italian, thirdly Negro, and then the mixes of all the other European countries. I'd always gone to a mixed school."

In later years, Elisabeth Welch's accent became decidedly upper-class British. Indeed, she sounded, and sometimes acted, much like the Queen Mother. She died in July 2003 at the age of ninety-nine.

While Americans in Britain were doing their part for the war effort, the British in Hollywood found themselves in a quandary. What to do, what not to do? Whether to stay or to return? The British Ambassador in Washington, D.C., advised that they stay in the comfort and security of Los Angeles, Bel Air, and Beverly Hills and do their "bit" for their country 6,000 safe miles

Lady Hamilton/That Hamilton Woman (1941), with Vivien Leigh and Laurence Olivier.

away. Some, including David Niven and Laurence Olivier, determined to return home as soon as contractually possible. Others pointed out that they were no longer British citizens, and had no obligation to the motherland. Herbert Wilcox and Anna Neagle returned to England. Alexander Korda and his wife, Merle Oberon, remained, although Korda did produce the patriotic film, *Lady Hamilton/That Hamilton Woman*, in which Olivier, as Lord Nelson, makes a speech of such magnificence that it has been suggested it was written by Winston Churchill. The latter and President Roosevelt viewed the film together one evening after dinner while in Newfoundland working on the Atlantic Charter. Alfred Hitchcock, who was too old to serve in the military, remained, and produced *Foreign Correspondent*, which also features a patriotic speech delivered by Joel McCrea.

The British colony was very much aware of negative publicity in England, particularly a May 1940 comment by distinguished actor Sir Seymour Hicks that Alfred Hitchcock, Charles Laughton, and Herbert Marshall star in a film titled *Gone with the Wind Up*. All three men, of course, were unfit for military service, most notably Marshall, with his wooden leg.

In August 1940, the *Los Angeles Times* printed a lengthy story in which producer Michael Balcon branded British actors and directors in Hollywood as "deserters" and "war profiteers." His most virulent comment was directed towards one director, easily identifiable as Alfred Hitchcock:

> I had a plump young junior technician in my studio whom I promoted from department to department. . . . Today he is one of our most famous directors and he is in Hollywood while we who are left behind short-handed are trying to harness the films to our great national effort.
>
> Some time ago this man is reported to have made an astonishing statement in an interview. He said he was anxious to come back to England and he sent his wife back to see what was doing in the film business. But after getting her report he decided to stay in Hollywood.
>
> According to the newspapers, this lady "saw one of the leading production companies which said it couldn't even offer our former salaries". . . . When you're called up for the army, navy or air force can you refuse because the pay isn't good enough?[18]

Another director whom Balcon might well have criticized was Robert Stevenson, who, along with his actress-wife Anna Lee, came to America in August 1939, like Hitchcock, at the invitation of producer David O. Selznick. Lee maintained that her husband was a pacifist and refused to return to his homeland. She did not agree with his views, and she was not particularly happy in Los Angeles. "I thought it a very plastic place and I certainly didn't want to work there," she told me. The actress visited the British Consul General but was told that no women with small children—the couple had daughter Venetia with them—were currently permitted to cross the Atlantic. She journeyed to Canada and tried, without success, to join the Red Cross. Eventually, Lee remained in America, and did her "bit" by joining the USO. She also had success with her third American production, *How Green Was My Valley*, produced in 1941, which secured her lasting acclaim.[19] There were some "dry" years in regard to her American career, but Lee's fame increased

Anna Lee at the height of her British film career in the mid-1930s.

and was assured with her long-term engagement as Lila Quartermaine in the ABC daytime soap opera, *General Hospital*, from 1978 through 2003, a year before her death.

Robert Stevenson, from whom Anna Lee was later divorced, became a highly successful Hollywood director, responsible for *Jane Eyre* (1944, with a young Elizabeth Taylor appearing as a friend of Jane Eyre at the film's beginning), and from 1956 onwards was associated with Walt Disney, directing two of the producer's best-known English-oriented films, *Mary Poppins* (1964) and *Bedknobs and Broomsticks* (1971).

Sidney Bernstein, founder of the Granada cinema chain in Britain, had been appointed Films Advisor to the British Government in 1940. One of his first tasks was to find a narrator for the Crown Film Unit's tribute to the British civilian facing the blitz in *London Can Take It*. As the film was intended for an American audience, Bernstein determined that an American narrator was needed and he found one in Quentin Reynolds, a writer for *Collier's* magazine. In 1941, Bernstein brought the film to America and was able to arrange its screening at some 12,000 theatres to an estimated audience of sixty million. In Hollywood, he met with Louis B. Mayer, who told him of plans for *Mrs. Miniver* and insisted on acting out the entire story after lunch, "taking first one part and then another, bustling from side to side, his round face rather raccoon-like creased into expressions of disdain, anguish or fear."[20] Bernstein urged that the film be made in Britain, but apparently Greer Garson refused to return to her homeland during the war. He also met with Charlie Chaplin and asked that, as part of the war effort, the comedian allow *The Great Dictator* to be shown to British forces in the Middle East on 16mm projectors. Chaplin refused, even after being offered the possibility of frozen currency in Britain being released to him. Bernstein was able to arrange that a limited number of British war propaganda films be released in the United States, beginning with *The 49th Parallel* (1942) under the American title of *The Invaders*. The plot concerns a German U-boat sinking off Canada's Hudson Bay and a group of Nazi sailors coming ashore, and the cast, under the direction of Michael Powell, includes Laurence Olivier, Leslie Howard, Anton Walbrook, Raymond Massey (a Canadian for the first time playing a Canadian), and a teenage Glyns Johns (who much later was to enjoy a career in Hollywood). As has been pointed out, none of the film actually takes place on the 49th parallel.

The attack by Michael Balcon on Alfred Hitchcock and his patriotism is totally without foundation or fact. Obviously, he was both too old and physically unsuited to the military. Unknown to his colleagues, he had also been recruited by Sidney Bernstein to work on British propaganda. In December 1943, the director returned to his country of birth and teamed up with screenwriter Angus MacPhail to make a short tribute to the French Resistance movement, titled *Bon Voyage*. A second Hitchcock short subject with a French theme was *Aventure Malgache* (1944), concerning the resistance movement on the French island of Madagascar. Returning to America, Hitchcock worked on three propaganda films, *The Fighting Generation* (1945), *Watchtower over Tomorrow* (1945), and a feature film on the Holocaust, *Memory of the Camps*, which was not publicly seen until 1984.

Ultimately, the best the British colony in Hollywood could do (again, without Chaplin's support) was to produce a patriotic film, *Forever and a Day*, released in America by RKO in March 1943. It is the story of a London home from the 1800s through the war, as seen through the eyes of an American reporter, played by Kent Smith. Cedric Hardwicke came up with the original idea—which is far from original—and it was developed by a group of celebrity British writers, including Charles Bennett, C. S. Forester, James Hilton, Christopher Isherwood, Frederick Lonsdale, R. C. Sheriff, and John Van Druten. Aside from René Clair, supposedly replacing Alfred Hitchcock, the directors handling various assigned scenes were all British: Edmund Goulding, Frank Lloyd, Victor Saville, Robert Stevenson, and Herbert Wilcox. The British colony provided the cast—both stars and "bit" players—including Brian Aherne, Nigel Bruce, Isobel Elsom, Patric Knowles, Elsa Lanchester, Charles Laughton, Anna Lee, Ida Lupino, Herbert Marshall, Jessie Mathews, Anna Neagle, C. Aubrey Smith, Dame May Whitty, and Roland Young.

None of the British contingent was paid, RKO made no profit on the distribution, and all profits went to various British and American charities. Michael Balcon was quick to point out that British Red Cross and others needed funds urgently, not at some time in the future when the profits were distributed: "These isolationists are being allowed to accumulate fortunes without sharing in any way the hardships which their fellow Britons endure gladly for our cause."[21]

In Hollywood, Britain's Ronald Colman read Edna St. Vincent Millay's "Poem & Prayer for an Invading Army" as part of NBC's twenty-four-hour D-Day broadcast of Tuesday, June 6, 1944.

The one group of Hollywood films that impresses and strangely moves one most, when viewed as a tribute to the British at war, is the Sherlock Holmes series, starring Basil Rathbone and Nigel Bruce, made quite cheaply at Universal between 1942 and 1946, beginning with *Sherlock Holmes and the Voice of Terror* and ending with *Dressed to Kill*. Rathbone and Bruce had already played Holmes and Dr. Watson in two 20th Century-Fox features, *The Hound of the Baskervilles* and *The Adventures of Sherlock Holmes*, both released in 1939. They were good, solidly constructed period pieces, and there was little to suggest that the actors might be called back for further films. But they were, not at 20th Century-Fox but at Universal, where the notion was to base the productions on the original stories by Sir Arthur Conan Doyle but to place them in the present, as Britain waged war with Germany.

Nigel Bruce and Basil Rathbone as Dr. Watson and Sherlock Holmes.

There were anachronisms galore, and often the screenwriters displayed an appalling lack of knowledge of the country in which the stories were set. Why Rathbone and Bruce never spoke up and pointed out such errors one will never know. The worst of the series is undoubtedly *Terror by Night* (1946), which smacks of cheapness and is primarily set on a train traveling between London and Edinburgh, a train it must be noted that leaves from the wrong London station and passes incorrect process plate scenery. Alan Mowbray is as good as always as the villain, but adding to the film's failings is leading lady Renee Godfrey, who appears to have no idea how to act convincingly.

The best of the series is the first, thanks to an incredibly moving speech at its conclusion, a speech lifted in its entirety from the story, "His Last Bow." Holmes and Watson are standing on a cliff looking out over the English Channel.

Holmes: "There's an east wind coming, Watson."

Watson: "No, I don't think so. Looks like another warm day."

Holmes: "Good old Watson—the one fixed point in a changing age. There's an east wind blowing all the same, such a wind as never blew on England yet. It will be cold and bitter, Watson, and a good many of us may wither before its blast. But it's God's own wind, nonetheless, and a greener, better, strong land will lie in the sunshine when the storm has cleared."

The speech works on many levels. It may be viewed as a veiled hint at Russian postwar expansion. (The film is co-scripted by Communist-leaning and Blacklisted John Bright.) More importantly, it suggests the Blitz, the bombings that are to come, and the wholesale destruction of working-class slums. It heralds a new post-Churchillian era, with a Labor government in power, the National Health Service about to come into existence, decent housing opportunities for the poor, an end to the old class system, and the start of a new democratic era. Of course, it never really happened the way Sherlock Holmes might have envisaged; after all, this is a Hollywood tale.

CHAPTER TWELVE

The Postwar Renaissance

THE POSTWAR ERA IN BRITAIN WAS BAD FOR THE BRITISH WITH SEVERE rationing, harsh weather conditions, and a far-from-triumphant return to peace and normalcy. The years were also initially bad for the American film industry in Britain. It was a period of confusing statistics and confusing legislation. British film production increased from twenty-four feature films in 1945 to forty-nine feature films in 1947. A new, grand period for British cinema was at hand. Historians generally agree that 1946 was the peak year for filmgoing in Britain with theatre admissions totally 121 million pounds.[1] The problem was that British cinemagoers, as in the 1930s, were more interested in seeing American films rather than British films on British screens.

The postwar British government was a Labor one, led by prime minister Clement Atlee. Winston Churchill may have fought the first battle of Britain during World War II, but Atlee fought a second battle against American filmmakers with film revenues on the front line. In August 1947, his government decreed that no more than 25 percent of box-office receipts from American films would be allowed to leave the country. In response, two days later, the Motion Picture Export Association of America announced that it would cease importing American films into the United Kingdom. The British government might be on the side of British producers and British financial interests, but the British public sided with America. It wanted American films and American stars.

The British government had the understandable notion that British theatre chains should show British films. The government was supported and encouraged in this by film magnate J. Arthur Rank, whose organization controlled Gaumont-British, Two Cities, Independent Producers, as well as the Denham and Pinewood Studios. The only major problem, perhaps unforeseen by the government or Rank, was not just the American response but also the issue of the major Odeon Theatres circuit being substantially owned by American distributor, United Artists. "We have reached a crisis," reported the British trade paper, *Kinematograph Weekly*, on October 2, 1947. "The result is a state of flux in the production industry, and a strong indication that this year's output will be very little in excess of 1946."

As a result of the American boycott, in March 1948, the British government basically capitulated. The Anglo-American Film Agreement, negotiated by future prime minister Harold Wilson in his capacity as president of the Board of Trade, allowed America to distribute 180 feature films in Britain and gave the producers the right to take out of the country $17 million of their earnings. Dated March 11, 1948, the British Board of Trade document with the long-winded title of *Memorandum of Agreement between His Majesty's Government in the United Kingdom of Great Britain and Northern Ireland and the Motion Picture Industry of the United States* divided US film rentals into remittable and non-remittable sterling.

As film historian Robert Murphy notes,

> In retrospect it appears an adroit settlement of what had developed into a futile and mutually harmful dispute. In view of the close political, military, and economic relations between Britain and America, an attempt to exclude American films permanently from the British market was unthinkable, especially as British film producers had revealed themselves as totally incapable of filling the vacuum which would exist if there were no more imports from Hollywood.[2]

What the British government also did in 1948 was to introduce a new quota system, under the Cinematograph Act of that year, requiring that 45 percent of films shown in British theatres should be British made. J. Arthur Rank did his part by informing 20th Century-Fox, RKO, Paramount, and United Artists, which had previously provided his theatre chains with over 100 films a year, that currently he had room on his release schedules for only twenty-five. Perhaps mindful of the manner in which British films in the 1930s had been relegated to the second half of a double bill on American screens, Rank offered to find space for additional films as the second half of a British film-dominated double bill.

If Alexander Korda, and to a lesser extent Herbert Wilcox, were the major British production figures involved in American cinema of the 1930s, it was J. Arthur Rank who dominated the 1940s. His trademark bodybuilder banging the gong at the start of a Rank film became a national symbol for British cinema. In 1945, Rank brought over to England David Hand, a top Disney animator who had been supervising director on *Snow White and the Seven Dwarfs* (1937) and *Bambi* (1941), and had him head an animation unit for a couple of years. As *Kinematograph Weekly* (April 5, 1945) reported,

> David Hand has already begun to supervise the production of cartoon-type films, both at the G.B. Instructional Studios in Soho Square and at G.B. Screen Services. There are at present about fifty artists at work, but Hand said that possibly he would have at least a hundred and fifty, with corresponding increase in other departments. "Artists are to be recruited from the Forces," he stated, "and this will be an all-British industry, providing jobs for hundreds of skilled men and women."
>
> As to the type of animated films to go into production, David Hand said that they would be medical, educational, instructional, industrial and comic, while a number would be made especially for children. In the latter category he is already co-operating with Mary Field. Children's cartoons would introduce new friends from the animal and human world, plus a story with a moral and the animations will include puppets as well as drawings. At the moment Mr. Hand is supervising a film dealing with sterility in cows, while a medical film dealing with plastic surgery and an historical film, containing a sequence dealing with Wat Tyler's rebellion, are other cartoons planned for early production.

They were ambitious plans, but even Hand's commercial films failed to find an audience in the United States, and in 1950, his studio was closed and Hand returned to America.

In an effort to become a worldwide distributor of British films, in 1944 Rank created Eagle-Lion Films, Inc., which was the parent company of the American PRC (Producers Releasing Corporation). In 1945, Rank began a relationship with International Pictures, which merged with Universal as Universal-International, and which distributed Rank's films in the United States.[3]

In June 1947, the five major US theatre chains guaranteed $10 million in bookings to J. Arthur Rank. As a result of this agreement, the trade paper *Variety* conducted a nationwide survey of American tastes vis-à-vis foreign films in general and British films in particular. Such films were successful in major metropolitan centers, such as New York, Los Angeles, San Francisco, and Boston, while "the midwest and south continue to be as much citadels of isolationism in their picture tastes as in their politics."[4] More than 50 percent of major New York theatres screened foreign films on a regular basis. In Chicago, "imported films are having a tough time catching on . . . except for the prestige British product,"[5] as exemplified by Laurence Olivier's *Henry V* (which ran for twenty-one weeks in the city). *Henry V* ran eight weeks in Pittsburgh, seven weeks in Cleveland, twenty-six weeks in Boston, and thirty-four weeks in San Francisco. Other British films noted in *Variety*'s survey are *Brief Encounter, Caesar and Cleopatra, A Matter of Life and Death/Stairway to Heaven*, and *The Seventh Veil*. At the same time, critical response to these films was not always totally positive; of *Caesar and Cleopatra*, for example, *Newsweek* (August 26, 1946) commented, "at its worst the film is a magnificent spectacle, at its best it leaves you wishing it were better." In the 1920s and 1930s, British films had often been relegated to "art-house" screenings in the United States, but in the 1940s, they could play in regular, mainstream theatres and many were helped to success thanks to their being presented as roadshow attractions.

As critic Bosley Crowther wrote in the *New York Times* (November 17, 1946), "an unrestricted give-and-take of films between the two English-speaking countries is most desirable both from the point of cultural contacts and of the sheer satisfaction it could bring. Only the most naïve could figure that nothing but national pride or whim might act as a restrictive barrier to the international circulation of films."

The quota was later reduced to 40 percent in 1949 and 30 percent a year later. The quota system was not abolished until 1983.

Just as in the 1930s, American companies and studios had begun the regular production of films in Britain to satisfy the quota system, so did the cycle begin again in the late 1940s. This time, however, rather than produce cheap, "B"-style pictures, the Americans determined to make major films, with major stars and often major American directors, for a worldwide market. The reason for a renaissance in American production in Britain may have been the quota system, but, ultimately, as Sue Harper and Vincent Porter have pointed out, the major studios "soon realized that there were economic and political advantages to using British studios."[6] In the 1950s, in fact, it is estimated there were approximately 150 US-British productions. "Runaway production," as it is generally described, was rampant not only in Britain, but also in other European countries, influenced in part by the demise of the Hollywood studio system, the advent of television, and the earlier Consent Decree in the United States, separating studios from their theatre holdings.

MGM maintained the largest studio in Britain, some 120 acres at Elstree/ Borehamwood in Hertfordshire, just outside of London. The former Amalgamated Studios had opened in 1935 and been given over to aircraft production during World War II. It was acquired by MGM in 1948, and the number of its stages increased to seven. The first film to be produced there by MGM was the screen adaptation of the play *Edward, My Son*, the story of a man's destructive devotion to his only child, which had starred on Broadway Robert Morley (who co-wrote the play with Noel Langley). Prior to production, according to *Variety* (June 15, 1948), MGM had agreed not to import any Hollywood technical talent in response to a proposal from the British film union, the Association of Cine-Technicians or ACT,[7] that for every Hollywood technician brought to the United Kingdom, one Britisher would be allowed to work for a comparable period of time in Hollywood.

MGM did bring over director George Cukor and had Donald Ogden Stewart prepare the screenplay. MGM contract star Spencer Tracy was assigned the role of Edward's father, with his nationality changed from English to Canadian because of Tracy's inability to adopt an English accent. Deborah Kerr, who had originated the role on the London stage, played Edward's mother, and supporting roles were played by Ian Hunter and Leueen McGrath, who had also appeared in the original stage production. Tracy lacks the polished presence that Robert Morley or a similar British actor might have provided, but the film opened to enthusiastic reviews following its British premiere at the Empire Theatre, Leicester Square, long the home of MGM releases, on March 3, 1949.

During the course of production, Tracy had become an ardent cricket enthusiast, and at the end of shooting, the crew provided him with a cricket bat as a souvenir of his time in England.

MGM's second British film was the anti-Communist propaganda production, *Conspirator*, starring Elizabeth Taylor in what was claimed to be her first adult role and directed by Victor Saville, but with the presence after a ten-year absence from Britain of American star Robert Taylor. The film was produced in late 1948, but not released until March 1950, indicative of its dubious worth.

Information on the financial success or more precisely failure of these first MGM British films does exist, thanks to a ledger kept by the staff of executive Eddie Mannix and archived at the Academy of Motion Picture Arts and Sciences. Between 1950 and 1958, only one film, *Knights of the Round Table*, shows a profit. With many costing well in excess of $1 million, and at least one, *The Miniver Story*, with a budget of over $3 million, the theoretical

Edward, My Son (1949), with Deborah Kerr and Spencer Tracy.

loss to the studio on these films is astounding. At the same time, it should be noted that studio accounting is notoriously unreliable and weighted towards loss rather than profit.

Following the 1950 production of *The Elusive Pimpernel*, an all-British production, released in the United States four years later as *The Fighting Pimpernel*, MGM returned to its past with a sequel to *Mrs. Miniver*, again starring Greer Garson and Walter Pidgeon, and titled *The Miniver Story*. H. C. Potter is the credited director, but he was actually replaced by Victor Saville. The film garnered poor reviews, with the *New York Times* (October 29, 1950) noting that it was made in the United Kingdom "though you'd

never know it from what you see." John McCarten in the *New Yorker* (November 4, 1950) provides both a critical comment and a synopsis of the storyline: "Miss Garson fumbles her way to the grave, after dealing lethargically with her own, her son's, and her daughter's problems." *The Miniver Story* marks the first appearance by Peter Finch in what is nominally an American film.

Some years earlier, MGM and producer Alexander Korda had embarked on a co-production deal, forming MGM-London Film Productions, Ltd., but only one film emerged from the partnership, *Vacation from Marriage*, shot at Elstree with location filming in Scotland in late 1944. The cast, headed by Robert Donat and Deborah Kerr, was British, as was the crew, headed by producer/director Alexander Korda. Korda had taken over direction from American Wesley Ruggles, with whose approach to this patriotic comedy-drama he disagreed. The film opened in London in August 1945 under the title of *Perfect Strangers*, and was released in the United States in November of the same year. Gossip columnist Louella Parsons was full of praise, describing it as the "most amusing picture ever to come out of England," continuing, "It's American, in spirit, fun and action."[8]

The Miniver Story (1950), with Greer Garson and Walter Pidgeon.

In the 1950s, MGM, like other American studios, took advantage of British scenery and British history with productions such as *Ivanhoe* (1952) and *Knights of the Round Table* (1953), both directed by Richard Thorpe (who had experience of working in Britain in the 1930s) and both starring Robert Taylor, and *Young Bess* (1953), directed by George Sidney and starring the then husband-and-wife team of Jean Simmons and Stewart Granger, two British actors making their mark in Hollywood. For the next three decades, there were many American directors at work at MGM Borehamwood, most notably Mark Robson (*Inn of the Sixth Happiness*, 1958), Robert Aldrich (*The Angry Hills*, 1959 and *The Dirty Dozen*, 1967), Robert Wise (*The Haunting*, 1963), Blake Edwards (*A Shot in the Dark*, 1964), and Jerry Lewis (*One More Time*, 1970). The studio closed in 1970.

American director Stanley Kubrick moved permanently to England in 1961, filming there a substantial body of work that is generally American in theme. Sometimes finished efforts can contain jarring inconsistencies, such as the very British suburban houses in *Lolita* (1962) or the glimpse of the Oxo Tower on the south bank of the Thames in the New York-located *Eyes Wide Shut* (1999). Kubrick shot two of his greatest works at MGM Borehamwood Studios, *2001: A Space Odyssey* (1968) and *A Clockwork Orange* (1971). Most of *The Shining* (1980) was filmed at EMI Elstree Studios, but for the scene in the maze, Kubrick returned to the former backlot of MGM Borehamwood.

The first postwar American film to be shot in Britain was *Escape*, filmed by 20th Century-Fox at Denham in September 1947 and released in the United States in July 1948. Directed by Joseph L. Mankiewicz, with a script by Philip Dunne, and starring British actress Peggy Cummins (who made a tremendous impact in the American production of *Gun Crazy* [1949]), *Escape* is a curious mix of American *film noir* and British social drama, based on a play by John Galsworthy. "Little in the way of thrills, excitement, or suspense," commented the *Hollywood Reporter* (May 26, 1948).

Other 20th Century-Fox British-based productions that followed include *I Was a Male War Bride*, which began production in September 1948, for August 1949 US release, directed by Howard Hawks, and starring Cary Grant and Ann Sheridan; *The Forbidden Street*, which began production at Shepperton Studios in July 1948 for May 1949 US release, directed by Jean Negulesco, and starring Dana Andrews; *The Black Rose*, which began production at Shepperton in April 1949 for September 1950 US release, directed by Henry Hathaway, and starring Tyrone Power and Orson Welles; and *The Mudlark*, which began production at Shepperton in May 1950 for December

1950 US release, directed by Jean Negulesco, with Nunnally Johnson as producer and screenwriter, and starring Irene Dunne as Queen Victoria. The best of the 20th Century-Fox British productions of this period is undoubtedly the London-based *film noir* of the British underworld, *Night and the City*, also filmed at Shepperton, beginning in July 1949, for June 1950 US release. The production owes much to director Jules Dassin and American stars Richard Widmark and Gene Tierney, brilliantly supported by Googie Withers and the superb Francis L. Sullivan, a far more talented version of the equally obese Sidney Greenstreet, here playing a nightclub owner.

In 1941, Paramount Pictures had filmed at Denham Studios an adaptation of A. J. Cronin's novel, *Hatter's Castle*, with Robert Newton in the title role of a wealthy Victorian hat maker who builds himself a mansion. The producer was American David E. Rose, who was managing director for Paramount in Britain. The crew, headed by director Lance Comfort, and the cast were all British. Perhaps wisely, Paramount delayed American release until the summer of 1948, by which time the co-stars, James Mason and Deborah Kerr, had become relatively well-known in the United States.

The first Paramount postwar British film was *So Evil My Love*, which began production at London's Lincoln's Inn Field in May 1947 for August 1948 US release. The Denham-based Victorian thriller garnered good reviews in both Britain and the United States. If not for the Hollywood studio behind it, *So Evil My Love* can scarcely be considered an American film, with director Lewis Allen heading an all-British crew and British-born Ray Milland starring.

Warner Bros.-First National Pictures, Ltd., was the British subsidiary of Warner Bros., whose first production, begun in December 1948 at Elstree was *The Hasty Heart*, based on the 1945 play by John Patrick, concerned with a group of soldiers in a Red Cross hospital in Burma. The script is by Ranald MacDougall, who, despite his very Scottish name, is American, as is director Vincent Sherman, leading lady Patricia Neal, and leading man Ronald Reagan (as if he needed ethnic identification). *The Hasty Heart* was produced in collaboration with Associated British Pictures Corporation (ABPC), which was partly owned by Warner Bros. through into the late 1960s. It was followed by *Stage Fright*, which began shooting at Elstree in May 1949 for February 1950 US release.[9] Jane Wyman stars under Alfred Hitchcock's direction, although many might argue that Marlene Dietrich is more responsible for the film's appeal. Later Warner Bros. productions filmed in England include *Captain Horatio Hornblower RN* (1951), *Where's Charley?* (1952), *The Crimson Pirate* (1952), and *His Majesty O'Keefe* (1954).

So Evil My Love (1948), with Ray Milland.

The Warner Bros.-British films were no longer shot at Teddington, but at the Associated British Pictures Corporation studios at Elstree. The studios had opened in 1927, with the first production being *Madame Pompadour*, starring Dorothy Gish. That same year, British International Pictures, which became Associated British Pictures Corporation, took over the studio, shooting Alfred Hitchcock's *Blackmail* there. Warner Bros. had been involved with the company as early as 1941, when it acquired a 25 percent interest not so much because it wanted use of the studio but because it wanted access to the sister company, ABC Cinemas, as a showcase for its films. In 1946, Warner Bros. became more actively involved in the studio and rebuilt

So Well Remembered (1947), Mangin (Reginald Tate) and Olivia (Martha Scott) congratulate George (John Mills) on his campaign oratory.

its stages. In time, the Warner Bros. connection with ABPC grew, with the formation of a new distribution company, Warner-Pathé. The studios were renamed EMI in 1968, and here a number of international successes, with varying degrees of American participation, were filmed, including *The Go Between* (1971), *Murder on the Orient Express* (1974), *The Shining* (1980), *Star Wars* (1977), and its various sequels.

The Walt Disney Company came to Britain with a definite plan to produce live-action feature films, for release by RKO, which took advantage of British locations and British stories. The two companies formed a new subsidiary, RKO-Walt Disney British Productions, Ltd., for what were in fact the first completely live-action films made by Disney; shooting took place at Denham Studios. The series began with *Treasure Island*, relatively faithful to the Robert Louis Stevenson novel, filmed in the summer and fall of 1949 for a July 1950 US release. The director, Byron Haskin, was American, as was the child star, Bobby Driscoll, and, as far as can be ascertained, veteran Disney producer, Perce Pearce. The remainder of the cast and crew were British, and it was the British Robert Newton who steals the film in the role of Long John Silver.

Treasure Island was followed by *The Story of Robin Hood* (1952), with a British director, Ken Annakin, a British cast, and British production crew. Richard Todd had the title role, and he, Perce Pearce, and Annakin worked together on the third Disney British film, *The Sword and the Rose* (1953). They would have made a fourth together, *Rob Roy, Highland Rogue* (1954), but at this time Annakin was under contract to J. Arthur Rank and was replaced by Harold French. The cast and crew on the films were all British.

J. Arthur Rank's Alliance Productions, Ltd., and RKO co-produced one film together, *So Well Remembered*, which began production at Denham in July 1946, and was released in the US in November 1947. John Mills stars as a newspaper editor under the direction of Edward Dmytryk, with American Martha Scott as his leading lady, and Trevor Howard elevated to stardom as the second male lead. Dmytryk further directed at Denham in 1949 *Give Us This Day*, also known as *Christ in Concrete* (the title of the novel upon which it is based) and released in the US in 1950 as *Salt to the Devil.* A highly political social drama, set in New York in the 1920s, the film was initially set for filming in New York by American producer Rod E. Geiger, but when the screenwriter Ben Barzman, star Sam Wanamaker, and Dmytryk were all blacklisted by the House Committee on Un-American Activities, the production moved to England.

It was the Hollywood blacklist that resulted in a new and different breed of American émigrés to Britain. They were well-educated, often multitalented, and their politics range from vaguely leftist-liberal to somewhat equally vague Communistic tendencies. The British were sympathetic to these blacklistees, offering them opportunities to both work and prosper. An editorial in the October 28, 1947, issue of the London *Evening Standard* reported,

> The Hollywood investigations now being conducted by the Congress Committee on un-American activities are only the latest stop on a witch-hunting process, whose torch the Committee has been carrying through the Union. To what depths of intolerance have its members sunk!

The blacklistees found a sympathetic household in that of Constance Cummings and her playwright-screenwriter husband, Benn Levy, who was later to become a Labor member of parliament. Several were recipients of financial support from the couple. Cummings recalled,

> The first I knew of it was when Paul Draper and Larry Adler came over. They were among the first. And then one began to hear about it. Benn spoke out about it, and so did I. We never stopped shooting our mouths off. . . . I think I would have written off America. But we did go back and forth all the time. I never had any trouble about it.
>
> There had been, after the First World War, an interest in Communism and what Russia was doing. And there were a lot of people here who felt this is something good that's happening. It's going to have a good effect. What happened in America was really a little too late to get sympathy here. McCarthy and [Roy] Cohn, they didn't have very good reputations. Over here, it was a much more relaxed thing, and certainly among the film and theatre world, I think there was much more shock than approval. Communism, you see, had really been rejected by all the left-wing people, all the liberal people. So while America was saying, have you ever been, I think the English people were a lot more sophisticated in their relation to this. We had quite a lot of friends who dipped their toes in the water of Communism and then suddenly said, No, this is a horrible thing. Their first impulse was to investigate, to find out about it, for a good reason. . . .
>
> In 1946, at the end of the war, there was a big landslide towards Labour. We were very excited. Now, we're in, big majority, we can fix things. It was too difficult to fix. Labour, Capitalism, Communism, they've all had their day, and none of them have quite worked. I don't think we've quite got the answer.[10]

An accomplished master of the harmonica, whose repertoire included both popular and classical music, Larry Adler had toured the US with dancer Paul Draper, before coming to Britain in 1949. His best-known British achievement is the score for the 1953 film *Genevieve*, with its evocative theme song. Despite the film's being released in the US with his name missing from the credits, Adler received an Academy Award nomination for his work. This did not constitute Adler's first involvement in British cinema; in 1938, he had played Constantine in the tribute to London buskers, *St. Martin's Lane/The Sidewalks of London*.

Writer-producer Carl Foreman went into self-imposed exile in Britain after writing *High Noon* in 1952. There, he was responsible for at least three major works, *The Bridge on the River Kwai* (1961), *The Guns of Navarone* (1961), and *The Victors*, which he also directed (1963). In 1958, he formed his own production company in London, Open Road Films, and became firmly ensconced as part of the British establishment, serving as a governor of the British Film Institute and accepting a CBE (Commander of the British Empire) in 1970.

Just as Foreman was never actually forced to flee the United States, there were others who came as part of a so-called graylist, including actors Phil Brown, Alexander Knox (actually Canadian) and his wife, Doris Nolan. Nolan never pursued a major career in Britain, joking sometimes that she took stage and television roles as American characters that her friend Constance Cummings rejected; she also worked as little more than an extra in a couple of Joseph Losey's productions. Both she and Phil Brown appear in Losey's 1975 film, *The Romantic Englishwoman*.

Doris Nolan recalled of the director:

> He was always very gloomy on the set. He didn't have much of a sense of humor. But he had wonderful taste. And Joe had a very good eye with the camera. His pictures always looked wonderful. But he didn't have much story sense.[11]

Arguably, the most important American to come to Britain as a result of the blacklist was Joseph Losey, who was, as British film historian Neil Sinyard has commented, "an artist among philistines. . . . He seemed, if you like, the British cinema's Orson Welles."[12] There can surely be no disagreement that his British films are far superior to the early ones he made in the United States. In Britain, Losey matured and grew as a filmmaker, contributing a number of classics to British cinema, including *The Servant* (1963) and *The Go-Between* (1971).

The most openly outspoken of American refugees during this period was Hannah Weinstein, a left-wing and probably Communist activist. After her arrival in London in 1952, she founded her own television production company and made a series of highly popular historical adventures, *The Adventures of Robin Hood*, with Richard Greene in the title role (1955–59), *The Buccaneers* (1956–57), *The Adventures of Sir Lancelot* (1956–57), and *Sword of Freedom* (1958–60). The series provided employment for a number of blacklisted writers, working under pseudonyms, and also Americans in exile, such as Doris Nolan. The latter was quite outspoken in her comments on Weinstein:

> They were backed by the American Communists. Dalton Trumbo had put money in and set up Hannah Weinstein. She was a friend of Dashiel Hammett, and he put up money as well. They had all these high-priced

> writers and Americans, and shipped them over. It was a Communist organization. I don't think Howard Koch was a Communist, but he came over.[13]

Hollywood studios might not have found time or space for American blacklistees, but, as in the 1930s, they did utilize the services of independent British production companies. For example, Coronado Productions (England), Ltd., whose managing director was American David E. Rose, who had been active earlier in Britain with Paramount, and whose board of directors included The Viscount Astor, produced *Saturday Island* (1952), with Linda Darnell, for RKO and *The End of the Affair* (1955), with Van Johnson, for Columbia.

Tempean Films, Ltd., was founded in 1948 by Monty Berman and Robert S. Baker, and in the 1950s it became relatively well-known as a British "B"-picture producer, using minor American leading players who had some name recognition but were more generally associated with American "B" pictures. The first was Mark Stevens as an American who is framed in Britain for a murder he did not commit in *The Lost Hours* (1952), released in the US as *The Big Frame*. Stevens was followed by Scott Brady, Arthur Kennedy, Rod Cameron, Forrest Tucker, Virginia Bruce, and John Carroll. Constance Smith and Kennedy starred in Tempean's 1955 production of *Impulse*, which is directed by blacklisted Cy Endfield, who enjoyed a successful British career as a director and writer after being hounded out of the United States in 1951. Helping Tempean locate potential stars was former Universal casting director Bob Goldstein.

The attitude of the American industry censorship board, the Production Code Administration, had always been surprisingly lenient towards British films released in the United States. This, despite its being headed by an Irish-American Catholic, Joseph Breen, whose anti-Semitism would often surface in his relationship with American producers. There were routine complaints from the Production Code Administration in regard to the amount of alcohol consumed in British films. Historical dramas, such as *Nell Gwyn* (1933), might raise issues as to the questionable morality on display, but, otherwise, the British producers and the Production Code Administration had a fairly cozy relationship.[14]

Following World War II, it was suggested that the Production Code set up an office in London to advise British producers on subject matter that might be considered inappropriate for the American market. Breen visited London in the fall of 1946 and was enthusiastic about such a proposal; "it would be good business to help English pix in any possible way to find a market here," it was explained.[15] However, Breen's boss, Eric Johnston, head of the Motion Picture Association, expressed no sympathy for the idea, his opinion being that "what goes into British pictures is strictly a British problem."[16]

Acting in British films was not necessarily an advantage for American performers. In June 1946, a new tax treaty had been ratified between Britain and the United States whereby American actors were subject to the British tax rate while working in Britain for less than six months, a rate considerably higher than they would have paid in their native land. Actors were the only group singled out to pay the British tax rate, with all others working in Britain paying tax to the US treasury.

With its control of the British Odeon Cinema chain (with which United Artists was also involved) and the former Paramount Cinema chain, the J. Arthur Rank Organization was very similar to many American studios, not only producing films but also owning theatres in which to exhibit them. In total, Rank controlled 619 theatres by the early 1940s. As early as December 1948, New York's Beacon Theatre had become a first-run house, and the first two films to play there were both Rank productions, *Don't Take It to Heart* and *Waterloo Road*. In the spring of 1957, Rank determined to create a chain of theatres in which its films might be shown in the United States. The flagship for Rank's American chain was the 600-seat Sutton Theatre in New York, which reopened on April 26, 1957, with *Reach for the Sky*. Earlier, the popular British vintage-car-themed *Genevieve* had played seventeen weeks at the Sutton. Outside of the Rank chain, the Exeter Theatre in Boston had become known as "the *doyen* of American cinemas specializing in British films,"[17] with everything from *Love on the Dole* to *Henry V* (its American premiere) finding a place on its screen.

For the British in Hollywood, the postwar years meant a gradual dwindling in their ranks until, by the 1950s, they were represented by the likes of Stewart Granger, Rex Harrison, James Mason, Robert Newton, Jean Simmons, and Michael Wilding. Charlie Chaplin, while never an ardent member of the British colony, was forcibly removed in September 1952, when his residency was revoked while he was at sea en route to England. In February 1983, Queen Elizabeth II became the first British monarch to visit Hollywood. As Sheridan Morley commented, "True, there were a few [British] actors left, but somehow they were no longer recognizably the Hollywood British; even Julie Andrews had by now taken to appearing in transvestite musicals, while Michael Caine would have been employed by Aubrey Smith as, at best, an under-gardener."[18] Although not actually living anymore in Los Angeles, Greer Garson and James Mason were brought in for a royal banquet at 20th Century-Fox. The British contingent in Hollywood was there represented by Michael Caine, Joan Collins, Samantha Eggar, Jean Marsh, Dudley Moore, director Tony Richardson, and Michael York.

In the 1980s, and later, those Britishers remaining in Hollywood and vicinity have become Americanized. Some, such as Anthony Hopkins, proudly boast of their American citizenship, while others keep quiet, maintaining two passports, British and American, and juggling their individual worth as they travel the globe. In later life, some, such as Anna Lee, find it easy to uphold so-called British standards while demeaning Great Britain. "It's very sad because England seems to be going to the dogs," she told me in 1994. "I hate this idea of becoming a European citizen."[19]

CHAPTER THIRTEEN

The New International Cinema

AT THE BEGINNING OF THE TWENTIETH CENTURY, THE UNITED STATES was arguably not the only dominant country in world cinema. The French and the British were also there at the forefront, and it has certainly been suggested that until World War I engulfed Europe, the French had as much influence in film production and distribution as the Americans. Europe went to war while America went to the movies, as has so often been claimed.

The argument throughout the modern age had always been that the British film industry could never become a recognized international success story. It failed to establish itself in the way that the British pop industry, led by the Beatles' invasion of America, or the British fashion industry had left their marks. Such commentary, of course, ignores the reality of how minor, and relatively unimportant, the British film industry is on a worldwide level. How can one little island in Europe compete with the vastness of the Hollywood film industry or even the output from such disparate countries as India and Hong Kong? It can compete with the likes of the French, German, or Italian film industries, and that should be adequate.

British attitudes towards America changed drastically from the 1960s onwards. As historian H. C. Allen has noted, for most of the century, "there was strong criticism of many of its aspects. Englishmen deplored the excessive commercialism of Americans and their lack of social and aesthetic taste; they disliked the high American divorce rate; they pointed to such social scandals as those depicted in *The Jungle* of Upton Sinclair; they never missed a lynching; above all, they still displayed a Dickensian mistrust of what they regarded as the extreme American worship of the Golden Calf."[1]

Professor Allen notes that long before the British musical invasion of America, it was American popular music that dominated. Between 1919 and 1933, eleven of the sixteen most popular songs in England were American. A 1936 study showed that British children gained their ideas about America from the motion picture, and to a large extent that source has not changed with the passing decades or even the turn of the century. Between 1908 and 1914, between 60 and 75 percent of all films shown in Britain were American in origin, rising by 1917 to 90 percent. "With the coming of the talkies the influence increased because it became aural as well as visual, and in 1933, 330 out of 476 important films shown in Britain were American."[2]

In the 1990s, some *very* British films found an extremely profitable market in the United States. Charles Crichton, a director associated earlier with Ealing, gave modern American audiences more than a hint of why those Ealing comedies were so popular with *A Fish Called Wanda* (1988), combining a British star, John Cleese, and an American star, Jamie Lee Curtis. Also in the Ealing tradition were *Four Weddings and a Funeral* (1994) and *Notting Hill* (1999), with scripts by Richard Curtis. *Notting Hill* introduced Julia Roberts to British films, and also provided cameo roles for two other Americans, Alec Baldwin and Matthew Modine. Definitely not in the Ealing tradition was Danny Boyle's *Trainspotting* (1996), which introduced American audiences to Ewan McGregor and Jonny Lee Miller and assured them of eventual international stardom.

However, in the late twentieth century and the first decade of the twenty-first century, Britain became part of an international trend. Certainly, a handful of honest British films continued to be made—thanks to directors such as Mike Leigh and Ken Loach—but basically there was no such entity as a truly British film production. If the film was made in England, with British talent, it was not necessarily a British film in that the funding came from other countries. Typifying this new trend was *Harry Potter and the Philosopher's Stone*, released in the United States as *Harry Potter and the Sorcerer's Stone* (2001), the first of the Harry Potter series, based on the novels of J. K. Rowling, and directed by American Chris Columbus. If nothing else, this first film seemed to indicate that American audiences would not understand what a philosopher was, and, more importantly, that here was a series that was to provide work (and international fame) for a hard-working and previously unappreciated group of British character players (whose primary place was on the stage rather than the cinema screen). *Harry Potter and the Philosopher's Stone* was nominally a British film, shot at a British studio, but released by an American company, Warner Bros., which had acquired the rights to the novel for a reported $1 million, and which had the financial backing to produce such an epic.

The blur between British and American films is no better illustrated than by two film franchises: James Bond, which began in 1960 with *Dr. No*, and Harry Potter. The James Bond series is actually produced by two Americans, Albert R. "Cubby" Broccoli and Harry Saltzman[3] (an American born in Canada), but both are on the surface very much British, with British authors (Ian Fleming and J. K. Rowling), substantial British casts, shooting in large part limited to British studios, and yet to the average moviegoer they are American series—they look, thanks to visual effects which heavily influence both, very Americanized. If truth be told, they are too sophisticated, too perfect to be British productions. Their appeal is international, and rightly so. Unlike British films of the 1930s, which tried desperately to look American, often with pathetic attempts at musical numbers badly copied from American routines, series such as *James Bond* and *Harry Potter* illustrate that here at least whatever America can do, Britain can do just as well.

Writing in the British *Sunday Times* in 1993, Angus Finney had argued that a well-financed European blockbuster could compete with anything Hollywood had to offer.[4] Yet the reality, it would seem, is that if world audiences want a European blockbuster, Hollywood will come to the United Kingdom and make it. Thus, in 1995, Mel Gibson directed and starred in *Braveheart*, a very Hollywood and distorted view of Scottish history. Similarly, Liam Neason and Jessica Lange starred in *Rob Roy*, dealing with a later period of Scottish history.

While not exactly in a foreign language, although American audiences may have had some problems with the Scottish burr, both *Braveheart* and *Rob Roy* are illustrative of what critic Vincent Canby in the *New York Times* (June 3, 1989) described as the "Berlitz era of movie making." He continued,

> If films are an accurate indicator of what is happening in Europe, it is clear that national identities—centuries of accumulated heritages—are under siege. The attackers are not the unruly, unwashed and the hungry who brought down the Bastille just 200 years ago. They are the tanned, well-fed bankers who finance movies and the once high-minded artists who are so desperate to make movies that they are succumbing to a fever of pan Europeanism.

A curious anomaly existed in the 1990s, when—thanks to government action to keep British studios active—it was determined that films made entirely in the country would be British. Thus, as has been pointed out, the Sylvester Stallone vehicle *Judge Dredd* (1995) is British, whereas *The English Patient* (1996), directed by Britisher Anthony Minghella, but with postproduction work handled overseas, is not.[5]

At the same time, financial lines are decidedly vague in regard to what film entity belongs to what country. An obvious example is Britain's independent production facility, Working Title Films, founded in 1983 by Tim Bevan and Sarah Radclyffe, and responsible for such prominent British films as *Four Weddings and a Funeral* and *Notting Hill* (both very much in the tradition of the Ealing comedies), as well as *Billy Elliott* (2000) and *Atonement* (2008). All were major successes in the United States. Working Title Films was financed in the early 1990s by the Anglo-Dutch company, PolyGram. In 1999, when PolyGram was purchased by Universal, Working Title also became part of the American studio, which was later, in turn, acquired by the French company, Vivendi.

Handmade Films, founded in 1978, may be British, responsible for such minor classics as *The Life of Brian* (1979), *Time Bandits* (1981), and *Withnail and I* (1987), and its formation has always been credited to former Beatle George Harrison. But Handmade Films was also co-founded by American businessman Dennis O'Brien.

Seven Arts Productions, UK, was a British company, headed by Kenneth Hyman, whose father, Eliot, had funded the American concern of the same name, in collaboration with Ray Stark, in 1957. It produced a number of British films, including *The Roman Spring of Mrs. Stone* (1961) and *Lolita* (1962). In November 1961, it partnered with Bryanston Films, headed by Michael Balcon, and produced *Sammy Going South/A Boy Ten Feet Tall* (1963), which concerns a young boy stranded in Port Said, who tries to reach his only living relative, an aunt in Durban, South Africa. The British film stars two Americans, Edward G. Robinson and Constance Cummings, and is directed by Alexander Mackendrick. Mackendrick is of some interest, not only because of the major Ealing comedies for which he was responsible, but because he was an American-born Scottish filmmaker, who initially returned to the United States in the mid-1950s and took up permanent residence there in 1969, when he became dean of the film school at the California Institute of the Arts.

American investment in the British film industry is substantial, and not always limited to the blockbuster. Among American-financed productions from the 1960s onwards have been *Tom Jones* (1963), *Dr. Dolittle* (1967), *Star!* (1968), *Goodbye Mr. Chips* (1969), *Mission Impossible* (1996),

Sammy Going South/A Boy Ten Feet Tall. Fergus McClelland in the title role cuts his birthday cake, with director Alexander Mackendrick behind him and star Edward G. Robinson far right.

The Wings of the Dove (1997), *The Full Monty* (1997), *Sliding Doors* (1998), and *Little Voice* (1999). *Tom Jones* cost $1.3 million to make, and its gross of $17 million persuaded United Artists to fund the first Beatles film, *A Hard Day's Night*, the following year. *A Hard Day's Night* was produced by San Francisco-born Walter Shenson, who had come to England in 1959 and made the amiable comedy, *The Mouse That Roared*. The Beatles film was directed by American Richard Lester, who had lived in Britain since 1953, and went on to direct the second Beatles film, *Help!* (1965). He also directed such quintessentially British films as *The Mouse on the Moon* (1963), *The Knack . . . and How to Get It* (1965), *How I Won the War* (1967), *Petulia* (1968), and *Robin and Marian* (1976). He even presented a 1993 BBC television series, *Hollywood U.K.*

More than 100 US films were produced in Britain between 1950 and 1970.[6] Between 1951 and 1960, some 257 British feature films, made with or without American money, were released in the United States. During the 1960s, all of the major American producers were active in the United Kingdom, with Universal producing some thirteen films there in the later part of the

Richard Lester.

decade. It was not so much a lack of commercial success for some of their British films—although quite a few did not do well—but rather a change in the economic climate back in Hollywood that brought an end to major US participation in British production. The Hollywood studios were running at a loss. In 1969, Universal ceased its activities in Britain and MGM closed its Borehamwood Studios. The Hollywood studios moved towards joint partnerships in Britain, with Columbia, Warner Bros., and EMI entering a joint distribution program, and Universal, Paramount, and MGM forming a new British distribution outlet, Cinema International Corporation (CIC).

As the twentieth century drew to a close, America remained a powerful player in the world film market, but times were changing. As the authors of *Global Hollywood* point out, "The number of big-budget pictures made overseas went from none in 1990 to twenty-four in 1998."[7] Hollywood was very much aware that the world market was highly critical to a film's success, as exemplified by *Titanic* (1997), with its British leading lady and American leading man, which made $1 billion outside of the United States.

In reaction to a perceived American takeover of British cinema, the British became nostalgic, celebrating the British class system and the British past, most notably on the big screen with *Chariots of Fire* (1981), a sentimental yet strongly political examination of British participation in the 1924 Olympics. It was a celebration of what Britain had been as much as was *Cavalcade* decades earlier, and, more recently, the television series *Upstairs, Downstairs* and *Downton Abbey*. As with *Chariots of Fire*, all are representative of a nostalgia for a Britain that was or might have been, or, rather, as Americans would like it to have been. As has been noted by others, *Chariots of Fire* is a strange hybrid in that it is written by two major supporters of the British Labor Party and yet it espouses what might certainly be considered a Thatcherite philosophy. Such an anomaly is presumably lost on American audiences.

Chariots of Fire won the Academy Award for Best Picture, as well as Best Costume Design, Best Music (the evocative theme song by Vangelis), and Best Writing. It was also nominated for Best Actor in a Supporting Role (Ian Holm), Best Directing, and Best Film Editing. One of the winners for Best Writing, Colin Welland, who had also written *Yanks* (1977), a British film starring Richard Gere, made the famous statement at the Academy Awards presentation, "The British Are Coming." It may have had some relevance during the American Revolution, but since then it is a phrase that has meant little, in or out of the film industry. For every Britisher coming to Hollywood, there has been an American filmmaker coming to Britain.

"These two great organizations of the English-speaking democracies, the British Empire and the United States, will have to be somewhat mixed up together in some of their affairs for mutual and general advantage," said Winston Churchill in an August 1940 speech. "For my part, looking out upon the future, I do not view the process with any misgivings. I could not stop it if I wished; no one can stop it. Like the Mississippi, it just keeps rolling along. Let it roll. Let it roll on full flood, inexorable, irresistible, benignant, to broader lands and better days." Those words, spoken at the height of war, resonate in the twenty-first century and in regard to twenty-first-century cinema. Today, the British and American motion pictures—more accurately and better defined as simply the international cinema of the English-speaking world—roll on as one, indivisible and united in a common cause: to entertain and to generate wealth for their respective countries.

NOTES

INTRODUCTION

1. Iris Barry, *Let's Go to the Movies*, p. 239.
2. Wim Wenders, *The Logic of Images: Essays and Conversations*, p. 98.
3. Myrtle Gebhart, "From Jolly Old England," p. 74.
4. Harold Weston, *The Art of Photo Play Writing*, p. 13.
5. Cecil M. Hepworth, "Director Points Out Defects in Production," p. 2647.
6. R. C. Buchanan, quoted in "British Exhibitors Denounce Famous Players and Hearst," p. 50.
7. James R. Quirk, "Speaking of Pictures," p. 118.
8. Kenneth Macpherson, "As Is," p. 9.
9. Ernest Marshall, "British Producers Take Heart with Their Latest Talking Pictures," p. 110.
10. Herbert Harris, "Those English Americans," p. 10.
11. Anthony Asquith, "The American Invasion," p. 78.
12. "Mr. Douglas Fairbanks Jr. Makes a Speech," p. 4.
13. Cedric Belfrage, "Hollywood Cocktail," p. 8.
14. Paul Rotha, *The Film Till Now*, p. 313.
15. Josie Lederer, "The Blindness of Britain," p. 8.
16. Joseph B. Walker and Juanita Walker, *The Light on Her Face*, p. 192.
17. Reported in *Film Weekly*, April 13, 1934, p. 7.
18. Sydney Howard, "The Tea Curse in British Studios," p. 10.
19. Anna Lee, interview with Anthony Slide, March 9, 1994.
20. Ibid.
21. John Russell Taylor, *Strangers in Paradise: The Hollywood Emigrés*, p. 15.
22. David Niven, *The Moon's a Balloon*, p. 207.
23. This anecdote was told to me by Norman Lloyd in the course of a conversation, March 5, 2014.
24. Quoted in John Russell Taylor, *Strangers in Paradise: The Hollywood Émigrés, 1933–1950*, p. 96.
25. James Fidler, "England Wants Its Hollywood Stars," p. 58.
26. "Ronald Colman as Cricketer," p. 7.
27. Jeffrey Richards, *Visions of Yesterday*, p.73.
28. Sir Cedric Hardwicke and James Brough, *A Victorian in Orbit*, p. 211. Primarily a stage actor, Hardwicke had made his British sound film debut in 1931 and his American

screen debut in 1935 with the first three-color Technicolor feature-length production, *Becky Sharp*.

29. "Introducing Darts to Hollywood," pp. 4–5.
30. There is at least one British film, a quota quickie, in which darts are featured, and that is *Darts Are Trumps*, released in the summer of 1938. Starring as a lowly clerk by day and a famous darts player at night is Eliot Makeham, of whom *Film Weekly* (July 9, 1938) wrote, "Putting Suburbia on the screen has been Eliot Makeham's job ever since he entered pictures. Since 1922, he's been playing down-trodden little city clerks, brow-beaten private secretaries, at an average of one every two months."
31. Mention should be made of the phenomenon of the football pools, on which vast numbers of Britishers gamble each week as to the scores of the various football games. There is at least one film on the subject, *The Penny Pool*, a surprisingly delightful Mancuian Films production from 1937, starring the much-underrated Duggie Wakefield.
32. Kenneth Macpherson, "As Is," pp. 8–9.
33. Dick Henderson, Jr., became a fairly popular entertainer in later years thanks to a number of television appearances.

CHAPTER 1

1. Blackton also founded the world's first fan magazine, the *Motion Picture Story Magazine*, in 1911, and so perhaps the British deserve credit for this cultural phenomenon.
2. Marian Blackton Trimble, *J. Stuart Blackton: A Personal Biography by His Daughter*, p. 68.
3. On the site stood an abandoned tavern that had belonged to Louis Blondeau.
4. Paul Mandell, "David Horsley, Pioneer Picturemaker," p. 51.
5. "The Father of Kinematography," p. 487.
6. Stephen Herbert and Luke McKernan, eds., *Who's Who in Victorian Cinema*, p. 144.
7. *Motion Picture News*, October 7, 1922, p. 1778.
8. Urban was elected a fellow of the Zoological Society.
9. He is the subject of an excellent website: http://www. Charlesurban.com.
10. H. C. Allen, *The Anglo-American Relationship Since 1783*, p. 54.

CHAPTER 2

1. Gene Gauntier, "Blazing the Trail," *Woman's Home Companion*, October 1928. Much the same attributes were applied to Olcott in the only fan magazine article devoted to his work, Pearl Gaddis, "Blazing a Trail in the Movies," *Photoplay*, September 1914, pp. 104–107.
2. Quoted in George Mitchell, "Sidney Olcott," *Films in Review*, p. 180; the original source is unidentified.
3. This story was told to me by Annie O'Sullivan during a conversation in Beaufort, County Kerry, in the spring of 1967. It was first recounted by me in "The O'Kalems," *Cinema Studies*, September 1967, pp. 77–79. Other anecdotes by O'Sullivan throughout this chapter come from that same meeting.
4. Gene Gauntier, "Blazing the Trail," *Woman's Home Companion*, December 1928.
5. Ibid.
6. Ibid.
7. Gene Gauntier claims the ship was the *Adriatic*, but according to *Moving Picture World*, June 3, 1911, p. 1242, it was the *Baltic*.

8. John J. (Jack) Clark (1876–1947) was an Irish-American, who married Gene Gauntier in 1912. The couple was divorced in Kansas City on January 30, 1918.
9. As far as I can ascertain, the name "The O'Kalems" was first used in *Moving Picture World*, July 1, 1911, p. 1506.
10. The play version was one of the biggest successes for actor Tyrone Power, Sr.
11. *The Colleen Bawn* had earlier been filmed in 1911 in a one-reel production by the Yankee Film Company.
12. "The Colleen Bawn," *Moving Picture World*, September 30, 1911, pp. 954, 956.
13. The score does not survive.
14. The trials and tribulations of filming the former in high seas are told by Gene Gauntier in "Taking Pictures under Difficulties," *Moving Picture World*, September 16, 1911, p. 784.
15. Agnes Mapes, "A Kalem Girl in Ireland," *Moving Picture World*, July 15, 1911, p. 31.
16. "O'Kalems Return," *Moving Picture World*, October 14, 1911, p. 136.
17. Advertisement in the company's house organ, *Kalem Kalendar*, June 15, 1912, p. 8.
18. "Kalem Sends Company to the Orient," *Moving Picture World*, December 16, 1911, p. 880.
19. J. P. McGowan, "O'Kalem Returns to Ireland," *Moving Picture World*, August 10, 1912, p. 537.
20. These letters, without dates, are reprinted in Robert S. Birchard, "Kalem Company: Manufacturers of Moving Picture Films," *American Cinematographer*, August/September 1984, p. 37.
21. There is a vague possibility that some of these titles may actually have been shot on the 1911 visit to Beaufort.
22. A mere 125-feet in length, *Conway the Kerry Dancer* was released on the same reel as *A Race with Time*, which is a non-Irish production.
23. This film may have been shot in Ireland or, perhaps, in North Wales, as the company would have left the ferry from Cork or Dublin in Holyhead in North West Wales prior to taking the train to London.
24. Kalem was not the only company to realize the potential audience for "Irish" films. On St. Patrick's Day, 1912, Carl Laemmle's IMP Company released *Shamus O'Brien*, based on the poem by Sheridan Le Fanu, and dealing with the 1798 rebellion.
25. See "Gauntier Feature Players," *Moving Picture World*, December 21, 1912, p. 1169.
26. Sometimes referred to as Sid Films.
27. The general assumption of the people of Beaufort was that Olcott was deeply in love with Gauntier, but because he was a devout Catholic and she was a divorced woman, a marriage was impossible.
28. George K. Hollister's wife, Alice, told me that shortly before Pat O'Malley's death, the two had got together and sat up all night talking of Beaufort. Pat O'Malley (1890–1966) is one of the few Irish-Americans actually born in Ireland—in Dublin.
29. Lewis Jacobs, *The Rise of the American Film: A Critical History, A Critical History*, p. 123.
30. *From the Manger to the Cross* opened in the United Kingdom prior to the coming into existence in January 1913 of the British Board of Film Censors. For information on censorship and *From the Manger to the Cross* in the UK, see James C. Robertson, *The British Board of Film Censors: Film Censorship in Britain, 1898–1950* (London: Croom Helm, 1985). For information on censorship and *From the Manger to the Cross* in Ireland, see Kevin Rockett, *Irish Film Censorship: A Cultural Journey from Silent Cinema to Internet Pornography* (Dublin: Four Courts Press, 2004).
31. Lee Shippey, "The Lee Side o' L.A.," *Los Angeles Times*, November 4, 1932, p. A4.
32. This anecdote appears in Gene Gauntier, "Blazing the Trail," *Woman's Home Companion*, January 1929, and was also told to me by Annie O'Sullivan. The term "tramp photographers" was used by Robert Vignola in a 1953 Radio Eireann interview.

CHAPTER 3

1. Hubert H. Tiltman, "Ireland—A Film El Dorado," p. 23.
2. *The Passing of the Third Floor Back* was remade in 1935 by director Berthold Viertel, with Conrad Veidt as The Stranger. While at times the story seems awkward, it is both moving and impressive.
3. Herbert Brenon notes, October 16, 1951, Anthony Slide Collection.
4. It is ironic that while making a propaganda film for the war, Brenon should also have made *The Passing of the Third Floor Back*, of which he said in the December 15, 1917, issue of the *Dramatic Mirror*, "It carries a message of hope and optimism which Americans—indeed people of every land—are seeking in these dark and troubled days. To me the message of loving kindness is the greatest message of *The Passing of the Third Floor Back*. I love the subject; it is full of sunshine, beauty and comedy, as well as drama of the finest order I am firmly convinced that not only will it be the most artistic achievement of my career, but the most popular. It fulfills to the highest extent one of the greatest functions of the screen—to spread the message of hope to the masses."
5. Helena Millais, interview with Anthony Slide, March 17, 1968.
6. Quoted in George Geltzer, "Herbert Brenon," p. 120.
7. *Film Weekly*, January 2, 1932, p. 4.
8. Brenon's British films of the 1930s are *Royal Cavalcade* (1935), *Honours Easy* (1935), *Living Dangerously* (1936), *Someone at the Door* (1936), *The Dominant Sex* (1937), *Spring Handicap* (1937), *The Live Wire* (1937), *The Housemaster* (1938), *Yellow Stockings* (1938), *Black Eyes* (1939), and *The Flying Squad* (1939).
9. Ian Hay to Herbert Brenon, February 8, 1938, Anthony Slide Collection.
10. Herbert Brenon notes, November 16, 1951, Anthony Slide Collection.
11. Herbert Brenon notes, November 17, 1951, Anthony Slide Collection.
12. Johnstone Craig, "The Dominant Race," p. 48.
13. Michael Troyan, *A Rose for Mrs. Miniver: The Life of Greer Garson*, p. 1.
14. Quoted in Sheridan Morley, *Tales from the Hollywood Raj*, p. 212.
15. Marsha Hunt and Samantha Eggar, in conversation with Anthony Slide, April 20, 2014.
16. Samuel Crowl, *The Films of Kenneth Branagh*, p. 7.
17. Ibid.
18. Gary Jenkins, *Daniel Day-Lewis: The Fire Within*, p. 158.

CHAPTER 4

1. Lynde Denig, "Larry Trimble Brings Turner Films," p. 1223.
2. Ibid.
3. L. C. Moen, "Florence Turner, First Star, Returns to U.S.," p. 2431.
4. "Miss Edna Flugrath," p. 1519.
5. Elizabeth Risdon enjoyed a film career in the US as a character actress through into the 1950s.
6. Why do the British seem incapable of coming up with attractive, enticing titles? Consider some of the films in which Gertrude McCoy appears: *Angle, Esquire* (1919), *Sam's Kid* (1922), *The Temptation of Carlton Earle* (1923), and *Chappy—That's All* (1924).
7. Jane Novak has another link to British cinema in that, after an eleven-year absence, she returned to the screen in 1940 in Alfred Hitchcock's *Foreign Correspondent*.
8. François Truffaut, *Hitchcock*, p. 28.

9. Joan Morgan, letter to Anthony Slide, undated.
10. Edwin Schallert, "Elated over London Trip," p. II14.
11. Herbert Wilcox, interview with Anthony Slide, February 22, 1971.
12. Ibid.
13. Rachael Low, *The History of the British Film, 1918–1929*, p. 135.
14. *Southern Love* was reissued in 1947 by New Realm, with a commentary by Lionel Gamelin, as a comedy-burlesque.
15. G. A. Atkinson, "British Films Made to Please America," p. 6.
16. Peter Stead, "Hollywood's Message for the world: The British Response in the Nineteen Thirties," p. 20

CHAPTER 5

1. The Plaza, one of the most prominent of London movie theatres, was opened by Famous Players-Lasky in the 1920s.
2. Hal Young also shot location scenes in London for the Samuel Goldwyn 1922 production of *Sherlock Holmes*.
3. Another American screenwriter who contributed scripts for Famous Players-Lasky British films was Margaret Turnbull, who also may not actually have visited the studio. Her films are *Appearances* (1921), *The Princess of New York* (1921), and *Beside the Bonnie Briar Bush* (1921). All three were directed by London-born Donald Crisp who always cultivated a persona in Hollywood that he was Scottish.
4. Iris Barry, *Let's Go to the Movies*, p. 234.
5. Guissart had also photographed Betty Balfour in *Paradise* (1928).
6. Quotes here and elsewhere in this chapter that appear without attribution were published originally in my 1986 article, "American Cinematographers in Britain." In the intervening years, my original notes have disappeared or are no longer accessible.
7. The silent films of Graham Cutts evidence his extraordinary directorial talent, and if there are those who might claim it is limited only to the 1920s, I would suggest they view Cutts's 1937 production of *Over She Goes*. The camerawork here in the "Side by Side" number is quite incredible to watch, with takes so long they seem impossible to be real.
8. Bernard Vorhaus, *Saved from Oblivion*, p. 18.
9. A British film of *The Return of the Soldier* was made in 1981. Bette Davis also, apparently, had wanted to star in a screen adaptation.
10. Nerina Shute, "Mary Pickford's 'Right Hand' in England," p. 15.
11. Rachael Low, *Film Making in 1930s Britain*, p. 136.
12. Phil Tannura, interview with Anthony Slide, July 20, 1972.
13. Tannura's other twenty films are *Service for Ladies* (1932), *Women Who Pay* (1932), *Channel Crossing* (1933), *A Cup of Kindness* (1934), *Lady in Danger* (1934), *Dirty Work* (1934), *Fighting Stock* (1935), *Stormy Weather* (1935), *Moscow Nights* (1935), *The Crimson Circle* (1936), *Wolf's Clothing* (1936), *Dishonor Bright* (1936), *Southern Roses* (1936), *Love from a Stranger* (1937), *For Valour* (1937), *Who's Your Lady Friend* (1937), *Break the News* (1938), *Stolen Life* (1939), *Poison Pen* (1939), and *Hell's Cargo* (1939).
14. William K. Howard directed a second but lesser film at Denham, *The Squeaker*, released in the summer of 1937, produced by Alexander Korda, based on the play by Edgar Wallace, and starring American Edmund Lowe. For American release, the film was retitled *Murder on Diamond Row*.

CHAPTER 6

1. *Sabotage* was dismissed by *Film Weekly* (June 27, 1936) as nothing more than "a typical Hollywood thriller."
2. *Seven Sinners* was promoted as a successor to Hitchcock's *The 39 Steps* and boasted Americanized dialogue. That did not help the film, directed by Albert de Courville, when it opened at New York's Roxy Theatre on August 21, 1936.
3. William K. Howard also directed *Fire over England* (1937), which Korda presented but which was produced by Erich Pommer.
4. Anthony Asquith, "The American Invasion," in Peter Noble, ed., *The British Film Yearbook, 1947–1948*, p. 78.
5. "The Trek to London," p. 3.
6. Peter Noble, *The British Film Yearbook*, p. 48.
7. Polish-born Pola Negri starred in one British film, Paul Czinner's 1930 production of *The Woman Scorned.*
8. Excluded from this group is Victor Varconi who appeared in two British films in the 1930s, but who, despite being an American silent leading man, even playing Lord Nelson in *The Divine Lady*, was actually born in Hungary. In Europe from 1933–35, Varconi also made films in Germany and Spain. There are other examples of actors primarily associated with American films but who were not born here and, therefore, excluded from this study: Danish-born Nils Asther, starring in five British films of the 1930s; German-born Marlene Dietrich, who came to the UK in 1937 to star in *Knight without Armour*; Trieste-born Paul Henreid, starring in two British films of the 1930s; Canadian-born Victor Jory, starring in two British films of the 1930s; Hungarian-born Bela Lugosi, starring in one British film of the 1930s; Hungarian-born Paul Lukas, starring in three British films of the 1930s; Canadian-born Raymond Massey, starring in five British films of the 1930s; and Norwegian-born Greta Nissen, starring in one British films of the 1930s. Marian Marsh, best remembered as Trilby opposite John Barrymore as Svengali in the 1931 film of the same, was actually born in Trinidad; she starred in two British semi-musicals from 1934, *Love at Second Sight* and *Over the Garden Wall*, and also went to Germany to appear opposite Luis Trenker in *Der Verlorene Sohn/The Prodigal Son* (1935). William Austin was also born in a British colony, British Guiana, and so his two British screen appearances—in *High Society* (1932) and *Three Men in a* Boat (1933)—cannot be discussed. I would love to write of H. B. Warner's British films of the 1930s. But I must remain silent, because Warner is as English as anyone born in the St. John's Wood area of London can be.
9. How galling it must have been for Corinne Griffith that when *Lilies of the Field*, in which she had starred in both a silent and early sound version, was remade in the UK in 1934, it was Winifred Shotter who had the leading role.
10. *The Bioscope*, June 19, 1929, p. 19.
11. W. D. Ormond, "Meet the Passengers on Rome Express," p. 13.
12. Mary Brian, interview with Anthony Slide, January 13, 1988.
13. The E. Phillips Oppenheimer novel had first been filmed by Cecil Hepworth in 1920 as a silent production starring Henry Edward and Chrissie White.
14. Ibid.
15. James Mason, letter to Dudley Nichols, undated, Anthony Slide Collection.
16. Rachael Low, *Film Making in 1930s Britain*, p. 261.
17. Jeanne Stein, "Edward Everett Horton," p. 37.
18. In review of *It's a Boy*, July 7, 1933, p. 32.

19. Davina Craig, interview with Anthony Slide, October 1969.
20. Alex Esway, "London and Hollywood," p. 41.
21. Fay Wray, interview with Anthony Slide, 1981.
22. The popular American composers Mack Gordon and Harry Revel also have credits on British films, but, in all probability, provided the songs from their home base of Hollywood.
23. Berthold Viertel, "Huston: The Man and the Actor," p. 9.
24. *Spectator*, March 27, 1936.
25. The other films are *Freedom of the Seas* (1934), *Give Her a Ring* (1934), *Spring in the Air* (1934), and *Joy Ride* (1935).
26. Jean Straker, "Rise of a Red-Head," p. 14.
27. Bushell's Hollywood career had started thanks to George Arliss's casting him as the juvenile lead in *Disraeli* (1929); his other Hollywood credits include *Three Faces East* (1930), *Five Star Final* (1931), *Vanity Fair* (1932), and Pola Negri's first talkie, *A Woman Commands* (1932).
28. Lupe Velez had come to London as early as November 1931, to "console" John Gilbert who was also in England at the time.
29. The *Hollywood Reporter* (June 18, 1937) commented that "Mary Ellis brings what conviction she can to an oddly-assorted role, and carries off the operatics with top honors."
30. Competing with Finlay Currie for roles as an American in British films is Hartley Power (1894–1966), who was New York-born but made his professional debut on the stage in Britain in 1911; he appears in many British films from 1931 onwards, most notably perhaps as the rival ventriloquist in *Dead of Night* (1945).
31. Released in the US as *The Playboy*, and when reissued in the UK in the 1940s, one of Harry Richman's songs was cut.
32. Walter Forde, interview with Anthony Slide, October 1, 1976.
33. Anthony Slide, *The Encyclopedia of Vaudeville*, p. 506.
34. James Agate, *Around Cinemas*, p. 172.
35. "Are British Directors Crazy?", p. 8.
36. Mayflower Pictures Corp. produced three films, all starring Laughton, *Vessel of Wrath/The Beachcomber* (1938, and the only film Pommer directed), *St. Martin's Lane/Sidewalks of London* (1938), and *Jamaica Inn* (1939). The company was resurrected and taken over by Maxwell Sefton and Aubrey Baring in 1949, and produced seven films, the last two of which have American associations: *The Golden Mask* (1953), with Van Heflin and Wanda Hendrix, and *They Who Dare* (1954), directed by Lewis Milestone. Erich Pommer had produced two films with Pola Negri in Hollywood in 1927, come to England from Germany in 1936, was in the United States during World War II, returned to his native Germany after the war, but eventually retired to California, where he died in 1966.
37. Peter Bogdanovich, *Allan Dwan: The Last Pioneer*, p. 97.
38. Goulding's other British films are *Honeymoon Merry-Go-Round* (1936), *One Good Turn* (1936), *Everything Is Rhythm* (1936), *Splinters in the Air* (1937), and *Sam Leaves Town* (1937).
39. They are *The Captain's Table* (1936), *David Livingstone* (1936), *Auld Lang Syne* (1937), *The Last Rose of Summer* (1937), *The Bells of St. Mary's* (1937), *A Dream of Love* (1938), *George Bizet, Composer of Carmen* (1938), and *The Life of Chopin* (1938).
40. Wendy L. Marshall, *William Beaudine: From Silents to Television*, pp. 171–72.
41. Aside from those mentioned here, Beaudine also directed *So You Won't Talk* (1935), *Two Hearts in Harmony* (1936), *Get Off My Foot* (1936), *Where There's a Will* (1936),

Windbag the Sailor (1937), *Educated Evans* (1937), *It's in the Bag* (1937), *Feather Your Nest* (1937), *Said O'Reilly to McNab* (1937), and *Transatlantic Trouble* (1938).

42. Charles Drazin, "Editing: Lean Cuts," p. 38.
43. Other British films directed by Bernard Vorhaus are *On Thin Ice* (1933), *Money for Speed* (1933), *Crime on the Hill* (1933), *The Broken Melody* (1934), *Night Club Queen* (1934), *Blind Justice* (1934), *Ten Minute Alibi* (1935), *Street Song* (1935), *Dark World* (1935), *Dusty Ermine* (1936), and *Cotton Queen* (1937). While Vorhaus is constantly lauded, I must mention that in the early 1970s, the legendary British-born American film historian William K. Everson loaned me a 16mm print of *Cotton Queen*, urging that I watch it because it was the worst British film ever made.
44. Walter C. Mycroft, *The Time of My Life*, p. 74.
45. Tim Whelan's other British films are *It's a Boy* (1933), *Aunt Sally* (1933), *The Camels Are Coming* (1934), *Two's Company* (1936), *The Mill on the Floss* (1936), *Farewell Again* (1937), *Action for Slander* (1937), *Smash and Grab* (1937), and *Ten Days in Paris* (1939).
46. Louella Parsons, syndicated column, August 12, 1969.
47. Richardson's British films are *We Dine at Seven* (1931), *Peace and Quiet* (1931), *Above Rubies* (1932), *Flat No. 9* (1932), *Don't Be a Dummy* (1932), *River House Ghost* (1932), *Going Gay* (1933), *For Love of You* (1933, producer only), *Money Mad* (1934), *Oh, What a Night* (1935), *The Howard Case* (1936), and *The Man Who Made Diamonds* (1937).
48. *Bait* should not be confused with an American film from the same period and of the same title.
49. It is ironic that Jeanette MacDonald's failure to come to London led to Elmo Williams's relationship with Wilcox. It was Wilcox who starred his wife, Anna Neagle, in the first screen version of *Bitter Sweet* (1933), and the reason the producer/director acquired the rights was because Fox, which had just produced Noel Coward's *Cavalcade* and had an option on *Bitter Sweet*, could not sign Jeanette MacDonald for the role. MacDonald did, of course, star in MGM's 1940 remake.
50. William Hornbeck, quoted in program notes by Michael Agee for the Academy of Motion Picture Arts and Sciences presentation, "A Tribute to William Hornbeck," February 6, 1984.

CHAPTER 7

1. Sarah Street, *British National Cinema*, p. 11.
2. Peter Noble, *The British Film Yearbook*, p. 47.
3. In 1931, Paramount made arrangements with Herbert Wilcox and British & Dominions Film Corporation to make twelve films at an average cost of 20,000 pounds each. After the success of Korda's first British film, *Service for Ladies* (1932), he was contracted to make six films for Paramount.
4. Lachman's BIP films are *Under the Greenwood Tree* (1929), *The Compulsory Husband* (1930), *Song of Soho* (1930), *The Yellow Mask* (1930), and *The Love Habit* (1931).
5. "Clive Brook Won't Work in England Yet," p. 6.
6. Quoted in Steve Chibnall, *Quota Quickies: The Birth of the British "B" Film*, p. 172.
7. "Lasky's Plans," p. 6.
8. Gloria Swanson, *Swanson on Swanson*, p. 427.
9. *Film Weekly*, June 15, 1934, p. 6.
10. Gloria Swanson, *Swanson on Swanson*, p. 429.
11. *Film Weekly*, April 7, 1933, p. 6.
12. They are *After Dark* (1932), *The Right to Live* (1933), *Rolling in Money* (1934), *The Third Clue* (1934), *The Riverside Murder* (1935), *White Lilac* (1935), *Late Extra* (1935), *Troubled*

Waters (1936), *Blind Man's Buff* (1936), *Strange Experiment* (1937), *The Five Pound Man* (1937), *There Was a Young Man* (1937), *Murder in the Family* (1938), and *Second Thoughts* (1938).

13. Ronald Neame, *Straight from the Horse's Mouth*, p. 135.
14. Joseph B. Walker and Juanita Walker, *The Light on Her Face*, p. 192.
15. *Kinematograph Weekly*, January 9, 1936, p. 114.
16. Rachael Low, *Film Making in 1930s Britain*, p. 265.
17. Roscoe Fawcett, "Murder at Teddington," p. 4.
18. *Film Weekly*, May 6, 1932, p. 12.
19. Another American-born director at Teddington, with three films to his credit—*High Society* (1932), *Lucky Ladies* (1932) and *Going Straight* (1933)—is Jack Rawlins.
20. They are *What's in a Name* (1934), *A Glimpse of Paradise* (1934), *Murder at Monte Carlo* (1935), *So You Won't Talk?* (1935, actor only), *Mr. What's His Name* (1935), *Rolling Home* (1935), *Crime Unlimited* (1935), *The Black Mask* (1935), *Jury's Evidence* (1936), *Twelve Good Men* (1936), *Goalbreak* (1936, also actor), *Fair Exchange* (1936), *Hail and Farewell* (1936), *The Vulture* (1937), *It's Not Cricket* (1937), *Side Street Angel* (1937), *The Perfect Crime* (1937, also actor), and *The Man Who Made Diamonds* (1937).
21. Michael A. Hoey, "Roy William Neill: The Master of Suspense," p. 29. I am grateful to Hoey for his article and for his extensive research into Neill.
22. Roy William Neill's Teddington films are *Gypsy* (1936), *The Viper* (1938), *Quiet Please* (1938), *Simply Terrific* (1938), *Double or Quits* (1938), *Thank Evans* (1938), *Many Tanks, Mr. Atkins* (1938), *Everything Happens to Me* (1938), *A Gentleman's Gentleman* (1939), *The Good Old Days* (1939), *Murder Will Out* (1939), *His Brother's Keeper* (1939), and *Hoots, Mon* (1939).
23. Walter Forde to Anthony Slide, May 25, 1972.
24. Jack L. Warner, letter to Doc Salomon, August 8, 1939, Jack L. Warner Collection, USC Cinematic Arts Library.
25. In 1942, at the height of the war, Associated British reported, "that at no time has there been any interruption in our film supplies from American producers; they have passed through all the rigours of Trans-Atlantic transport; and for that, tribute should be paid to the men and ships who have brought them here. Mr. Milder, who has just returned from a short visit to the United States, reports that there is no indication that America's entry into the war will lead to curtailment in production in the United States for some time to come so there is no reason at present to anticipate any diminution of first-class American films in our cinemas."
26. Max Milder died in Surrey, England, on August 1, 1948, at the young age of fifty-seven. In July of that year, he had resigned from Warner Bros. owing to ill health.
27. Jack L. Warner, memorandum to entire staff, July 7, 1944, Jack L. Warner Collection, USC Cinematic Arts Library.
28. "Trends by the Thames," p. 140.
29. Irving Asher, letter to Jack L. Warner, July 23, 1935. Warner Bros. Archive, USC.
30. Jack L. Warner, letter to Irving Asher, November 17, 1936, Warner Bros. Archive, USC.
31. Many of the films produced at Teddington were made at a loss. For example, *Educated Evans* (1936) cost 28,980 pounds and grossed 34,040; *The Man Who Made Diamonds* (1937) cost 14,243 and grossed 10,794; *Thank Evans* (1938) cost 25,864 and grossed 21,475; *They Drive by Night* cost 24,689 and grossed 35,246; *Hoots Mon* cost 18,895 and grossed 13,996; *The Prime Minister* (1941) cost 90,215 and grossed 64,119; *Atlantic Ferry/Sons of the Sea* (1941) cost 97,355 and grossed 88,418; and *Flying Fortress* (1942) cost 107,362 and grossed 174,978. Grosses are as of October 1948. Information from the Warner Bros. Archive, USC.

32. *Film Weekly*, February 20, 1937, p. 5.
33. Laura La Plante, interview with Anthony Slide, June 8, 1972.
34. Ibid.
35. Irving Asher, letter to Jack L. Warner, March 1, 1938, Warner Bros. Archive, USC.
36. Jack L. Warner, letter to Sam E. Morris, March 3, 1938, Warner Bros. Archive, USC.
37. Jack L. Warner, letter to Doc Salomon, August 9, 1938, Jack L. Warner Collection, USC Cinematic Arts Library.
38. Doc Salomon, letter to Jack L. Warner, undated, Jack L. Warner Collection, USC Cinematic Arts Library.
39. Max Milder, letter to Jack L. Warner, February 2, 1942, Jack L. Warner Collection, USC Cinematic Arts Library.
40. Ibid.
41. Jack L. Warner, letter to Doc Salomon, February 12, 1942, Jack L. Warner Collection, USC Cinematic Arts Library.
42. Max Milder, letter to Jack L. Warner, November 16, 1942, Jack L. Warner Collection, USC Cinematic Arts Library.
43. Others killed were Harry Brayfield, who was working the reception desk, and a Miss Reeves of the dispatch department.
44. Rachael Low, *Film Making in 1930s Britain*, p. 212.
45. "Queen Mary Sees Movie," *New York Times*, February 22, 1930, p. 19.
46. News item, *New York Times*, November 30, 1930, p. X6.
47. Joanne D'Antonio, *Andrew Marton*, p. 83.
48. Ibid., p. 96.
49. Rock was not in the United States when the Academy Awards were presented. It was not until 1963 that he asked for his Oscar, only to be told there was no proof on the film that he was the producer. After legal wrangling, and without any fanfare, Rock finally collected the Academy Award in 1973.
50. Thornton Freeland, "Elstree Tunes in to Hollywood," p. 8.
51. Marilyn Ann Moss, *Raoul Walsh: The True Adventures of Hollywood's Legendary Director*, p. 155.
52. Ernest Marshall, "British Producers Take Heart with Their Latest Talking Pictures," p. 110.
53. "British Army Co-operates in Making Picture," *Los Angeles Times*, February 14, 1937, p. C3.
54. "Mr. Douglas Fairbanks Jr. Makes a Speech," p. 3.
55. Douglas Fairbanks, Jr., *The Salad Days*, p. 245.
56. Ibid., p. 157.
57. *The Return of the Scarlet Pimpernel* deserves recognition as the first feature film to be televised live in the United States—on May 31, 1938.
58. Sam Eckman, Jr. (1892–1976) was born and died in New York, but he spent forty years in Britain, being appointed vice president and managing director of MGM, Ltd., London, in 1927, becoming its chairman in 1957. In 1947, he was given an OBE. After leaving MGM, Eckman worked for other American companies in London, most notably Stanley Kramer Productions. Eckman achieved some fame in 1933 when he announced that he would not allow any MGM film to be shown in a British cinema with a program of more than three hours duration. "We hope that the filmgoer will support him," editorialized *Film Weekly* (December 15, 1933).
59. The British male lead, as Paul Beaumont, is Griffith Jones. A talented, handsome, and virile leading man, with a nice pair of legs, as shown in this film, Jones was one of the best British leading men of the 1930s and it is a mystery why he was never signed to a Hollywood contract. He is the father of actress Gemma Jones.
60. Jeffrey Richards, ed. *The Unknown 1930s: An Alternative History of British Cinema, 1929–1939*, p. 70.
61. "Donat and Dr. Manson," p. 3.

CHAPTER 8

1. Karol Kulik, *Alexander Korda: The Man Who Could Work Miracles*, p. 135.
2. Quoted in Anthony Aldgate and Jeffrey Richards, *Best of Britain: Cinema and Society from 1930 to the Present*, p. 135.
3. Charles Davy, ed., *Footnotes to the Film*, p. 64.
4. Robeson quoted in Marie Seton, *Paul Robeson*, p. 108.
5. *Film Weekly*, March 3, 1933, p. 6.
6. Elisabeth Welch, interview with Anthony Slide, October 20, 1985.
7. Basil Dean, *Mind's Eye: An Autobiography, 1927–1972*, p. 67.
8. Marjory Collier, "The Chinese Girl: East Meets West in Anna May Wong," pp. 26–27.
9. Ibid., p. 219.
10. "Those Unwanted Villains," p. 6.
11. Luke McKernan has compiled a very good listing of women silent filmmakers in Britain, available on his website.
12. Copy in her biography file at the Margaret Herrick Library of the Academy of Motion Picture Arts and Sciences.
13. Ibid.
14. Her work is documented in Mary Field, *Good Company: The Story of the Children's Film Foundation, 1943–1950*, Longmans Green, 1952.
15. Nerina Shute, "Jacqueline Logan Defies Convention," p. 11.
16. Sometimes erroneously identified as Naomi.
17. This and other highly amusing, if at times inappropriate, stories may be found in Nigel Ostrer's self-published 2010 volume, *The Ostrers and Gaumont British*.
18. Information on Wikipedia is incorrect.

CHAPTER 9

1. Unless otherwise indicated, this and other quotes are taken from my article, "*Wings of the Morning*, an Important Film."
2. Harold Schuster, interview with Anthony Slide, February 11, 1984.
3. Glyn Roberts, "What Shall We Make for America?", p. 14.
4. "Wax Models of Films stars Costing 2,000 Pounds," p. 3.
5. A role for which Gregory Peck, James Mason, and Laurence Olivier had also been considered.
6. Peter Noble, *The British Film Yearbook*, p. 78.
7. Sid Field died in February 1950 at the age of forty-five. He is virtually unknown in the United States despite being compared to Chaplin. There is certainly a surrealistic quality to his humor, as for example in "The Golf Lesson" sketch, in which he circles the golf ball, asking, "Get behind the ball?"
8. Justin Bowyer, *Conversations with Jack Cardiff: Art, Light and Direction in Cinema*, p. 44.

CHAPTER 10

1. James Fidler, "England Wants Back its Hollywood Stars," p. 58.
2. John Sedgwick, "Michael Balcon's Close Encounter with the American Market, 1934–1936," p. 347.
3. I have written extensively on the subject of British silent films in the United States in an essay of the same title included in *Silent Topics* (Lanham, MD: Scarecrow Press, 2005), pp. 1–19.
4. Cecil Hepworth, *Came the Dawn: Memories of a Film Pioneer*, p. 89.

5. The film was remade in Britain in 1932 under the title *Let Me Explain Dear.*
6. In the *Observer* (February 19, 1933), C. A. Lejeune wrote, "*Cavalcade* is the best British film that has ever been made, and it was made in America."
7. David Niven, *The Moon's a Balloon*, p. 345.
8. Walter Butler was played by Lionel Barrymore in D. W. Griffith's *America* (1924) and appears as one of the "jury of the damned" in William Dieterle's *The Devil and Daniel Webster* (1941).
9. Walter Forde to Anthony Slide, May 25, 1972.
10. Walter Forde, interview with Anthony Slide, October 1, 1976.
11. It was reported that when Betty Balfour arrived in Los Angeles in February 1933 to reunite with her composer husband, Jimmy Campbell, writer of "Try a Little Tenderness" and "Show Me the Way to Go Home," she was considering a Hollywood career.
12. *Film Weekly*, April 1, 1929. P. 6.
13. Sheridan Morley, *Tales from the Hollywood Raj*, p. 164.
14. W. H. Mooring, "What America Thinks of British Films," p. 10.
15. Quoted in Glyn Roberts, "What Shall We Make for America?", p. 30.
16. *Forever and a Day*, released in March 1943, raised money for British and American war charities, and boasted a stellar cast of British expatriates, including Victor McLaglen, Cedric Hardwicke, Herbert Marshall, Charles Laughton, C. Aubrey Smith, Dame May Whitty, Anna Neagle, Brian Aherne, and Elsa Lanchester.
17. H. Kingsley Long, "Hollywood Can't Tempt Me Says Gracie Fields," p. 12.
18. Jeffrey Richads, "Gracie Fields, The Lancashire Britannia," p. 27.
19. Charlotte Greenwood, "Making the World Laugh," p. 28.
20. Cicely Courtneidge, *Cicely*, p. 118.
21. Ibid.
22. Anthony Slide, "An Interview with Anna Neagle," p. 27.
23. Glyn Roberts, "What Shall We Make for America?", p. 30.
24. James Fidler, "England Wants Back Its Hollywood Stars," p. 58.

CHAPTER 11

1. Douglas W. Churchill, "A British Invasion of Hollywood," p. X5.
2. The film opened at New York's Rialto Theatre on July 18, 1939, to enthusiastic reviews.
3. Republic productions were released in the United Kingdom under the name of British Lion-Republic. As *Film Weekly* (February 19, 1938) commented, "British Lion make cheap but entertaining second features in England as Republic do in Hollywood."
4. Charlot's papers are at the Department of Special Collections of UCLA, and are worthy of serious study and research.
5. Anthony Aldgate and Jeffrey Richards, *Britain Can Take It: The British Cinema in the Second World War*, p. 286.
6. Joyce Howard, interview with Anthony Slide, March 26, 2003.
7. Formby's last Ealing film in 1941, prior to the Columbia contract was *Turned Out Nice Again*.
8. "The Lancashire Buffoon," p. 168.
9. Information from Warner Bros. Archve at USC.
10. Peter Noble, ed., *The British Film Yearbook*, p. 72.
11. Louella Parsons, syndicated column, September 15, 1944.
12. Charles Davy, ed., *Footnotes to the Film*, p. 27.
13. This and all other quotes, Constance Cummings, interview with Anthony Slide, September 12, 1997.

14. "Bebe Daniels in Conversation with Ben Lyon and Anthony Slide," n. pag.
15. Vic Oliver was a Viennese-born comedian who was very popular in Britain; he was married from 1936–45 to Winston Churchill's daughter, Sarah, which caused something of a sensation because of Oliver's being a Jew.
16. Ibid.
17. These and all other quotes from Elisabeth Welch, interview with Anthony Slide, October 20, 1985.
18. "British Actors Called Slackers," p. 1.
19. Aside from Anna Lee, *How Green Was My Valley* features a number of British players, Donald Crisp, Roddy McDowall, John Loder, and Patric Knowles, as well as at least four Irish players, Maureen O'Hara, Sara Allgood, Barry Fitzgerald, and Arthur Shields. If any film is guaranteed to make the Welsh, which it is about, feel inferior, *How Green Was My Valley* is it.
20. Caroline Moorehead, *Sidney Bernstein: A Biography*, p. 133.
21. "British Actors Called Slackers," p. 1.

CHAPTER 12

1. Paul Swann, *The Hollywood Feature Film in Postwar Britain*, p. 36.
2. Robert Murphy, *Realism and Tinsel: Cinema and Society in Britain, 1939–1948*, p. 223.
3. The first batch of Universal-International releases consisted of *The Wicked Lady*, *The Rake's Progress*, *London Town*, *The Magic Bow*, *The Seventh Veil*, *The Man in Grey*, *Madonna of the Seven Moons*, *They Were Sisters*, *Dad of Night*, *Love Story*, *Brief Encounter*, *This Happy Breed*, *The Years Between*, *The Captive Heart*, *I Know Where I'm Going*, *Johnny Frenchman*, *A Matter of Life and Death*, *Odd Man Out*, and *The Upturned Glass*.
4. "Stix Still Nix British Pix," p. 16.
5. *Ibid.*
6. Sue Harper and Vincent Porter, *British Cinema of the 1950s: The Decline of Deference*, pp. 135–36.
7. Now the Broadcasting Entertainment Cinematograph & Theatre Union or BECTU.
8. Louella Parsons, syndicated column, January 19, 1946.
9. *Stage Fright* was the last of three films produced by Transatlantic Pictures Corp., a company formed at the end of World War II by Alfred Hitchcock and British producer Sidney Bernstein. Its first two films were *Rope* (1948), shot in Hollywood, and *Under Capricorn* (1949), which began production at Elstree in July 1948 but was completed at the Warner Bros. studios in Burbank, California.
10. Constance Cummings, interview with Anthony Slide, September 12, 1997.
11. Doris Nolan, interview with Anthony Slide, October 1996.
12. Ian Mackillop and Neil Sinyard, *British Cinema of the 1950s: A Celebration*, p. 122.
13. Doris Nolan, interview with Anthony Slide, October 1996.
14. I have discussed the censorship of British films in America in my book *Banned in the USA: British Films in the United States and Their Censorship, 1933–1960*.
15. "Johnston's Hands-Off on British Pix Standards Puzzles the Trade," p. 29.
16. Ibid., p. 3.
17. Richard Roud, "Britain in America," p. 122.
18. Sheridan Morley, *Tales from the Hollywood Raj*, p. 261.
19. Anna Lee, interview with Anthony Slide, March 9, 1994.

CHAPTER 13

1. H. C. Allen, *Conflict and Concord: The Anglo-American Relationship Since 1783*, p. 113.
2. Ibid., p. 112.
3. Harry Saltzman also co-founded Woodfall Film Productions with Tony Richardson and John Osborne in the late 1950s, and deserves some credit for such quintessentially British films as *Look Back in Anger* (1959) and *Saturday Night and Sunday Morning* (1960).
4. Angus Finney, "Continental Drift," p. 13.
5. Toby Miller, Nitin Govil, John McMurria, and Richard Maxwell, *Global Hollywood*, p. 73.
6. Justine Ashby and Andrew Higson, eds., *British Cinema, Past and Present*, p. 53.
7. Toby Miller, Nitin Govil, John McMurria, and Richard Maxwell, *Global Hollywood*, p.59.

BIBLIOGRAPHY

Agate, James. *Around Cinemas.* London: Home & Van Thal, 1946.

Aldgate, Anthony, and Jeffrey Richards. *Best of British: Cinema and Society from 1930 to the Present.* London: I. B. Tauris, 1999.

———. *Britain Can Take It: The British Cinema in the Second World War.* Oxford: Basil Blackwell, 1986.

Allen, H. C. *Conflict and Concord: The Anglo-American Relationship Since 1783.* New York: St. Martin's Press, 1959.

"American Movie Firm Backs British Concern." *Christian Science Monitor*, August 20, 1926, p. 3.

"Are British Directors Crazy?" *Film Weekly*, March 25, 1932, p. 8.

Ashby, Justine, and Andrew Higson, eds. *British Cinema, Past and Present.* London: Routledge, 2000.

Asher, Irving. "Sorting Out the Stars." *Film Weekly*, March 31, 1933, p. 10.

Asquith, Anthony. "The American Invasion." In *The British Film Yearbook, 1947–1948*, edited by Peter Noble. London: Skelton Robinson, n.d., pp. 78–80.

Atkinson, G. A. "British Films Made to Please America." *Daily Express*, March 18, 1927, p. 6.

Balcon, Michael. *Michael Balcon Presents . . . A Lifetime of Films.* London: Hutchinson, 1969.

Baldwin, Oliver. "The People Make British Pictures: Irving Asher." *Picturegoer*, August 12, 1939, pp. 12–13, 32.

Ball, Edward. *The Inventor and the Tycoon.* New York: Doubleday, 2013.

Barber, Sian. *The British Film Industry in the 1970s: Capital, Culture and Creativity.* London: Palgrave Macmillan, 2013.

Barr, Charles, ed. *All Our Yesterdays: 90 Years of British Cinema.* London: BFI Publishing, 1986.

Barry, Iris. *Let's Go to the Movies.* New York: Payson & Clarke, 1926.

"Bebe Daniels in Conversation with Ben Lyon and Anthony Slide." *Silent Picture*, Spring 1971, n. pag.

Belfrage, Cedric. "Hollywood Cocktail." *Film Weekly*, October 22, 1928, p. 8.

Bernds, Edward. *Mr. Bernds Goes to Hollywood.* Lanham, MD: Scarecrow Press, 1999.

Blackwell, Carlyle. "Star-Making in England." *Film Weekly*, April 26, 1930, p. 7.

Bodeen, DeWitt. "Evelyn Brent, 1899–1975." *Films in Review*, June 1976, pp. 339–60.

Bogdanovich, Peter. *Allan Dwan: The Last Pioneer.* New York: Praeger, n.d.

Bourne, Stephen. *The Black Garbo: Nina Mae McKinney.* Duncan, OK: BearManor, 2011.

———. *Black in the British Frame.* London: Cassell, 1998.

———. *Elisabeth Welch: Soft Lights and Sweet Music.* Lanham, MD: Scarecrow Press, 2005.

Bowyer, Justine. *Conversations with Jack Cardiff: Art, Light and Direction*. London: Batsford, 2003.

Brenon, Herbert. "Is Sensation Killing the Film?" *Film Weekly*, July 8, 1932, p. 11.

"Brenon Places Great Faith in Forbes-Robertson Picture." *Dramatic Mirror*, December 15, 1917, p. 14.

"Brenon Proves Himself a Screen Generalissimo." *Motion Picture News*, May 20, 1916, p. 3073.

"British Actors Called Slackers." *Los Angeles Times*, August 26, 1940, p. 1.

"British Exhibitors Denounce Famous Players and Hearst." *Variety*, July 18, 1919, p. 50.

Brown, Geoff, and Laurence Kardish, eds. *Michael Balcon: The Pursuit of British Cinema*. New York: Museum of Modern Art, 1984.

Burrows, Jon. *Legitimate Cinema: Theatre Stars in Silent British Films, 1908–1918*. Exeter, UK: University of Exeter Press, 2003.

Casella, Donna R. "Ireland a Nation: A Celebration of All Things Irish-American." *Post Script*, Summer 2013, pp. 27–43.

Caute, David. *Joseph Losey: A Revenge on Life*. London: Faber and Faber, 1994.

Chapman, James. *The British at War: Cinema, State and Propaganda, 1939–1945*. London: I. B. Tauris, 1998.

Chibnall, Steve. *Quota Quickies: The Birth of the British "B" Film*. London: BFI Publishing, 2007.

Churchill, Douglas W. "A British Invasion of Hollywood." *New York Times*, October 29, 1939, p. X5.

"Clive Brook Won't Work in England Yet." *Film Weekly*, September 26, 1931, p. 6.

Collier, Marjory. "The Chinese Girl: East Meets West in Anna May Wong." *Picturegoer*, May 1930, pp. 26–27.

Courtneidge, Cicely. *Cicely*. London: Hutchinson, 1953.

Craig, Johnstone. "The Dominant Race." *Photoplay*, October 1918, pp. 48, 112.

Crowl, Samuel. *The Films of Kenneth Branagh*. Westport, CT: Praeger, 2006.

Cummings, Constance. "Hullo, England!" *Film Weekly*, March 3, 1933, p. 7.

Daniels, Bebe, and Ben Lyon. *Life with the Lyons*. London: Odhams Press, 1953.

Danischewsky, M. [Monja]. *Michael Balcon's 25 Years in Films*. London: World Film Publications, 1947.

Davy, Charles, ed. *Footnotes to the Film*. New York: Oxford University Press, 1937.

Dean, Basil. *Mind's Eye: An Autobiography, 1927–1972*. London: Hutchinson, 1973.

Del Rio, Dolores. "This Visit to England Is My Big Chance." *Film Weekly*, April 25, 1936, p. 7.

Denig, Lynde. "Larry Trimble Brings Turner Films." *Moving Picture World*, August 19, 1916, p. 1223.

Dickinson, Margaret, and Sarah Street. *Cinema and State: The Film Industry and the British Government, 1927–1984*. London: British Film Institute, 1985.

"Donat and Dr. Manson." *Film Weekly*, February 19, 1938, p. 3.

Drazin, Charles. "Editing: Lean Cuts." *Sight and Sound*, July 2008, p. 38.

Esway, Alex. "London and Hollywood." *Hollywood Reporter*, June 30, 1937, pp. 41, 62.

Fairbanks, Douglas, Jr. *A Hell of a War*. New York: St. Martin's Press, 1993.

———. *The Salad Days*. New York: Doubleday, 1988.

Farrell, Charles, "Making My First British Picture." *Film Weekly*, June 22, 1934, pp. 8–9.

"The Father of Kinemacolor." *Moving Picture World*, February 10, 1912, pp. 487–88.

Fawcett, Roscoe. "Murder at Teddington." *Film Weekly*, January 16, 1932, p. 4.

Fidler, James. "England Wants Back Its Hollywood Stars." *Movie Classic*, June 1933, pp. 30–31, 58.

Finney, Angus. "Continental Drift." *Sunday Times*, December 12, 1993, Section 9, p. 13.

Freeland, Thornton. "Elstree Tunes in to Hollywood." *Film Weekly*, November 16, 1934, pp. 8–9.

Friedman, Lester, ed. *Fires Were Started: British Cinema and Thatcherism*. Minneapolis: University of Minnesota Press, 1993.

"The Gangplank Man," "Greeting the Stars When They Arrive in Britain." *Film Pictorial*, Christmas Extra, 1937, pp. 44–45.

Gartside, Michael Roy. *For All Seasons: The Story of Stage and Screen Actress Constance Cummings*. Bognor Regis, UK: Lauremar, 1999.

Gebhart, Myrtle. "From Jolly Old England." *Picture Play*, September 1926, pp. 74, 105.

Geltzer, George. "Herbert Brenon." *Films in Review*, March 1955, pp. 116–25.

"George Tucker Succeeding in England." *Moving Picture World*, December 19, 1914, p. 1700.

Gifford, Denis. *The British Film Catalogue, 1895–1985: A Reference Guide*. New York: Facts on File, 1986.

———. *Entertainers in British Films: A Century of Showbiz in the Cinema*. Westport, CT: Greenwood Press, 1998.

———. *The Golden Age of Radio: An Illustrated Companion*. London: B. T. Batsford, 1985.

Glancy, Mark. *Hollywood and the Americanization of Britain from the 1920s to the Present*. London: I. B. Tauris, 2014.

Gledhill, Christine. *Reframing British Cinema, 1918–1928: Between Restraint and Passion*. London: British Film Institute, 2003.

Greenwood, Charlotte. "Making the World Laugh." *Film Weekly*, May 26, 1933, p. 28.

Griffith, Corinne. "You English Are Blindfolded!" *Film Weekly*, May 6, 1932, pp. 7, 25.

Hanson, Patricia King, ed. *The American Film Institute Catalog of Motion Pictures Produced in the United States: Feature Films, 1931–1940*. Berkeley: University of California Press, 1993.

———. *The American Film Institute Catalog of Motion Pictures Produced in the United States: Feature Films, 1941–1950*. Berkeley: University of California Press, 1999.

Hardwicke, Sir Cedric, and James Brough. *A Victorian in Orbit*. Garden City, NY: Doubleday, 1961.

"Harold Shaw to Direct in London." *Moving Picture World*, May 24, 1913, p. 821.

Harper, Sue, and Vincent Porter. *British Cinema of the 1950s: The Decline of Deference*. Oxford: Oxford University Press, 2003.

Harris, Herbert. "Those English Americans." *Film Weekly*, February 10, 1933, p. 10.

Hepworth, Cecil. *Came the Dawn: Memories of a Film Pioneer*. London: Phoenix House, 1951.

———. "Director Points Out Defects in Production." *Motion Picture News*, p. 2647.

Herbert, Steve, and Luke McKernan, eds. *Who's Who in Victorian Cinema*. London: British Film Institute, 1996.

Hill, John. *British Cinema in the 1980s: Issues and Themes*. Oxford: Clarendon Press, 1999.

Hoey, Michael W. "Roy William Neill: The Master of Suspense." *Monsters from the Vault*, Winter 2011, pp. 26–34.

Howard, Sydney. "The Tea Curse in British Studios." *Film Weekly*, February 3, 1933, p. 10.

"Introducing Darts to Hollywood." *Film Pictorial*, May 15, 1937, pp. 4–5.

Jackson, Stuart. "'The American Venus' Goes British." *Film Weekly*, July 22, 1932, p. 10.

Jacobs, Lewis. *The Rise of the American Film: A Critical History*. New York: Harcourt, Brace, 1939.

Jenkins, Gary. *Daniel Day-Lewis: The Fire Within*. New York: St. Martin's Press, 1994.

"Johnston's Hands-Off on British Pix Standards Puzzles the Trade." *Variety*, October 30, 1946, pp. 3, 29.

Kulik, Karol. *Alexander Korda: The Man Who Could Word Miracles*. London: W. H. Allen, 1975.

"The Lancashire Buffoon." *New York Times*, December 8, 1940, p. 168.

"Lasky's Plans." *Film Weekly*, August 15, 1936, p. 6.

Laurel, Stan. "We Want to Thank British Filmgoers." *Film Weekly*, February 17, 1933, pp. 8–9.

Leach, Jim. *British Film*. Cambridge, UK: Cambridge University Press, 2004.

Lederer, Josie. "The Blindness of Britain." *Film Weekly*, November 5, 1928, p. 8.

Lee, Anna, and Barbara Roisman Cooper. *Anna Lee: Memoir of a Career on General Hospital and in Film*. Jefferson, NC: McFarland, 2007.

Lejeune, C. A. "The Film Scene Along the Thames." *New York Times*, April 21, 1946, p. 51.

Leslie, Cecilie. "Dark Deeds at Teddington Studios." *Film Weekly*, January 9, 1932, p. 10.

Littlefield, Joan. "Trends by the Thames." *New York Times*, August 1, 1937, p. 140.

Locke, Richard. "Why Lupe Came to London." *Film Weekly*, November 14, 1931, p. 9.

Long, H. Kingsley. "Hollywood Can't Tempt Me Says Gracie Fields." *Picturegoer Summer Annual*, n.d. [1932], pp. 12–13.

Love, Bessie. *From Hollywood with Love*. London: Elm Tree Books, 1977.

Low, Rachael. *Film Making in 1930s Britain*. London: George Allen & Unwin, 1985.

———. *The History of the British Film, 1914–1918*. London: George Allen & Unwin, 1950.

———. *The History of the British Film, 1918–1929*. London George Allen & Unwin, 1971.

Mackie, Doris. "Laura La Plante Talks." *Film Weekly*, August 25, 1933, p. 12.

Macpherson, Kenneth. "As Is." *Close Up*, July 1927, pp. 5–15.

Mandell, Paul. "David Horsley, Pioneer Picturemaker." *American Cinematographer*, March 1989, pp. 44–52.

Marriot, A. J. *Laurel & Hardy: The British Tours*. Blackpool, UK: The Author, 1993.

Marshall, Ernest. "London Film Notes." *New York Times*, February 2, 1930, p. 110.

Marshall, Wendy L. *William Beaudine: From Silents to Television*. Lanham, MD: Scarecrow Press, 2005.

Matthews, Jessie. *Over My Shoulder*. London: W. H. Allen, 1974.

McFarlane, Brian, and Anthony Slide. *The Encyclopedia of British Film*. Manchester, UK: Manchester University Press, 2013.

McGann, William. "A Film-Maker Looks at the Stars." *Film Weekly*, April 1, 1932, p. 9.

McKernan, Luke. *Charles Urban: Pioneeering the Non-Fiction Film in Britain and America, 1897–1925*. Exeter, UK: University of Exeter Press, 2013.

———. *A Yank in Britain: The Lost Memoirs of Charles Urban Film Pioneer*. Hastings, UK: The Projection Box, 1999.

McKillop, Ian, and Neil Sinyard, eds. *British Cinema of the 1950s: A Celebration*. Manchester: Manchester University Press, 2003.

McNab, Geoffrey. *J. Arthur Rank and the British Film Industry*. London: Routledge, 1992.

Meehan, Thomas. "Those Old Movie Travelogues, Or, 'As the Sun Sinks Slowly in the West, We Bid Farewell . . .'" *New York Times*, November 28, 1971, pp. XX1, XX15.

Menjou, Adolphe, and M. M. Musselman. *It Took Nine Tailors*. New York: Whittlesey House, 1948.

Miller, Toby, Nitin Govil, John McMurria, and Richard Maxwell. *Global Hollywood*. London: BFI Publishing, 2001.

"Miss Edna Flugrath." *Moving Picture World*, September 12, 1914, p. 1519.

"Mr. Douglas Fairbanks Jr. Makes a Speech." *National Board of Review Magazine*, May 1936, pp. 3–4.

Mitchell, George. "Sidney Olcott." *Films in Review*, April 1954, pp. 175–81.

Moen, L. C. "Florence Turner, First Star, Returns to U.S." *Motion Picture News*, May 24, 1924, pp. 2430–31, 2433.

Moorehead, Caroline. *Sidney Bernstein: A Biography*. London: Jonathan Cape, 1984.
Mooring, W. H. "What America Thinks of British Films." *Film Weekly*, January 15, 1938, pp. 9–10, 24.
Morley, Sheridan. *Tales from the Hollywood Raj: The British in California*. London: George Weidenfeld & Nicholson, 1983.
Moss, Marilyn Ann. *Raoul Walsh: The True Adventures of Hollywood's Legendary Director*. Lexington, KY: University Press of Kentucky, 2011.
Murphy, Robert. *Realism and Tinsel: Cinema and Society in Britain, 1939–1948*. London: Routledge, 1989.
Murphy, Robert, ed. *The British Cinema Book*. London: British Film Institute, 1997.
———. *British Cinema of the 90s*. London: British Film Institute, 2000.
Mycroft, Walter C. *Walter Mycroft: The Time of My Life: The Memoirs of a British Film Producer*. Lanham, MD: Scarecrow Press, 2006.
Napper, Lawrence. *British Cinema and Middlebrow Culture in the Interwar Years*. Exeter, UK: University of Exeter Press, 2009.
Neame, Ronald. *Straight from the Horse's Mouth*. Lanham, MD: Scarecrow Press, 2003.
Newton, David. "Britain Leads in Equipment." *British Studio Newsletter*, April 1948, pp. 6–7.
Niven, David. *Bring on the Empty Horses*. New York: G. P. Putnam's Sons, 1975.
———. *The Moon's a Balloon*. New York: G. P. Putnam's Sons, 1972.
Noble, Peter. *The British Film Yearbook*. London: British Yearbooks, n.d.
———. *The British Film Yearbook, 1947–1948*. London: Skelton Robinson, n.d.
Omand, W. D., "Meet the Passengers on Rome Express." *Film Weekly*, February 3, 1933, p. 13.
Park, James. *British Cinema: The Lights That Failed*. London: B. T. Batsford, 1990.
Parkinson, David, "Hitchcock at War." *Empire*, August 2010, pp. 124–25.
Perry, George. *The Great British Picture Show: From the 90s to the 70s*. New York: Hill and Wang, 1974.
Petrie, Duncan. *The British Cinematographer*. London: British Film Institute, 1996.
———. *Creativity and Constraint in the British Film Industry*. New York: St. Martin's Press, 1991.
Phillips, M. D. "That Imported Talent." *Picturegoer*, May 14, 1932, p. 5.
"Plain Speaking About 'Quota' Pictures." *Film Weekly*, June 29, 1934, p. 3.
Quirk, James R. "Speaking of Pictures." *Photoplay*, September 1926, pp. 27, 118.
Ralston, Esther. *Some Day We'll Laugh: An Autobiography*. Metuchen, NJ: Scarecrow Press, 1985.
Ramsaye, Terry. "*Cavalcade*." *Motion Picture Herald*, January 14, 1931, p. 16.
Rawton, Steve. *Kicking the Moon Around: The Story of Ambrose and His Orchestra*. Folkestone, UK: Kamuscio, 2007.
Reeves, Nicholas. *Official British Film Propaganda during the First World War*. London: Croom Helm, 1986.
Renshaw, Charles, Jr. "Carlyle Blackwell's Delayed Romance." *American Weekly*, June 6, 1948, p. 19.
Richards, Jeffrey. *The Age of the Dream Palace: Cinema and Society in Britain, 1930–1939*. London: Routledge & Kegan Paul, 1984.
———. *Films and British National Identity: From Dickens to Dad's Army*. Manchester, UK: Manchester University Press, 1997.
———. "Gracie Fields, The Lancashire Britannia." *Focus on Film*, August 1979, pp. 27–35.
———. *Visions of Yesterday*. London: Routledge & Kegan Paul, 1973.
Richards, Jeffrey, ed. *The Unknown 1930s: An Alternative History of the British Cinema, 1929–1939*. London: I. B. Tauris, 1998.
Roberts, Glyn. "What Shall We Make for America?" *Film Weekly*, July 9, 1938, pp. 14, 30.

Robertson, James C. *The Hidden Cinema: British Film Censorship in Action, 1913–1972*. London: Routledge, 1989.

"Ronald Colman as Cricketer." *Film Weekly*, July 19, 1930, p. 7.

Rotha, Paul. *The Film Till Now*. London: Vision Press, 1949.

Roud, Richard, "Britain in American." *Sight and Sound*, pp. 119–23.

Russell, Frederick. "Hollywood Wants the Other Lawton Now." *Film Pictorial*, May 12, 1934, p. 12.

Ryall, Tom. *Britain and the American Cinema*. London: Sage Publications, 2001.

"Sam (Eckman) Picks Up His Musket." *Film Weekly*, December 15, 1933, p. 3.

Sargeant, Amy. *British Cinema: A Critical History*. London: British Film Institute, 2005.

Saville, Victor, and Roy Moseley. *Evergreen: Victor Saville in His Own Words*. Carbondale, IL: Southern Illinois University Press, 2000.

Schallert, Edwin. "Elated over London Trip." *Los Angeles Times*, November 12, 1920, p. II14.

Sedgwick, John. "Michael Balcon's Close Encounter with the American Market, 1934–1936." *Historical Journal of Film, Radio and Television* 16, no. 3, 1996, pp. 333–48.

———. *Popular Filmgoing in 1930s Britain: A Choice of Pleasures*. Exeter: University of Exeter Press, 2000.

Seton, Marie. *Paul Robeson*. London: Dennis Dobson, 1958.

Seymour, Miranda. *Chaplin's Girl: The Life and Loves of Virginia Cherrill*. London: Simon & Schuster, 2009.

Shute, Nerina. "Jacqueline Logan Defies Convention." *Film Weekly*, September 19, 1931, p. 11.

———. "Mary Pickford's 'Right Hand' in England." *Film Weekly*, March 4, 1929, p. 15.

Slide, Anthony. "American Cinematographers in Britain." *American Cinematographer*, November 1986, pp. 36-40.

———. *Banned in the USA: British Films in the United States and Their Censorship, 1933–1960*. London: I. B. Tauris, 1998.

———. *The Big V: A History of the Vitagraph Company*. Metuchen, NJ: Scarecrow Press, 1987.

———. *The Cinema and Ireland*. Jefferson, NC: McFarland, 1988.

———. *The Encyclopedia of Vaudeville*. Jackson, MS: University Press of Mississippi, 2012.

———. *Frank Lloyd: Master of Screen Melodrama*. Albany, GA: BearManor Media, 2009.

———. *The Kindergarten of the Movies: A History of the Fine Arts Company*. Metuchen, NJ: Scarecrow Press, 1980.

———. "Old World, New Cinema." *Queen's Quarterly*, Summer 1995, pp. 357–74.

———. "*Wings of the Morning*, an Important Film." *American Cinematographer*, February 1986, pp. 36–40.

Stead, Peter. "Hollywood's Message for the World: The British Response in the Nineteen Thirties." *Historical Journal of Film, Radio and Television* 1, no. 1, 1981, pp. 19–32.

Stein, Jeanne. "Edward Everett Horton." *Focus on Film*, January/February 1970, pp. 30–49.

"Stix Still Nix British Pix." *Variety*, June 18, 1947, pp. 1, 16, 18.

Straker, Jean. "Rise of a Red-Head." *Film Weekly*, October 12, 1934, p. 14.

Street, Sarah. *British National Cinema*. London: Routledge, 1997.

———. *Colour Films in Britain: The Negotiation of Innovation, 1900–55*. London: British Film Institute, 2012.

———. *Transatlantic Crossings: British Feature Films in the USA*. New York: Continuum, 2002.

Swann, Paul. *The Hollywood Feature Film in Postwar Britain*. New York: St. Martin's Press, 1987.

Swanson, Gloria. *Swanson on Swanson*. New York: Random House, 1980.

Tannura, Phil. "Looking Back at Ten Years in Europe." *Cine-Technician*, October–December 1940, pp. 84–85.

Taylor, John Russell. *Strangers in Paradise: The Hollywood Emigrés, 1933–1950*. New York: Holt, Rinehart and Winston, 1983.

Taylor, Philip M., ed. *Britain and the Cinema in the Second World War*. New York: St. Martin's Press, 1988.

"Those Unwanted Villains." *Film Weekly*, May 23, 1931, p. 6.

Tiltman, Hubert H. "Ireland—A Film El Dorado." *Picture Plays*, January 10, 1920, p. 23.

"The Trek to London." *Film Weekly*, March 31, 1933, p. 3.

Trimble, Marian Blackton. *J. Stuart Blackton: A Personal Biography by His Daughter*. Metuchen, NJ: Scarecrow Press, 1985.

Troyan, Michael. *A Rose for Mrs. Miniver: The Life of Greer Garson*. Lexington, KY: University Press of Kentucky, 1999.

Truffaut, François. *Hitchcock*. New York: Simon and Schuster, 1967.

Underhill, Duncan. "Reformed Vagabonds." *Motion Picture Magazine*, August 1944, pp. 58. 84.

Varconi, Victor, and Ed Honeck. *It's Not Enough to Be Hungarian*. Denver: Graphic Impressions, 1976.

"Vast Pix Saving in New Brit. Pact." *Variety*, June 5, 1946, pp. 5, 29.

Vazzana, Eugene Michael. *Silent Film Necrology*. Jefferson, NC: McFarland, 2001.

Viertel, Berthold. "Huston: The Man and the Actor." *Film Weekly*, March 14, 1936, p. 9.

Vorhaus, Bernard. *Saved from Oblivion*. Lanham, MD: Scarecrow Press, 2000.

Walker, Alexander. *Hollywood UK: The British Film Industry in the 1960s*. New York: Stein and Day, 1974.

Walker, John. *The Once & Future Film*. London: Methuen, 1985.

Walker, Joseph, and Juanita Walker. *The Light on Her Face*. Los Angeles: The ASC Press, 1984.

Walsh, Raoul. *Each Man in His Time*. New York: Farrar, Strauss and Giroux, 1974.

Wearing, J. P. *The London Stage, 1930–1939: A Calendar of Plays and Players*. Metuchen, NJ: Scarecrow Press, 1990.

———. *The London Stage, 1940–1949: A Calendar of Plays and Players*. Metuchen, NJ: Scarecrow Press, 1991.

Wenders, Wim. *The Logic of Images: Essays and Conversations*. London: Faber and Faber, 1991.

Weston, Harold. *The Art of Photo Play Writing*. London: McBride, Nast, 1916.

Wilcox, Herbert. *25,000 Sunsets*. London: The Bodley Head, 1967.

Williams, Elmo. *A Hollywood Memoir*. Jefferson, NC: McFarland, 2006.

Winnington, Richard. *Drawn and Quartered: A Selection of Weekly Film Reviews and Drawings*. London: The Saturn Press, n.d.

Wong, Anna May. "I Protest." *Film Weekly*, p. 11.

Wray, Fay. *On the Other Hand: A Life Story*. New York: St. Martin's Press, 1989.

"*A Yank at Oxford*." *Picturegoer's* Famous Films Supplement, September 3, 1938.

Yule, Andrew. *Fast Fade: David Puttnam, Columbia Pictures, and the Battle for Hollywood*. New York: Delacorte Press, 1989.

Zouary, Maurice H. *DeForest: Father of the Electronic Revolution*. Self-published, 2000.

INDEX

ABC Cinemas, 255
Absinthe, 57
Accused, 155
Across the Atlantic, 57
Action for Slander, 101
Adams, Robert, 166
Adam's Apple, 92, 131
Addinsell, Richard, 220
Adler, Larry, 9, 258
Adventures of Robin Hood, The, 259
Adventures of Sherlock Holmes, The, 243
Adventures of Sir Lancelot, The, 259
Adventures of Tartu, The, 163
African Americans, 164–70, 236–38
After the Ball, 110
Agate, James, 125, 126
Aherne, Brian, 93, 210, 243
Akins, Zoe, 155
Aldrich, Robert, 253
Allan, Elizabeth, 161, 162, 174
Allen, H. C., 33, 263, 264
Allen, Lewis, 254
Allgood, Sara, 112
Alliance Productions, Ltd., 257
Alvarado, Don, 105, 109
Amateur Gentleman, The, 155
Amazing Quest of Mr. Ernest Bliss, The, 111
Ambler, Eric, 221
Ambrose, Bert, 125
AmerAnglo Corporation, 199
American Overseas Artists, 236
American Prisoner, The, 92
Among the Irish Fisherfolk, 41
Andrews, Dana, 253
Angel Street, 226, 227
Angelus, Muriel, 140
Anglo-American Film Agreement, 247
Angry Hills, The, 253
Animation in Britain, 248
Annabella, 100, 102, 182, 187, 189
Annakin, Ken, 257
Aoki, Tsuru, 78
Apfel, Oscar, 80
"Are You Really Mine?," 82
Aren't We All?, 135
Argyle, John, 113
Argyle-British Studio, 113
Arlen, Richard, 109
Arliss, George, 109, 142, 144, 159, 211
Arrah-Na-Pogue, 39, 41
Arsenal Stadium Mystery, The, 15
Arthur, George K., 7, 72–73, 210
Artlee Pictures, 199
As You Like It, 102
Asher, Irving, 123, 142, 143, 144–48, 156, 163
Ashley, Lady Sylvia, 158
Asquith, Anthony, 7, 15, 107, 221
Associated British Pictures Corporation, Ltd., 143, 254, 255, 256
Associated Talking Pictures, 139
Association of Cine-Technicians, 250
Astaire, Fred, 212
Astor, Viscount, 260
Ates, Roscoe, 144
Atlantic, 171
Atlantic Ferry, 228
Atlantic Films, 118
Atlee, Clement, 246
Atoll K., 122
Atonement, 266
Aubrey, Jimmy, 15, 206
Austin, William, 15

Autumn Crocus, 178
Aventure Malgache, 242
Aylmer, Felix, 220
Ayre, George, 141

Babb, Sanora, 103
Baggot, King, 57
Bairnsfather, Bruce, 198
Bait, 132
Baker, Kenny, 190
Balcon, Michael, 78, 81, 85, 110, 158–60, 173, 184, 192, 198, 228, 240, 242, 243
Balcon-Saville-Freedman, 85
Balfour, Betty, 98, 199, 208
Bankhead, Tallulah, 77
Banks, Leslie, 102, 166, 187, 210, 231
Banks, Monty, 92, 131, 156, 213, 214, 230
Barnaby Rudge, 71
Barnato, Leah, 81
Barnes, Barry K., 157
Barnes, Binnie, 205
Baroud, 54
Barry, Iris, 3, 31, 91
Barrymore, John, 83
Barrymore, Lionel, 77, 102
Barthelmess, Richard, 108–9
Bartholomew, Freddie, 15, 160, 210
Barzman, Ben, 257
Batchelor, Harold, 192
Battle Cry of Peace, The, 28
Battle of the Sexes, The, 233
B.B.C. the Voice of Britain, 169
Beacon Theatre, New York, 261
Beaudine, William, 125, 129–30
Beauford, Ireland, 39, 42, 45, 46, 47, 48
Bedrock, 82
Beery, Noah, 117–18
Belfrage, Cedric, 7
Bell, Monta, 127
Belle of North Wales, The, 45
Beloved Vagabond, The, 80–81
Bennett, Charles, 243
Bennett, Compton, 153
Bennett, Constance, 114
Berger, Ludwig, 189
Bergman, Ingrid, 226
Bergner, Elizabeth, 102, 103, 114, 127
Bernds, Edward, 140
Bernstein, Sidney, 242–43
Better 'Ole, The, 198
Bevan, Billy, 205
Beyond the Stars, 82
Bickford, Charles, 105
Big Fella, 167
Big Frame, The, 260
Bill of Divorcement, A, 77
Billy Elliott, 266
Binney, Constance, 77
Biro, Lajos, 197
Blaché, Alice Guy, 26
Blaché, Herbert, 26
Black Eyes, 120
Black Narcissus, 192
Black Rose, The, 253
Black Waters, 111, 201
Blacklist, 9, 257–60
Blackmail, 201, 255
Blackton, J. Stuart, 27–30, 81, 93, 94, 209
Blackton, Marion, 94
Blackwell, Carlyle, 80–82
Blaisdell, George, 200
Blame the Woman, 116
Bland, R. Henderson, 43
Blane, Sally, 112–13, 144
Blarney Stone, The, 46
Blinkhorn, Albert "Blinkie," 198
Blithe Spirit, 149, 193, 222, 232–33
Blore, Eric, 114, 210
Blythe, Betty, 81, 83, 86, 92, 199
Bodeen, DeWitt, 221
Bohemian Girl, The, 92, 198
Bold Emmett, Ireland's Martyr, 47
Bon Voyage, 242
Bond Street, 109
Bondman, The, 97
Bonnie Prince Charlie, 192
Booth, Margaret, 160
Borden, Olive, 109
Borehamwood Studios, 249, 253, 268
Bouchier, Chili, 106, 146, 147
Boucicault, Dion, 40, 44, 45
Boy Ten Feet Tall, A, 266, 267
Boyer, Charles, 226
Boyle, Danny, 264
Boyle, John, 100
Brabin, Charles, 207
Brackett, Charles, 14
Brady, Scott, 260

Branagh, Kenneth, 64
Brat, The, 93
Braveheart, 207, 265
Breen, Joseph, 260
Brenon, Herbert, 44, 55–61, 77, 120
Brent, Evelyn, 79–80, 92
Brian, Mary, 110–12, 201
Bridge, Joan, 192
Bridge on the River Kwai, The, 258
Brief Encounter, 249
Bright, John, 245
British & Colonial, 77
British & Dominions Film Corporation, 89, 109, 127, 135, 136, 200
British Empire Film Institute, 5
British Film Institute, 4
British Instructional Films, Ltd., 199
British International Pictures, 199, 255
"British National War Film," 58
British Sound Film Productions, Ltd., 89
British Talking Pictures, Ltd., 89
British War Relief, 14
Brody, Estelle, 209–10
Brokaw, Francis Seymour, 184
Broken Blossoms, 96
Brook, Clive, 7, 15, 78, 80, 85, 86, 135, 205, 210, 211, 223
Brown, Phil, 9, 259
Browne, Irene, 205
Bruce, Nigel, 11, 13, 118, 142, 143, 210, 243, 244
Bruce, Virginia, 260
Brunel, Adrian, 123
Bryan, John, 192
Bryanston Films, 266
Buccaneers, The, 259
Buchanan, Jack, 91, 93, 103–4, 119, 120, 135
Bucquet, Harold, 163
Bulldog Drummond, 80
Bulldog Jack, 119
Bunny, John, 28, 45–46
Bunny at the Derby, 46
Burke, Johnny, 194
Burnside, William, 187
Busch, Mae, 83
Bushell, Anthony, 121, 122
Bushman, Francis X., 109
Busman's Holiday, 162–63
Butler, Alexander, 200
Butler, Lawrence, 192
Butler, Walter, 7, 207
Byng, Douglas, 111
Byron, Walter, 207

Caesar and Cleopatra, 192, 249
Caine, Hall, 58, 75, 83
Caine, Michael, 261, 262
Calendar, The, 127
Call of Youth, The, 91
Calvert, Catherine, 77
Calvert, Phyllis, 135
Campbell, Colin, 207
Campbell, Eric, 15, 206
Canterbury Tale, A, 225
Captain Horatio Hornblower, RN, 254
Captivation, 107–8
Cardiff, Jack, 187, 196
Carnival, 198
Carpentier, Georges, 94
Carroll, John, 260
Carroll, Madeleine, 82, 92, 106, 159
Carry On in the Legion, 9
Carstairs, John Paddy, 136
Caste, 71
Catherine the Great, 156, 202
Cavalcade, 15, 204–6
Cavalcanti, Alberto, 232
Ceballos, Larry, 124
Celestial City, The, 77
Centaur Film Company, 30
Chandler, Helen, 121
Channel Crossing, 230
Chaplin, Charlie, 10, 121, 211, 242, 243, 261
Chaplin, Syd, 10, 92, 198, 199, 211
Chapman, Edward, 167–68
Chariots of Fire, 269
Charlot, André, 110, 220–21
Charteris, Leslie, 219
Chatterton, Ruth, 120, 202
Chepstow, 57
Cherrill, Virginia, 112
Cherry Kearton Films, 152
Chester, 58
Chinese characterizations, 174–75
Christ in Concrete, 257
Christian, The, 83
Christopher Columbus, 193
Chu Chin Chow, 86, 173–74, 192, 197, 198

Church Mouse, The, 145, 148
Churchill, Diana, 60, 153
Churchill, Winston, 3, 10, 239, 269, 246
Churchill's Island, 224
Cinema International Corporation, 268
Cinematograph Films Act (1927), 134
Cinematograph Films Act (1938), 221
Circle of Chalk, The, 170
Citadel, The, 161, 163
Clair, René, 243
Claire, Bernice, 112
Clark, Jack, 38, 39, 40, 41, 42, 43, 44, 46, 47, 49
Clark, Petula, 195, 196
Cleese, John, 264
Clive, Colin, 136, 137
Clockwork Orange, A, 253
Clouds over Europe, 148
Clyde, June, 111
Cohn, Harry, 140
Cohn, Roy, 258
Colin, Jean, 190, 191
Colleano, Bonar, 222
Colleen Bawn, The, 39, 40, 41, 47
Collier, Constance, 85, 92, 118, 210
Collier, William "Buster," Jr., 147
Collins, Joan, 262
Colman, Ronald, 6, 7, 10, 11, 13, 119, 243
Columbia Pictures, 8, 118, 140, 148, 222, 223, 226, 229, 260
Columbus, Chris, 264
Come Out of the Pantry, 119
Comfort, Lance, 221, 228, 254
Comin' thro' the Rye, 199
Compson, Betty, 83, 85–86
Compton, Betty, 144
Compton, Fay, 72
Compton, Juliette, 78
Con the Shaughraun, 44
Confetti, 91
Conspirator, 250
Constant Nymph, The, 178
Conway, Jack, 160
Conway, the Kerry Dancer, 45
Cook, Clyde, 123
Cooke lenses, 23–24
Cooper, Gladys, 76, 92
Coronado Productions (England), Ltd., 260
Cortez, Ricardo, 109
Counsel's Opinion, 128
Courtneidge, Cicely, 106, 214–16
Coward, Noel, 83, 103, 149, 192, 204, 205
Craig, Davina, 114
Crawford, Anne, 149
Crespinel, William T., 93
Crichton, Charles, 264
Cricket, 12–14, 250
Crime on the Hill, 144
Crimson Pirate, The, 254
Crisp, Donald, 210
Criterion Film Productions, 155–56
Croker, Richard, 37, 48–49
Cromwell, Richard, 118
Crooked Billet, The, 82
Crouching Beast, The, 115
Cukor, George, 226, 250
Cummings, Constance, 9, 163, 193, 229–33, 257–58, 259, 266
Cummins, Peggy, 253
Curry, Finlay, 125
Curtis, Jamie Lee, 264
Curtis, Richard, 264
Cutts, Graham, 78, 82, 84–86, 95
Czinner, Paul, 102, 103, 127

Dall, Evelyn, 125
Dance Band, 110, 111
Dandy Dick, 129
Dandy Donovan, the Gentleman Cracksman, 75–76
Dangerous Moonlight, 220
Daniels, Bebe, 233–36
D'Arcy, Alexander, 109
Dark Journey, 101
Dark Sands, 167
Dark Tower, The, 150
Darnell, Linda, 260
Darts, 14
Dassin, Jules, 254
Daw, Marjorie, 78
Day-Lewis, Daniel, 64–66
de Courville, Albert, 231
de Mille, Agnes, 194
Dean, Basil, 139, 170, 174, 213
Death Drives Through, 120
Decameron Nights, 77
DeForest, Lee, 89
DeForest Phonofilms, 89

Del Rio, Dolores, 155, 157
Dell, Jeffrey, 107
Denham Studios, 102, 152, 160, 161, 184, 187, 190, 192, 247, 253, 254
Denny, Reginald, 210
Desert Victory, 224
Desmond, Florence, 126
Detective Lloyd, 140
Diamond Cut Diamond, 116
Diana of Dobson's, 76
Dickinson, Thorold, 15, 174, 225
Dickson, W. K. L., 23, 25–26
Dietrich, Marlene, 101, 254
Dinner at the Ritz, 100
Dirty Dozen, The, 253
Divorce of Lady X, The, 101, 128, 132, 189, 197
Dix, Richard, 83, 109
Dmytryk, Edward, 257
Donaldson, Arthur, 39, 40, 42
Donat, Robert, 22, 23, 102, 145, 160, 161, 162, 163, 203, 252
Donlevy, Brian, 113
Don't Take It to Heart, 261
Doro, Marie, 58, 72, 77
Dors, Diana, 14
Douglas Fairbanks Jr. Presents, 157
Down Our Street, 135
Dr. Strangelove or: How I Learned to Stop Worrying and Love the Bomb, 223
Dr. Syn, 142
Draper, Paul, 258
Dreaming Lips, 103
Driscoll, Bobby, 256
Drum, The, 189
Duke, Ivy, 200
Dunne, Irene, 254
Dunne, Philip, 253
Dupont, E. A., 98, 170, 172, 173
Durante, Jimmy, 126
Dvorak, Ann, 226, 227–28
Dwan, Allan, 128

Eagle-Lion Films, Inc., 248
Ealing Studios, 139
Earle, Josephine, 78–79
East Is East, 71
Ebb Tide, 128
Edge of the World, The, 154–55
Edison Film Company, 72, 73, 75, 99
Edward, My Son, 250, 251
Edwards, Blake, 253
Edwards, Henry, 70, 71, 141
Eggar, Samantha, 64, 262
Eichberg, Richard, 170, 173
18 Minutes, 128
Eilers, Sally, 108, 233
Elephant Boy, 127
Ellington, Duke, 236
Ellis, Mary, 124–25
Elsom, Isabel, 243
Elstree Calling, 173
Elstree Studios, 124, 131, 133, 136, 140, 252, 254, 255
Elusive Pimpernel, The, 251
Elvey, Maurice, 2, 108, 119
Emil and the Detectives, 153
Empire Theatre, Leicester Square, 143, 250
End of the Affair, The, 260
Endfield, Cy, 260
England's Menace, 73
English Patient, The, 266
ENSA, 236
Escape, 253
Escape Me Never, 127
Escape to Danger, 228
Esway, Alexander, 176
Evans, Edith, 71
Evans, Madge, 108
Evensong, 178
Everybody Dance, 106
Everything Is Thunder, 114
Exeter Theatre, Boston, 261
Eyes Wide Shut, 253

Fairbanks, Douglas, Jr., 7, 63, 137, 155–56
Fairbanks, Douglas, Sr., 137, 158
Falling in Love, 108
Famous Players-Lasky, 5, 91, 95
Far from Erin's Eye, 41
Far from the Madding Crowd, 70
Farewell Again, 102
Farnham, Allen, 39, 40, 43, 46
Farnum, Dorothy, 178–81
Farrell, Charles, 108
Farrell, Glenda, 144
Fassbender, Michael, 66
Fegte, Ernst, 194
Feminine Touch, The, 196

Fenton, Leslie, 219, 226, 227–28
Feuchtwanger, Lion, 178, 181
Feuillere, Edwige, 220
Feyder, Jacques, 101
Field, Mary, 176–77, 248
Field, Sid, 195, 196
Fields, Gracie, 100, 113, 212–14
Fighting Generation, The, 242
Fighting Pimpernel, The, 251
Finch, Flora, 28
Finch, Peter, 251
Finlayson, Jimmy, 123
Fire over England, 102, 103, 197
Fish Called Wanda, A, 264
Fishermaid of Ballydavid, The, 41
Fitzgerald, Geraldine, 132
Fitzmaurice, George, 91
FitzPatrick, James A., 129
Flaherty, Robert, 127
Flames of Passion, 85, 92
Flight from Folly, 150
Florence Turner Impersonates Film Favorites, 70
Flugrath, Edna, 72–74
Flying Fortress, 151
Flying Squad, The, 61
Flynn, Errol, 146
Follow That Camel, 9
Fonda, Henry, 184, 188
Football, 14–15
For Ireland's Sake, 47
Forbes, Ralph, 4–5, 7, 210
Forbes Robertson, Sir Johnston, 16, 57–58
Forbidden Street, The, 253
Forbidden Territory, 153
Ford, Hugh, 91
Ford, John, 11
Ford, Wallace, 14, 124, 155, 167
Forde, Walter, 110, 119, 125, 143, 173, 207–8
Foreman, Carl, 9, 258–59
Foreman Went to France, The, 232
Forest, Ann, 77
Forester, C. S., 243
Forever and a Day, 212, 213
Formby, George, 130, 223–24
49th Parallel, The, 242
Four Dark Hours, 127
Four Feathers, The, 189, 202
Four Weddings and a Funeral, 264, 266
Fox British Pictures, 139, 152
Fox Farm, 95
Francis, Alec B., 210
Franciscan Friars of Killarney, The, 41
Franklin, Sidney, 160, 161
Frederick, Pauline, 77
Freedman, John, 85
Freedom Radio, 223
Freeland, Thornton, 167, 190
French, Harold, 220, 257
Friese-Greene, William, 22, 23
From the Manger to the Cross, 43, 46, 48
Furniss, Harry, 75
Fyffe, Will, 125, 135

Gail, Jane, 75
Gallagher, Skeets, 106
Gang Show, The, 128
Gangelin, Paul, 144
Garcia, Rosita, 54, 56
Gardiner, Reginald, 11, 210
Gardner, Cyril, 137
Gargan, William, 106
Garmes, Lee, 103–4
Garson, Greer, 62–64, 161, 163, 224, 262
Garvey, Marcus, 166
Gaslight, 225–26
Gaumont-British, 114, 158, 160, 167, 178, 180, 199
Gauntier, Gene, 35–47
Gay Love, 125
Gaye, Howard, 211
Geiger, Rod E., 257
Gene Gauntier Feature Players, 46, 47
Genevieve, 258, 261
Gentleman's Gentleman, A, 114
Geoffrey, Walter, 140
Geraghty, Carmelita, 80
Gering, Marion, 118
Ghost Camera, The, 131
Ghost Goes West, The, 102, 114, 202
Gibson, Mel, 207, 265
Gibson, Wynne, 115
Gilliat, Sidney, 231
Gillie, Jean, 220
Girl in Possession, The, 148
Gish, Dorothy, 83, 86–89, 91, 255
Gish, Lillian, 83, 84
Give Us This Day, 257

Glamorous Night, 124
Gleason, James, 125
Glorious Adventure, The, 93, 94, 209
Glyn, Elinor, 98
Go Between, The, 256, 259
Goddard, Paulette, 193
Godfrey, Renee, 244
Goetz, William, 159, 160
Goldstein, Bob, 260
Goldwyn, Sam, 6, 13, 61, 83
Good Deeds, 208
Goodbye, Mr. Chips, 63, 161–62
Goodhart, Al, 119
Gordon, Harry Pirie, 94
Gorman, Charles, 30
Goulding, Alfred, 128
Goulding, Edmund, 201, 243
Gowland, Gibson, 207
Graetz, Paul, 130
Graham, J. C., 135
Graham, Sheilah, 6
Grahame-White, Claude, 57
Granger, Stewart, 153, 220, 261
Grant, Cary, 10, 111–12, 210, 253
Grant, Eldon, 167
Grant, Valentine, 47, 49
Granville, Bonita, 206
Granville, Fred Leroy, 81, 200
Gray, Gilda, 170, 171, 172, 173
Gray, Sally, 219, 220
Great Barrier, The, 108
Great Day, 221
Great Day, The, 91
Great Dictator, The, 242
Great Love, The, 83
Great Mr. Handel, The, 192
Green, Guy, 104
Green, Martyn, 190
Green Cockatoo, The, 128
Green Spot, The, 141
Greene, Max, 221
Greenwood, Charlotte, 125, 214
Gréville, Edmond, 109
Griffith, Corinne, 136
Griffith, D. W., 61, 83, 84, 95, 96, 108
Groves, George, 141
Guest, Val, 194
Guissart, René, 92–93
Gullan, Campbell, 200
Gunning, Fred, 47
Guns of Navarone, The, 258
Gwenn, Edmund, 100, 160, 174, 210
Gynt, Greta, 195, 220
Gypsy Blood, 124
Gypsy Cavalier, A, 93, 94
Gypsy Melody, 124

Haas, Dolly, 96
Hagen, Julius, 108, 113–14, 131, 139
Hagenbeck Films, 152
Hale, Alan, 155
Hale, Sonny, 195, 196
Hall, Adelaide, 236–37
Hall, Charles D., 210
Hall, Emmett Campbell, 44
Hallard, C. M., 200
Hamilton, Neil, 109
Hamilton, Patrick, 225
Hammond, Kay, 232
Hanbury, Victor, 221
Hand, David, 248
Handmade Films, 266
Hard Day's Night, A, 267
Harding, Ann, 116, 117
Hardwicke, Cedric, 13, 72, 110, 125, 167, 180, 211, 243
Hardy, Oliver, 122–23
Harker, Gordon, 111
Harris, Henry, 94, 95
Harrison, George, 266
Harrison, Kay, 184
Harrison, Rex, 153, 203, 232, 261
Harron, Robert, 83
Harry Potter series, 152, 264–65
Harvey, Lilian, 227
Haskin, Byron, 256
Hasty Heart, The, 254
Hate Ship, The, 92
Hathaway, Henry, 253
Hatter's Castle, 254
Haunted Honeymoon, 163
Haunting, The, 253
Havelock-Allan, Anthony, 136
Hawks, Howard, 253
Hawks, William, 230
Hawley, Wanda, 77
Hay, Ian, 60, 61
Hay, Will, 123, 129, 166

Hayakawa, Sessue, 78
Head Office, 124
Heads We Go, 230
Hearst, William Randolph, 5, 198
Hearts of the World, 83
Heller, Otto, 109
Helm, Brigitte, 114
Henderson, Dick, 15, 205
Henry V, 192, 249, 261
Hepworth, Cecil, 5, 69, 71, 198, 199
Hepworth American Film Company, 198
Her First Affaire, 128
Her Imaginary Lover, 147
Herzig, Sid, 194
Hey! Hey! U.S.A., 123
Hi Gang!, 234
Hicks, Bert, 237
Hicks, Sir Seymour, 60, 142, 207, 240
High Seas, 93
Hildyard, Jack, 99
Hillier, Erwin, 194
Hilton, James, 243
Hindle Wakes, 209
His House in Order, 77
"His Last Bow," 244
His Majesty O'Keefe, 254
Hiscott, Leslie, 92
Hitchcock, Alfred, 4, 80, 82, 92, 95, 101, 105, 180, 239–40, 254, 255
Hobson, Valerie, 155
Hoffman, Al, 119
Hollister, Alice, 39, 43
Hollister, George K., 37, 39, 43, 49
Hollywood Cricket Club, 12, 15
Holmes, Phillips, 60, 121
Homolka, Oscar, 146
Honeymoon Abroad, 131
Hope, Bob, 211
Hopkins, Anthony, 262
Hopkins, Miriam, 105, 117
Hopper, Hedda, 6
Hopper, Victoria, 178
Hornbeck, William, 117, 133
Horney, Brigitte, 109
Horsley, David, 30–31
Horsley, William, 31
Horton, Edward Everett, 6, 113–14, 117
Hotel Reserve, 221
Hound of the Baskervilles, The, 243
Housemaster, The, 59–61, 120–21
Howard, Joyce, 86, 223
Howard, Leslie, 8, 13, 101, 102, 135, 211
Howard, Sydney, 8, 97
Howard, Trevor, 221
Howard, William K., 102, 103
Howe, James Wong, 102–3
Howes, Bobby, 93
Hubert, René, 117, 184, 189
Hulbert, Claude, 144, 147, 194, 196
Hungry Hill, 220
Hunt, Marsha, 64
Hunter, Ian, 62, 144, 213, 250
Hunter, Kim, 193, 225
Hunter, T. Hayes, 127
Hunting Tower, 91
Hurst, Brian Desmond, 220
Huston, John, 120
Huston, Walter, 108, 120
Hutchinson, Charles "Hutch," 77
Hyland, Peggy, 71, 200
Hyman, Kenneth, 266

I Claudius, 127
I Didn't Do It, 223
I Killed the Count, 234
I Met a Stranger, 153
I Spy, 128, 233
I Was a Male War Bride, 253
Ideal Husband, An, 14, 192
If Winter Comes, 83, 208
Imperfect Lady, The, 215
In the Name of the Father, 66
In Which We Serve, 224
Ince, Ralph, 141, 142
Incident in Shanghai, 136
Independent Producers, 246
Ingram, Rex, 44, 54–55, 135
Inn of the Sixth Happiness, 253
Insult, 135
International Pictures, 248
Invader, The, 123
Invaders, The, 242
Invasion of Britain, The, 58
Ireland, 34–49, 50–67, 83, 85
Ireland a Nation, 51–52
Ireland the Oppressed, 45
Irene, 133
Irish Honeymoon, An, 37, 39

Irish in America, The, 47
Irish Luck, 83
Irish Rebel, The, 47
Isherwood, Christopher, 243
Isle of Man, 83
It's a Bet, 121
It's a Boy, 113
It's in the Air, 224
It's You I Want, 142
Ivanhoe (1913), 57
Ivanhoe (1952), 253

Jackson, Jerome, 148
Jamaica Inn, 101
James Bond series, 265
Jane Eyre, 241
Jarman, Derek, 238
Jassy, 192
Java Head, 174
Jean, the Vitagraph Dog, 69
Jeans, Isabel, 95, 146
Jeans, Ursula, 205, 206
Jericho, 14, 100, 167
Jew Suss, 178–81
Johnny in the Clouds, 221–22
Johnson, Nunnally, 254
Johnson, Van, 260
Johnston, Eric, 261
Jones, Griffith, 161, 228
Journey's End, 201
Joyce, Alice, 59, 78
Judge Dredd, 266
Jump for Joy, 63, 155

Kalem Company, 34–49
Kalmus, Dr. Herbert T., 184–85, 189
Kalmus, Natalie, 185, 188–89, 192
Kane, Robert T., 102, 127, 152, 184, 189
Kanin, Garson, 222
Karloff, Boris, 13, 20
Kathleen Mavourneen, 112
Kaye, Danny, 152
Keaton, Buster, 123
Keeping Love Alive, 238
Kellermann, Annette, 57
Kellino, Pamela, 153
Kellino, Roy, 153
Kendall, Kay, 194, 195, 196
Kennedy, Arthur, 260
Kennedy, Edgar, 123
Kentucky Minstrels, 169
Kerr, Deborah, 250, 251, 252, 254
Kerry Gow, The, 44
Kesson, David, 96–98
Kicking the Moon Around, 125
Kinemacolor, 32
King, George, 152, 200
King in New York, 121
King of the Damned, 118
King Solomon's Mines, 99, 153, 167
Kipps, 72
Kirkwood, James, 111, 201
Kitty, 198, 201, 209
Knight without Armour, 101, 117
Knights of the Round Table, 250, 253
Knoles, Harley, 92
Knowing Men, 98
Knowles, Patric, 146, 243
Knox, Alexander, 9, 259
Korda, Alexander, 14, 16, 33, 98, 101, 102, 114, 117, 127, 128, 130, 132, 133, 135, 156, 158, 165, 184, 189, 190, 192, 202–3, 247, 252
Korda, Zoltan, 127, 166, 189
Kortner, Fritz, 114, 115, 146
Krauss, Werner, 146, 147
Kruger, Otto, 60, 117, 120–21, 124
Kubrick, Stanley, 223, 253

La Plante, Laura, 145, 147–48, 156
La Rue, Jack, 117
Lachman, Harry, 127, 135
Lad from Old Ireland, The, 37, 47
Lady Comes Across, The, 212
Lady Hamilton, 78, 133, 217, 239
Lady Is Willing, The, 140
Lady Killers, The, 196
Lady of the Lake, The, 129
Lady Peggy's Escape, 45
Lady with the Lamp, The, 217
Lamont, Molly, 177–78, 220
Lanchester, Elsa, 10, 220, 243
Land of Hope and Glory, 92
Landi, Elissa, 155
Lang, Matheson, 198
Langdon, Harry, 123–24, 234
Langley, Noel, 250
Lansbury, Angela, 227
Larraine, Harry, 141

Lasky, Jesse L., 136
Last Journey, The, 131
Late Extra, 112
Lauder, Harry, 91
Laughing Lady, 192
Laughton, Charles, 10, 127, 203–4, 240, 243
Launder, Frank, 231
Laurel, Stan, 10, 122–23
Lawrence, Gertrude, 203
Lawton, Frank, 204
Laye, Evelyn, 6, 178
Le Breton, Flora, 82, 209
Lean, David, 131, 173, 174
Leavesden Studios, 152
Lederer, Josie, 7
Lee, Anna, 8, 10–11, 64, 167, 240–41, 243, 262
Lee, Arthur A., 199
Lee, Mike, 264
Lee, Rowland V., 117
Lee Miller, Jonny, 264
Lee-Bradford Corporation, 199
Leigh, Vivian, 102, 149, 160, 211, 239
Lester, Richard, 267, 268
Let George Do It, 224
Levy, Benn, 9, 229, 232, 257, 258
Lewis, Jerry, 253
Life and Death of Colonel Blimp, The, 192, 225
Life with the Lyons, 235
Lilac Sunbonnet, The, 5
Lily Christine, 108, 135–37
Limelight, 126
Lion Has Wings, The, 101
Little Bit of Fluff, A, 92, 93, 199
Little Damozel, The, 86
Little Spreewald Maiden, The, 37
Litvak, Anatole, 153
Living Dangerously, 120
Lloyd, Doris, 211
Lloyd, Frank, 205, 206, 243
Lloyd of the C.I.D., 140
Loach, Ken, 264
Lockwood, Margaret, 100, 126, 142, 220
Loder, John, 167
Lodger, The, 82
Loftus, Cecelia, 76
Logan, Jacqueline, 175–78
Lohr, Marie, 142
Lolita, 253, 266
London, 89
London & District Cinemas, Ltd., 154
London Can Take It, 242
London Film Company, 74
London Scrapbook, 228
London Town, 193–96
Long Day's Journey into Night, 233
Longfellow, Malvina, 76–77
Lonsdale, Frederick, 243
Looking on the Bright Side, 213
Lorna Doone, 178
Losey, Joseph, 9, 259
Lost Hours, The, 260
Love, Bessie, 228, 230
Love from a Stranger, 117
Love in Morocco, 54–55
Love on the Dole, 261
Loves of Robert Burns, 97
Love's Old Sweet Song, 89
Low, Rachael, 99, 113, 152
Lowe, Edmund, 105
Lucky Number, The, 15
Ludwig, Otto, 139
Lugosi, Bela, 9
Lukas, Paul, 100
Lupino, Ida, 128, 243
Lye, Len, 124
Lynn, Vera, 223
Lyon, Ben, 124, 149, 228, 233–36
Lyons, Harry Agar, 32

Macbeth, 15
MacDonald, David, 149, 156
MacDonald, J. Farrell, 108
MacDougall, Ranald, 254
Mackaill, Dorothy, 211
Mackendrick, Alexander, 266, 267
Macnamara, Walter, 50–52
MacPhail, Angus, 242
Mad about Money, 124, 233–34
Madame Pompadour, 89, 91, 255
Mademoiselle from Armentieres, 209
Magic Box, The, 22, 23, 125
Mahoney, Will, 125
Malleson, Miles, 137
Man from Home, The, 91
Man in the Mirror, The, 113–14
Man of Aran, 127
Man of Mayfair, 135

Man of the Moment, 148, 156
Man Who Could Work Miracles, The, 102, 180
Man Within, The, 192
Mankiewicz, Joseph L., 253
Manners, Lady Diana, 81
Mannheim, Lucy, 221
Mapes, Alice, 39, 40
Marion, Frances, 117
Marmont, Percy, 129, 147, 208
Married to a Mormon, 80
Marsh, Jean, 262
Marsh, Mae, 83–85, 92, 95
Marshall, Herbert (actor), 211, 240, 243
Marshall, Herbert (writer), 168
Marton, Andrew, 153
Mason, James, 112, 139, 153, 221, 254, 261, 262
Massey, Raymond, 102, 127, 166
Matter of Life and Death, A, 192, 193, 225, 249
Matthews, Jessie, 99, 159, 212, 213, 243
Maude, Arthur, 207
Maxwell, John, 199
Mayer, Louis B., 54, 63, 159, 160, 242
Mayfair Girl, 144
Mayflower Pictures Corp., 127
Mayor from Ireland, The, 45
McCarthy, Joseph, 258
McCormack, John, 187
McCoy, Gertrude, 72
McGann, William, 141–42
McGowan, J. P., 39, 43, 44, 45
McGrath, Leueen, 250
McGregor, Ewan, 264
McKernan, Luke, 32, 33
McKinney, Nina Mae, 168–70
McLaglen, Victor, 7, 85, 94, 113, 156
McRae, Duncan, 72
McRae, Henry, 140
McWilliams, Glenn, 99
Meighan, Thomas, 75, 83
Melford, George, 39
Men Are Not Gods, 98, 105, 117
Men of Tomorrow, 100
Men of Two Worlds, 192
Mendes, Lothar, 180, 181
Menjou, Adolphe, 6, 116
Memory of the Camps, 242
Menzies, William Cameron, 127–28
Mercer, Beryl, 205
Merkel, Una, 89
Merry Comes to Town, 126
Merwin, Bannister, 75
MGM, 23, 116, 134, 135, 148, 160–63, 178, 198, 202, 215, 219, 227, 249
MGM-London Film Productions, Ltd., 252
Michael McShane, Matchmaker, 46
Middle Watch, The, 175
Mikado, The, 190–91
Milder, Max, 143, 149, 150
Miles, Bernard, 220
Milestone, Lewis, 140
Millais, Helena, 58
Milland, Ray, 125, 211, 254, 255
Miller, Arthur C., 91
Miller, Gilbert, 140
Miller, Max, 130
Mills, John, 221, 255, 257
Mimi, 156
Minghella, Anthony, 266
Miniver Story, The, 250, 251–52
Minter, Mary Miles, 54
Money Mad, 112
Montgomery, Douglass, 86, 114–15, 221, 222
Montgomery, Robert, 163
Moonlight Sonata, 180
Moore, Dudley, 262
Morals of Marcus, The, 124
Moreno, Antonio, 89
Morgan, Frank, 215, 216
Morgan, Joan, 82
Morgan Productions, 124
Moriarty, 83
Morley, Robert, 128, 163, 250
Morris, Sam E., 148
Mother Riley Meets the Vampire, 9
Motion Picture Export Association of America, 246
Moulin Rouge, 199
Mountain Eagle, The, 80
Mountbatten, Lord Louis, 10, 148, 150, 156
Mouse That Roared, The, 267
Mowbray, Alan, 211
Mr. Cinders, 121
Mr. Cohen Takes a Walk, 130
Mr. Drake's Duck, 157
Mr. Emanuel, 220
Mr. Satan, 106

Mr. Wu, 200
Mrs. Miniver, 63–64, 224, 242, 251
Mudlark, The, 253
Mundin, Herbert, 205, 216
Murder at Monte Carlo, 146
Murder in Soho, 117
Murder in the Night, 117
Murder on the Orient Express, 256
Murder on the Second Floor, 141
Murder Will Out, 149
Murphy, Joseph, 44
Musuraca, Nick, 93
Muybridge, Eadweard, 23, 24–25
My Heart Goes Crazy, 196
My Irish Molly, 113
My Left Foot, 66
My Old Dutch, 70–71
Mycroft, Walter, 131
Mystery of the Marie Celeste, The, 9

Naldi, Nita, 80
Namara, Marguerite, 124
Nares, Owen, 76
Nathan, George Jean, 87
Neagle, Anna, 133, 139–40, 191, 216–17, 218, 221, 239, 243
Neal, Patricia, 254
Neame, Ronald, 104, 131, 139
Negulesco, Jean, 253, 254
Neilan, Marshall, 96, 97, 201
Neill, Roy William, 141, 142–43, 149
Nell Gwynne, 78, 86–88, 91
Nelson, 72, 76
Nestor Film Company, 30
Newall, Guy, 95, 200
Newton, Robert, 254, 261
Niblo, Fred, 116
Night and the City, 237, 254
Nissen, Greta, 105
Niven, David, 11, 13, 100, 192, 205
Nixon, Marion, 235
No, No, Nanette, 133
Nobody Ordered Wolves, 107
Nolan, Doris, 259
Nolan, Mary, 59, 60
North, William, 28
Not Wanted on Voyage, 233
Notting Hill, 264, 266
Novak, Jane, 77
Novello, Ivor, 85, 92, 139, 153, 178, 198, 201–2, 238
Noy, Wilfred, 207
Nurse Edith Cavell, 133, 140, 217, 218

Oberon, Merle, 13, 16, 21, 101, 157, 158, 189, 190, 202, 203
O'Brien, Dennis, 266
O'Connor, Cavan, 126
O'Connor, Una, 205, 206
Odeon Cinemas, 247, 261
O'Hara, Maureen, 112, 125, 132
O.H.M.S., 155–56
O'Kalems, 34–49
O'Kalems Visit to Killarney, The, 39
Olcott, Sidney, 34–49, 50
Old Bones of the River, 166
Old Wives' Tale, The, 72
Oliver, Vic, 234
Olivier, Laurence, 22, 102, 137, 138, 149, 170, 189, 192, 217–18, 233, 239, 249
O'Malley, Pat, 47
On Velvet, 169
One Exciting Night, 223
One More Time, 253
One of Our Aircraft Is Missing, 225
O'Neal, Zelma, 121, 122
O'Neill, The, 41, 45, 47, 48
Open Road Films, 258
Orders Is Orders, 125
Orry-Kelly, 194
Oscar Wilde, 128
O'Shea, Tessie, 195
Ostrer, Pamela, 180
O'Sullivan, Alice, 39, 41, 42, 49
O'Sullivan, Maureen, 102, 160, 161
O'Sullivan, Patrick, 39, 41
Our Fighting Navy, 118
Outsider, The, 135
Over Night, 117
Over the Moon, 101, 190
Overbaugh, Roy, 91, 95
Owen, Byron, 146
Owen, Reginald, 211
Owen, Seena, 77

Paddy-the-Next-Best-Thing, 85, 92
Palmer, Ernest, 100
Panama Hattie, 235

Paramount Cinemas, 261
Paramount-British, 135–36
Parker, Albert, 112, 139
Parkes, Alexander, 23
Parsons, Louella, 16, 132, 228, 252
Pascal, Gabriel, 192
Passing of the Third Floor Back, The, 57–58
Passionate Adventure, The, 78
Pastor Hall, 225
Paul, Elliot, 194
Paul, Robert W., 198
Pearce, Perce, 257, 258
Pearson, George, 198
Perfect Gentleman, The, 215, 216
Perfect Strangers, 163, 252
Perfect Understanding, 137–38
Périnal, Georges, 102
Perpetua, 91
Peter Pan, 59
Peters, House, 207
Phantom Ship, The, 9
Piccadilly, 170–73
Piccadilly Pictures, 82
Pickwick Papers, 46
Piggot, Tempe, 205
Pilbeam, Nova, 208, 217
Pinewood Studios, 247
Pirates of the Seven Seas, 189
Pitts, ZaSu, 126
Pleasure Garden, The, 80
Poacher's Pardon, The, 44
Polygram, 266
Pomeroy, Roy, 210
Pommer, Erich, 127
Porter, Cole, 238
Potter, H. C., 251
Poulton, Mabel, 208
Powell, David, 207
Powell, Michael, 154, 189, 192, 225
Power, Tyrone, 253
Powers, Tom, 69, 71
Present from Margate, A, 147
Pressburger, Emerich, 192, 225
Price, Dennis, 220
Price, Kate, 28
Price of Things, The, 98
Prisoner of Zenda, The, 75
Private Life of Don Juan, The, 158
Private Life of Henry VIII, The, 197
Private Secretary, The, 113, 114
Prizma Color, 81, 93
Producers Releasing Corporation, 248
Production Code Administration, 260
Proud Valley, The, 99, 166, 167–68
Prude's Fall, The, 95
Pygmalion, 101

Q Planes, 132, 148
Queen's Affair, The, 133
Queer Cargo, 189
Quirk, James R., 6
"Quota Quickie," 134

Radio City Music Hall, 197, 202
Radio Parade of 1935, 121
Radio Romeo, 208
Raffles, 13
Raft, George, 117
Rains, Claude, 119, 211
Raise the Roof, 93
Ralston, Esther, 109–10
Ramsaye, Terry, 98
Rank, J. Arthur, 193, 246, 247–49, 257, 261
Rat, The, 85, 95
Rathbone, Basil, 11, 117, 142, 143, 211, 243, 244
Ratoff, Gregory, 8, 128
Raymond, Jack, 59
Reach for the Sky, 261
Reader, Ralph, 128
Reader, Ronald A., 27
Reagan, Ronald, 254
Red Shoes, The, 102
Red Wagon, 105
Reed, Carol, 222
Reed, Philip, 113
Reeves, Kynaston, 60–61
Reisner, Charles "Chuck," 106
Reisner, Charles, Jr., 106
Rembrandt, 202
Rennahan, Ray, 186
Rennie, James, 86, 108
Repton College, 161
Republic Pictures, 131, 220
Reserved for Ladies, 135
Return of Carol Deane, The, 233, 234
Return of the Rat, The, 95
Return of the Scarlet Pimpernel, The, 157
Return of the Soldier, 97

Reville, Alma, 92
Reynolds, Quentin, 242
Rhodes of Africa, 120
Rhythm Serenade, 223
Rich, Lillian, 93
Richards, Jeffrey, 13, 213, 221
Richardson, Frank A., 132
Richardson, Ralph, 127, 166, 174, 189
Richardson, Tony, 262
Richman, Harry, 125
Ringer, The, 48
Risdon, Elizabeth, 75
RKO, 139, 217, 228, 247, 260
RKO-Walt Disney British Productions, Ltd., 256–57
Road to London, The, 82–83
Rob Roy, 257, 265
Roberts, Desmond, 205
Roberts, Julia, 264
Robertson, John S., 77
Robeson, Paul, 100, 164–69, 238
Robinson, Edward G., 118, 266, 267
Robson, Flora, 102, 103
Robson, Mark, 253
Rock, Joe, 154–55
Rogers, Charles "Buddy," 110, 111
Rogers, Will, 89
Rolling Road, The, 82
Roman Spring of Mrs. Stone, The, 266
Romance of Lady Hamilton, The, 76
Romantic Englishwoman, The, 259
Rome Express, 110
Rooke, Irene, 97
Rooney, Mickey, 160
Roosevelt, Eleanor, 225
Rory O'More, 38, 39, 40, 42, 47, 49
Rose, David E., 254, 260
Rosen, Phil, 153
Rosher, Charles, 30, 117
Rosmer, Milton, 114, 123
Rosson, Arthur, 128, 207
Rosson, Harold (Hal), 102, 160
Rosza, Miklos, 105, 118
Rotha, Paul, 7
Rough Sea at Dover, 26
Royal Cavalcade, 59–60
Ruben, J. Walter, 174
Ruggles, Wesley, 193–96, 252
Ruggles of Red Gap, 203–4
"Runaway Production," 249
Runnin' Wild, 237
Rupert of Hentzau, 75
Russell, Rosalind, 161, 163
Rutherford, Margaret, 232–33

Sabotage, 105
Sabotage Agent, 163
Sabu, 203
Sagan, Leontine, 100
Said O'Reily to McNab, 125
Saint series, The, 219–20
Sally Bishop, 72, 77
Salomon, Ananda Max (Doc), 143–44, 148–52
Sammy Going South, 266, 267
Samuelson, G. B., 86, 200
San Demetrio, London, 228
Sanders, George, 219, 220
Sanders of the River, 165–67, 168
Santa Monica, 10
Saraband for Dead Lovers, 192
Sargent, Malcolm, 124
Saturday Island, 260
Saunders, John Monk, 120
Saville, Victor, 85, 101, 160, 163, 201, 243, 250, 251
Sayers, Dorothy L., 162
Scarlet Pimpernel, The, 102, 133
Schach, Max, 99
Schertzinger, Victor, 190
School for Husbands, 153
Schuster, Harold, 182, 185–86, 189
Scott of the Antarctic, 192
Sea Urchin, The, 95
Seastrom, Victor, 102
Secret Agent, 105, 106
Secret Lives, 109
Secret of Stamboul, The, 153
Secret of the Loch, The, 207
Seid, George, 140
Selznick, David O., 4, 101, 240–41
Sergava, Katharine, 128
Servant, The, 259
Service for Ladies, 135
Seven Arts Productions, UK, 266
Seven Sinners, 105, 231
Seventh Veil, The, 249
Shadows, 176

Shaun Rhue, 44
Shaunraun, The, 45
Shaw, Harold, 73–75
Shaw, Montague, 205
She, 81, 86
Shea, William, 28
Shenson, Walter, 267
Shepherd's Bush Studios, 231
Shepperton Studios, 253
Sheridan, Ann, 253
Sheriff, R. C., 243
Sherlock Holmes, 83
Sherlock Holmes and the Voice of Terror, 243–45
Sherlock Holmes series, 142–43, 243–45
Sherman, Vincent, 254
Sherwood, Robert, 118
Shining, The, 253, 256
Shot in the Dark, A, 253
Shuffle Along, 236
Sid Olcott International Features, 47
Sidewalks of London, The, 132, 258
Sidney, George, 253
Sidney, Sylvia, 105
Siepman, Eric, 107
Silent Barriers, 108
Silvers, Phil, 9
Simmons, Jean, 253
Simple Sinner, A, 77
Sinclair, Hugh, 219, 220
Sistrom, William, 219
Sixty Glorious Years, 139–40, 191, 216
Skall, William V., 191
Skirts, 92, 199
Sky's the Limit, The, 104
Sleeping Car, 153
Sloman, Edward, 207
Smith, Albert E., 27–30
Smith, Constance, 260
Smith, Percy, 33
Smith, Sir C. Aubrey, 10, 11, 12–13, 92, 261
So Evil My Love, 254, 255
So Well Remembered, 257
Soccer, 14–15
Soldiers of the King, 113
Somewhere in France, 232
Song of Freedom, 166–67, 169, 238
Song You Gave Me, The, 233
Sono Art World Wide Studios, 201
Sons of the Sea, 228
Sophisticated Lady, 237
Sorrell and Son, 59, 83
Sound City Studios, 141, 195
South Riding, 101
Southern Love, 86, 92
Southern Maid, A, 233
Spanish Jade, 91
Sparks, Ned, 111
Splinters, 97
Sporting Venus, The, 96
Spy in Black, The, 148
Spy of Napoleon, The, 109
Squadron Leader X, 228
Squandered Lives, 200
Squeaker, The, 105
St. Martin's Lane, 132, 258
Stage Fright, 254
Stairway to Heaven, 192, 193, 225, 249
Stallone, Sylvester, 266
Star Wars, 104, 256
Stars and Stripes, The, 234
State Secret, 157
Stein, Paul, 136, 220
Stevens, Mark, 260
Stevenson, Robert, 240, 243
Stewart, Donald Ogden, 250
Stoll, Sir Oswald, 200
Stoll Film Corporation of America, 200
Stonehenge, 96
Story of Robin Hood, The, 257
Stradling, Harry, 100–101, 160
Strange Case of Murder, A, 226
Strangers on a Honeymoon, 118, 119, 231
Street Singer, The, 126
Strictly Business, 176–78
Strictly in Confidence, 123
Stuart, Binkie, 113
Stuart, John, 201, 209
Suicide Squadron, 220
Sullivan, Francis L., 254
Sunny, 133
Swanson, Gloria, 136–39
Sweet, Blanche, 96–97
Sweet, John, 225
Sweet Devil, 93
Sword and the Rose, The, 257
Sword of Freedom, 259
Sydney, Basil, 124

Tannura, Phil, 98–100, 189
Target for Tonight, 224
Tauber, Richard, 100
Tawny Pit, 220
Taylor, Elizabeth, 241, 250
Taylor, Gilbert, 104
Taylor, Rex, 131
Taylor, Robert, 102, 160, 161, 250
Taylor, Taylor & Hobson, Ltd., 23
Taylor, William Desmond, 53–54
Tea Breaks, 8, 19–21
Tearle, Conway, 107–8
Technicolor, 140, 170, 182–96
Teddington Studios, 141–52
Tembi, 152
Tempean Films, Ltd., 260
Tempest, The, 238
Ten Days in Paris, 148
Ten Minute Alibi, 121
Tennyson, Pen, 168
Terror by Night, 244
Terry, Alice, 54
Terry, Ellen, 58
Tess of the D'Urbevilles, 96
That Hamilton Woman, 78, 133, 217, 239
That Night in London, 117
There's a Future in It, 228
Thesiger, Ernest, 98
They Came by Night, 135
They Drive by Night, 144, 224
They Flew Alone, 217, 221
Thief of Bagdad, The, 127, 132, 133, 202, 225, 237
Things to Come, 127
39 Steps, The, 180
This England, 232
This Happy Breed, 192
This Man Is News, 149
This Was Paris, 228
Thomas, Jameson, 78, 89, 92, 170, 172, 173, 207
Thompson, Emma, 64
Three Live Ghosts, 91
Thumbs Up, 220
Thunder in the City, 118
Thurmwood, Theodore, 92
Tierney, Gene, 253
Tiffany-Stahl Studios, 86
Tiger Bay, 173
Tip Toes, 89, 91
Titanic, 269
To Hell with Hitler, 224
Tobin, Genevieve, 6, 114, 137
Todd, Richard, 257
Tom Jones, 267
Tommy Atkins, 199
Too Many Millions, 144
Torrance, Ernest, 11
Torres, Raquel, 105
Tottenham, Merle, 205
Tovar, Lupita, 123
Tracy, Arthur, 126
Tracy, Spencer, 250, 251
Traffic in Souls, 50–51, 75
Trainspotting, 264
Transatlantic Tunnel, 108
Trapped by the Mormons, 80
Travers, Henry, 211
Treasure Island, 256
Tree, Sir Herbert Beerbohm, 15–16
Trimble, Larry, 45, 46, 69–71
Trimmingham, Ernest, 164
Triumph of the Rat, The, 82, 95
Trouble in Store, 123
Troubled Waters, 112
True Glory, The, 222
Trumbo, Dalton, 259
Tryon, Glenn, 185
Tucker, Forest, 260
Tucker, George Loane, 74, 75
Tucker, Sophie, 125
Tudor Rose, 217
Tunnel, The, 108
Turner, Florence, 28, 68–72
Turner Films, 70
Twelve-Ten, 77
Two Cities Films, 220, 221, 246
Two Hearts in Harmony, 112
2001: A Space Odyssey, 253
Two White Arms, 116
Two's Company, 111

Under the Red Robe, 102
Unfinished Symphony, The, 121
United Artists, 108, 141, 247, 261
Universal Pictures, 140–41
Universal-International, 248
Universal-Wainwright Studios, 153

Unsell, Eve, 91
Unsworth, Geoffrey, 99
Urban, Charles, 31–33

Vacation from Marriage, 163, 252
Vagabond Queen, The, 98
Valley of Decision, The, 62
Valli, Virginia, 80
Van Druten, John, 243
Van Enger, Charles, 141
Van Heusen, Jimmy, 194
Vananger, Willard, 141
Varney, Anthony, 129
Veidt, Conrad, 102, 114, 118, 125, 159, 180, 203
Velez, Lupe, 124, 234
Victoria the Great, 139, 216
Victors, The, 258
Victory and Peace, 58
Vidor, King, 160
Vignola, Robert, 43, 49
Vinson, Helen, 108
Virgin Queen, The, 81, 93, 94
Vitagraph Company of America, 27–30, 45–46
Vorhaus, Bernard, 130–31
Vortex, The, 198
Vosper, Frank, 117, 141

Wainwright, Richard, 152–53
Walbrook, Anton, 139, 149, 191, 216, 220, 226, 227
Walker, Alexander, 66–67
Walker, Joseph, 8
Walls, Tom, 99–100
Walpole, Hugh, 202
Walsh, Raoul, 155
Walt Disney Company, 256–58
Wanamaker, Sam, 257
Warburton, John, 205
Wardour Films, 105
Ware Case, The, 157
Warner, H. B., 13, 59, 118, 211
Warner, Jack L., 143, 147, 148, 149, 152, 212
Warner Bros.-First National Pictures, Ltd., 254
Warner Bros.-First National Productions, Ltd., 141–52
Warner Theatre, 143, 150
Warner-Pathé, 256
"Warsaw Concerto," 220
Warwick Trading Company, 31
Washburn, Bryant, 82–83
Watchtower over Tomorrow, 242
Waterloo in Wardour Street, 107
Waterloo Road, 261
Way to the Stars, 221–22
Webster, Ben, 16
Weinstein, Hannah, 259–60
Welch, Elizabeth, 167, 168, 169–70, 236–38
We'll Meet Again, 223
Welland, Colin, 269
Welles, Orson, 253, 259
Welsh Singer, A, 71
We're Going to Be Rich, 113
West, Rebecca, 97
Western Approaches, 192
Whale, James, 201
What Happened to Harkness, 123
Whelan, Tim, 21, 111, 131–32, 189
When Knights Were Bold, 119, 132
Where's Charlie?, 254
While Paris Sleeps, 94
White, Merrill, 133
White Rose, The, 85
White Shadow, The, 86
White Sheik, The, 92
Whitty, Dame May, 16
Whom the Gods Destroy, 29
Widmark, Richard, 253
Widow from Monte Carlo, The, 147
Widow's Might, 148
Wilcox, Herbert, 59, 77, 84–89, 91, 95, 97, 111, 133, 135, 139–40, 158, 191, 200, 216, 221, 239, 243, 247
Wilcoxon, Henry, 167, 211
Wilding, Michael, 261
Williams, Elmo, 132–33
Williams, Emlyn, 96
Williams, J. D., 88, 199
Wills, J. Elder, 173
Wilson, Harold, 247
Wings, 233
Wings and the Woman, 221
Wings of the Morning, 152, 182–89, 197
Winning a Continent, 74
Wise, Robert, 253
Wise Guy, 124
Withers, Googie, 254

Wodehouse, P. G., 13
Wolf's Clothing, 153
Wolves, 89
Woman Hater, 220
Woman in Command, The, 113
Woman in White, The, 97
Woman to Woman, 78, 85–86, 198
Womanhood, the Glory of a Nation, 29
Women filmmakers, 175–78
Women Who Pay, 128
Wong, Anna Mae, 170–74
Wood, Sam, 161
Woods, Arthur, 234
Working Title Films, 266
World, the Flesh and the Devil, The, 32
World War II, 11, 101, 219–45
World-Wide Films, Ltd., 199
Wray, Fay, 118–20
Wrecker, The, 82
Wuthering Heights, 217
Wyman, Jane, 254
Wynyard, Diana, 15, 162, 205, 223, 226

Yank at Eton, A, 160
Yank at Oxford, A, 102, 120, 160
Yankee Doodle Dandy, 150
Yanks, 269
Yellow Canary, 221
Yellow Mask, The, 174
York, Michael, 262
You Can't Do without Love, 223
You Remember Ellen, 41
You're in the Army Now, 155
Young, Hal, 47, 85, 91, 94–95
Young, Robert, 105, 106
Young, Roland, 102, 167, 211
Young, Terence, 220

Zinnemann, Fred, 9